Books

PORTRAIT OF MAX

THE WORCESTER ACCOUNT

DUVEEN

BY S. N. BEHRMAN

Plays

BUT FOR WHOM CHARLIE

LORD PENGO

THE COLD WIND AND THE WARM

FANNY (with Joshua Logan)

JANE (from Somerset Maugham)

I KNOW MY LOVE (from Achard)

DUNNIGAN'S DAUGHTER

JACOBOWSKY AND THE COLONEL (with Franz Werfel)

THE PIRATE

THE TALLEY METHOD

NO TIME FOR COMEDY

WINE OF CHOICE

AMPHITRYON 38 (adapted from the French)

END OF SUMMER

RAIN FROM HEAVEN

BIOGRAPHY

BRIEF MOMENT

METEOR

SERENA BLANDISH

THE SECOND MAN

THE
SUSPENDED
DRAWING
ROOM

S. N. Behrman

𝔖𝔇 STEIN AND DAY
PUBLISHERS / NEW YORK

ABIGAIL E. WEEKS MEMORIAL LIBRARY
UNION COLLEGE
BARBOURVILLE, KENTUCKY

814.52
B421

COPYRIGHT © 1939, 1940, 1944, 1945, 1946, 1947, 1965, BY S. N. BEHRMAN

The Public Trustee, as Trustee of Bernard Shaw's Estate, has granted permission for use of the letters written by Bernard Shaw to Gabriel Pascal appearing in this book, but disclaims all responsibility for the accuracy of the conversations described.

The following chapters appeared originally in *The New Yorker:* "The Suspended Drawing Room"; "It's Cold at Lady Windermere's"; "Hyper or Hypo?"; "Old Monotonous"; "The Red and the Blue"; "Playwright."

"Zion Comes to Culver City" was first published in *Chaim Weizmann,* edited by Meyer W. Weisgal, Dial Press, 1944.

LIBRARY OF CONGRESS CATALOG CARD NO. 65–22989

ALL RIGHTS RESERVED.

PUBLISHED SIMULTANEOUSLY IN CANADA BY SAUNDERS OF TORONTO, LTD.

DESIGNED BY JOAN STOLIAR

PRINTED IN THE UNITED STATES OF AMERICA

STEIN AND DAY/PUBLISHERS/7 EAST 48 STREET, NEW YORK, N.Y. 10017

IN MEMORY OF
HAROLD ROSS
· · · · · · · ·
· · · · · · · ·
· · · · · · · ·
· · · · · · · ·
· · · · · · · ·

Contents

Preface

HAROLD ROSS:

A Recollection

THE LAST TASK THAT HAROLD Ross, the founder and first editor of *The New Yorker*, worked on was a profile I wrote of a baffling and fascinating character named Gabriel Pascal. Pascal had achieved sudden fame because, in some mysterious way, he had persuaded Bernard Shaw to give him the exclusive rights to film his plays. The various theories to account for this remarkable arrangement are described in the profile itself, which appears in this volume. However, it is a fact that Shaw made the arrangement—a dazzling and ultimately inexplicable fact. Pascal's own account of it varied with his mood, as his accounts of everything varied with his moods. Every great film company in the world—at a time when there *were* great film companies—had been importuning Shaw for years to sell them these rights. The terms they offered had been fabulous. He nevertheless gave them, finally, to Pascal, a penniless and obscure Hungarian adventurer whom, evidently, he found irresistible. When I was working with Ross on this profile, in 1951, I did not realize how very ill he was. My last conference with Ross on Pascal took place in Ross's rooms in the Algonquin Hotel, a week before his death.

This is not the place for a memoir of Ross. I hope, one day, to write one. I will simply say that what I have read about him—including Thurber's book—seems to me very wide of the mark. He is, for example, generally described as "protean," as having been all things to all men—mercurial, unpredictable, capricious. Actually, Ross was one of the most single-minded, dedicated, and coherent men I have ever known. He was always the same. He was himself incapable of affectation and quick to detect it. He had one passion, and it animated his every action and thought: to maintain the excellence of *The New Yorker*. No artist absorbed in a work-in-progress could be more passionate than Ross was in the perfection of his magazine. Wolcott Gibbs once told me that when Ross wrote, opposite a paragraph Gibbs had written, "Is this interesting?" Gibbs was invariably forced to admit to himself, after he had got over his preliminary irritation, that the paragraph really wasn't very interesting. In 1944, Ross practically forced me to go to London, where the V-2s were falling, to write an impression of wartime England ("The Suspended Drawing Room," which is also contained in this volume). In 1946, he asked me to go again. I protested. "But

Ross," I said, "I've been. I've done it." "Write me a cold piece on London," he said. I went. London was indeed cold. The resulting piece was called "It's Cold at Lady Windermere's." It was a singular mission: to register frigidity. Ross's instinct was sound.

No one I have ever known had a shrewder sense of his own limitations. But Ross had no intention of allowing *The New Yorker* to be hemmed in by these limitations. His own "social conscience"—as an abstraction—was not acute. When he found himself badgered by radio-bullying on commuter trains, his rebellion crystallized in a successful crusade in *The New Yorker* columns to free the captive audience. But, for example, the Spanish Civil War did not impinge on him. Somewhere in his consciousness he felt that perhaps it should, but it didn't. He felt that *The New Yorker* must reflect the moral sense it abraded in others. He therefore nurtured one of the most sensitive social consciences in this country, that of E. B. White, and gave him the run of the magazine in matters involving social conscience. In effect, he substituted E. B. White's conscience for his own. As long as the conscience of *The New Yorker* was all right, he rested easy.

Several years before I had worked on the Pascal, Ross had been after me to do another project: a profile of Chaim Weizmann, who was to be the first President of Israel. I had seen as much as I could of Dr. Weizmann during his frequent visits here in the years before the State of Israel came into being. I had talked a lot about him to Ross, and had told him of my fascination with this extraordinary man. The Near East was no more in Ross's purview than was Spain. He was not a Zionist—he was not even a non-Zionist. About all that his mind was *tabula rasa*. But he sniffed something important in the ambiance of Weizmann, some portent. He began urging me to write a profile of this statesman without portfolio, this phenomenal man who went about the world, as Sir Isaiah Berlin has pointed out, with the authority and the dignity of a head of state, although he had no army, no navy, and no state. Ross never let up on Weizmann.

"You can let it run as long as you like," he said. I had many letters from him on the subject. One reached me in Hollywood. "For God's sake," he wrote, "get out of Hollywood and come to Zion." It was a singular plea to receive from a man who was not even a non-Zionist. As it happened, Dr. Weizmann was in Hollywood when Ross's letter arrived. I showed it to him. He was amused. He consented to sit for me and invited me to accompany him to Arrowhead, where he was spending the weekend. This weekend I have described in the piece on Dr. Weizmann contained in this book. The piece never appeared in *The New Yorker;* it was printed in the *Festschrift* volume presented to Dr. Weizmann on his seventieth birthday. But it had its genesis with Ross. Because of his insistence, I had begun taking notes for a profile long before that weekend in Arrowhead.

Professor Harold Laski, of the London School of Economics, was a friend of mine, and I always visited him when I was in London. Like many of his colleagues at the University, Laski was a great admirer of *The New Yorker.* The University, apparently, could afford only one copy; by unwritten law, equal time was allotted each member of the faculty. One day, Laski told me, a colleague came up to him, panting with indignation, and said, "Professor X has had it for more than an *hour!*" On one of his visits here, Laski asked to meet Ross. The meeting was arranged for a lunch at 21. Ross came in all spruced up and tidy, as is becoming when you are meeting a professor. Somewhere in his past, Ross had picked up and read a volume of *The Autobiography of Herbert Spencer,* and he mentioned this feat casually. "I happened to be reading the autobiography of Herbert Spencer the other day," said Ross dreamily—an opening he felt appropriate for a professor. Laski's eyes lit up behind his glasses. He sized up Ross at once as a Herbert Spencer man. He warmed to Ross and plunged at once into an intimate discourse, as one Spencerian to another. I saw panic in Ross's eyes as it dawned on him that Spencer had written other books besides the auto-

16

biography and that, regrettably, Laski seemed to be familiar with them. When Laski stopped for breath, Ross switched abruptly to a visit he had had the day before from Noel Coward. By this sudden shift of terrain, Ross forced Laski to the defensive, since Laski was less at home in Coward than he was in Spencer. As a result of this lunch, with all its ups and downs, Ross got a book review out of Laski.

Another Englishman, a friend of Laski's, equally eminent but considerably different, also asked to meet Ross. This gentleman is one of the most brilliant talkers in the world, but his utterance has a breakneck velocity and a uniqueness of intonation that force you to hang onto his sentences as they race by, as to a rope on an Alpine climb. At one point, Ross asked to shift chairs so as to be nearer his guest, but, alas, proximity did not bring clarification. As I walked away from the restaurant with Ross, he said mournfully, "I didn't understand a goddam word your friend said, but he can write anything for us that he likes."

The profile of Pascal was one I had begun many years before Ross's death. I had promised Gabby, as he was known to his innumerable acquaintances, that I would not publish it without letting him see it and without getting his approval. I had made such promises to profile subjects before. Theretofore, without exception, these subjects had proved amenable. Usually, they were so pleased to be written about at all that they did not hear whatever overtones of denigration there may have been. But Pascal was hurt by my portrait of him. I reported this to Ross, who brushed it aside. "It's a very friendly profile," he said. "Let me meet Pascal. I'll fix it up with him." I arranged for the three of us to have dinner in the Oak Room at the Plaza. I had been telling Ross all this time how genial Gabby was. And he usually was. He had a fluorescent smile, which slowly lit up the wide expanse of his swarthy face, till it reached the tips of his ears. But there was nothing fluorescent about Pascal when he came to our table at the Plaza. His expression was grim. I introduced

17

him to Ross. It was like the first encounter between Lord Halifax and Molotov in San Francisco—Lord Halifax smiling, Molotov stony-faced. I could see that Ross was taken aback. Pascal and I were on a first-name basis; he pronounced mine "Som." Before even sitting down, Pascal delivered himself of a short address: "Schopenhauer say it is fine dividing-line which separate charla-*tan* from genius. Som has put me on the wrong side of line."

It was inauspicious. Ross looked at me, an expression of bewilderment in his blue eyes. "Where is the genial character you have been telling me about?" he seemed to be asking. During the meal, Pascal never brightened. His vanity was inordinate, and I had wounded it by suggesting that the first Shavian film he had made, *Pygmalion,* had really been directed not by him—although it had been so announced in the credit-titles—but by Leslie Howard, who played Higgins. I had not made this statement lightly. I had talked to everyone connected with the filming of *Pygmalion,* and this was the consensus. Pascal vehemently rejected this notion. "I would hate for Charlotte to see this," he said. He was referring to Shaw's wife. I could see that what I had written was a threat to him. The first solid ground under his feet that he had ever known was this relationship he had achieved with Shaw. He felt that it was being eroded. I knew that Mrs. Shaw did not entirely share her husband's delight in Gabby. I offered at once to delete the offending sentence. Pascal was momentarily appeased, but he was not really comforted. He began to harangue Ross with a list of his achievements from early childhood—all intended to persuade him that he was not char-la-*tan,* as I had invidiously suggested. "When I was sixteen, I was already genius," he assured Ross. In the course of this persuasion, he dropped the names of his friends and prospective collaborators on films—Sir Basil Zaharoff, Eamon De Valera, and Gandhi. Among several lavish offers he had already made to me were proposals that we go to see these eminent pals of his with a view to filming their lives. I could see Ross stumbling to find a pathway through the thicket of Pascal's ecumenical projects. All

Ross wanted to do was to persuade Pascal that my piece was "friendly." Pascal remained obdurate. He insisted that he couldn't bear the idea of having Charlotte see what I had written. He didn't mind so much about "the sweet Irish Pope" (his sobriquet for GBS); it was Charlotte he was sensitive about. I suppose he felt sure that nothing any scribbler wrote could possibly dislodge the love and esteem Shaw felt for him but that my hints might give Mrs. Shaw a talking-point. I saw myself depriving Pascal of a lifeline. In my mind, right then, I gave up the project. The dinner was certainly a failure. Ross and I both promised to have another go at the piece, and to see whether we could get it into such shape that it would not disillusion Charlotte Shaw. Years passed, and both Shaw and his wife died, but Ross continued to be enthusiastic about the Pascal project. To the end, Ross insisted that Pascal must come to see that my piece on him was friendly. Had Ross lived for another meeting with him, perhaps Pascal would have yielded.

When I got out of college, I tried for years to make my living as a prose writer. I contributed to various magazines—especially to *The Smart Set,* edited by H. L. Mencken and George Jean Nathan. But there was no living in it. One day, in a moment of despair, I dramatized a short story of mine that had appeared in *The Smart Set.* The play opened and was a success. I was then caught up in a whirl of motion-picture writing and in other plays. All this time it was a frustration for me that I wasn't writing prose. One day—I don't precisely remember where or when—I met Ross. He asked me to write for him. I did a short, juvenile profile of George Gershwin, which he accepted. From then on, I was seeing him all the time and writing for him the pieces now contained in this book. He released for me a dammed-up means of expression. I am greatly indebted to him, also, for the exhilaration and delight of his company, from the moment I met him to the evening I spent with him a week before his death.   —S. N. B.

Time and Place

THE
SUSPENDED
DRAWING
ROOM

1945

TO ARRIVE IN LONDON IN A SAT-
urday twilight late in 1944, after
having been away since before the
war began, was to experience a
sinking of the heart for which
even the destruction in the suburbs, visible from the windows of
the train, had not prepared me.
The suburban wash, hung amply
across the gaps made by the
bombs in the rows of workers'
houses, stirred a quick, sympathetic awareness of human adapta-

bility, and so did the window curtains and flower pots in the truncated dwellings that remained—the persistent, vivid, still-life ameliorations. But these things I somewhat expected, though even here there was a shocking discrepancy between what one has written off as history and what was actually still contemporary. I accepted the neat erasures in the long rows of houses, and even the vestiges of normality in the partially demolished ones. And I wondered about the displaced inhabitants of the houses that were gone. Where, on that darkening afternoon, were they warming their feet and how were they going to kill the unpromising evening?

London was something else again. Nothing in the outworks had quite suggested the lowered atmosphere in the citadel itself. It was not merely the almost deserted railway station. I had arrived late in the day, and the British government official who met me remarked casually that the first V-2s had fallen earlier. They had made deep craters, my host said, but had been far less destructive than had been anticipated. There were no instructions about how to behave if you were out walking when the V-2s came, he said, because there were no alerts. You just strolled along, daydreaming, till you were hit. The instructions about what to do when you heard the sirens for the V-1s were very simple: fall flat on your face. My host, who was going to give me a lift to Claridge's, where I was to stay, asked me if I'd mind detouring to the Savoy to drop two other visitors who had arrived on the same train. In the curved areaway of the Savoy, off the Strand, I got out for a few minutes while the others went in to register and I walked onto the Strand. It was very still. For reassurance, I sought the entrance to the Savoy Grill. Sandbags were piled up against it. I peeped inside. There were a few people sitting around having tea. If, in the old days, there was a vivacious room in Europe, it was the Savoy Grill. It was the nerve center of bohemian and artistic London. I remembered an evening there: Paderewski, Yvonne Printemps, Sacha Guitry;

24

Chaliapin blowing kisses at large. (On the plane coming over, I had heard an anecdote about Guitry. When, recently, he arrived in a French prison for collaborationists, he was told, to cheer him up, that his first wife was there. The effect was the opposite. Guitry threw up his hands. "Everything I can endure," he groaned, "but this!") That evening was millennially far away. What had made me feel that the Savoy Grill would keep up its tempo forever I did not know, but I must have felt that, because I was so struck by the change. My Englishman came back and we resumed our drive to Claridge's. He asked about America. He had been an Oxford debater and had travelled through forty-seven of our states. He was wistful about that forty-eighth state, one of the Dakotas. He wanted me to tell him about it. As I had never been in it either, I couldn't help him much. With a careful detachment, he asked about "the election." In the ensuing eight weeks of my stay, I was to observe that no matter where a conversation started, it always ended up with speculation about the forthcoming election. I may add that I never heard a word against Dewey from any Englishman. That all came from the Americans.

Down the Strand, past the Admiralty Arch, and across Piccadilly Circus, with its boxed-up Eros, I kept my eyes—while I consoled my companion for having missed North or South Dakota—at the windows, watching the familiar streets and the people on the sidewalks. The streets, with distressing elisions, were still there, but they were subdued and very shabby, and so were the pedestrians. There was an air about the buildings and the people of being on the defensive. London, it was apparent at once, had endured unbelievably and was still enduring unbelievably. Thirty-six hours before, I had left an America simmering with the exhilaration of a boom; England was tense in the paroxysm of a death struggle. When I left New York, the end of the war was imminent—"in the bag," as people said—but here it was being fought out.

ABIGAIL E. WEEKS MEMORIAL LIBRARY
UNION COLLEGE
BARBOURVILLE, KENTUCKY

An English editor I met on the plane had told me that the day after I arrived would provide one of the biggest news stories of the war: London, for the first time in five years, was to have light. That night, however, the blackout was still to be on, and I deposited my fifty-five pounds of luggage in Claridge's and went for a walk while there was still some daylight. I made for Berkeley Square. Soldiers and sailors, English and American, were walking with their girls in a faint, intermittent drizzle. Most of the women wore no stockings. I had been seeing this all summer in New York. But the American legs were tanned and agreeable, whereas these English ones were muddy and streaked bluish and red with the cold. (A young woman later told me that she was embarrassed at having to go without stockings. "I hate the unusual," she said. As she had been going barelegged for five years, I wondered how long it took for the unusual to become the usual.) The façades of the houses leading into the square have a strangely quiet look; at a casual glance, you might think the houses were shut up for the weekend, but a closer inspection shows you that they have been shut up for longer than that. I peered in through a grimy, narrow, leaded window at the side of a fine oaken street door. Behind it was a great, obscene shambles of shattered brick and mortar and twisted iron. A huge sheet of what had been a fluted ceiling lay against a section of stairway, as if propped up on one elbow. I looked down the row. Several places in the long vista of wreckage had been cleared for the pools—for emergency use against incendiaries—which are now a common feature of the London scene. These dark, liquid oblongs, fine-meshed in the rain, reflected jagged back walls and gargoyles of contorted pipes. I remembered going out to the set in Hollywood where Leslie Howard was making the motion picture of *Berkeley Square*. Those reproductions of eighteenth-century façades had not much less behind them than this one had.

I looked up. On the third story of a house on the corner, following accurately the theatrical convention of the missing fourth wall, was an exquisite, suspended drawing room: delicately tinted blue walls, molded cornices, the curved, rifted ceiling, with a beautifully shaped oval where the center chandelier had been. All but the framework of the rest of the house was gone, but there it hung, this upstairs drawing room, elegant and aloof. I thought of Henry James. Here was his Mayfair, crisply anatomized. What would he have done with that room? With what malevolent ghosts would he have peopled it? What seedlings of social casuistry would have sprouted beneath that nonexistent chandelier, simmered along those pastel walls? An acute English critic speaks of James as the harbinger of decay and says that he described the final throes of a society he knew was done with. But James did not, I am sure, anticipate quite this finale. He must have visualized a long, slow inanition—the inhabitants of these drawings rooms giving up eventually because of their inability to sustain their own attitudes, to save face before their own pretensions. Certainly he could not have anticipated such rude visitations as there have been, cutting short the tortuous inhibitions, freezing the slow molds of refinement. Inescapably the Cassandra wails of our prophets, who are fond of reminding us that our civilization, like earlier ones, may disappear, somehow became very plausible. Ordinarily, when we become aware of moral rifts, we believe we can surmount them. Here disintegration was a physical actuality.

Later, I was to have this same feeling in drawing rooms still intact. I visited an august Englishman who has had a career of the highest distinction in English public life. He took me upstairs to show me his books—some of which he had written—and then into his shrouded drawing room. The long salon was musty and denuded. He lifted a linen hood from the head of a lovely statuette of a young girl. The girl smiled ravishingly, as if in sudden relief at her unveiling. He had bought her in Spain years ago. "We cannot, of course," he said, "keep these rooms open any longer." He walked about, uncovering other precious objects. "England," he said in the standard summary, "will never be the

27

same again." He then made a rueful acknowledgment that there would be another England, but he felt that his had vanished. Fashionable London, upper-class London, is a vast, urban Cherry Orchard.

While I was still staring up at the Jamesian drawing room, I was gradually swallowed up by darkness. Before I knew it, the suspended drawing room had disappeared, together with the framework which suspended it. Suddenly there were no buildings, no streets, no squares. There was darkness. I started back to the hotel in something of a panic, knowing that a sense of direction was not my strong point. A few taxis went by and I hailed them, because I had not yet learned that it was no use whatever to hail a taxi in a London street. I was told afterward that in a poll taken to discover what people considered the greatest hardship of the war, the blackout won hands down. I didn't wonder. This blackout was inhuman; it was too literal, it couldn't take a joke. We had had a blackout in New York that gave you a break. I remembered it, on that perilous walk back to Claridge's, as a flaming incandescence, a pillar of fire by night, a civic bonfire. Cars passed by—little points of blue light dragging darkness after them but leaving blackness behind. I made it finally, but I had aged. When I did get to Claridge's, I didn't know it for a minute —not till the doorman flashed his torch to light a guest across the sidewalk. When I got through the swinging door into the lighted lobby, I gasped with relief.

The next night was no better, or any night thereafter. The promised illumination did not come. The government didn't go through with the moderation of the blackout, nor did it make an explanation. About this there was much grumbling. Why, since the bombs that were coming over were pilotless, was the blackout necessary at all? The common explanation, that it was necessary to save fuel, did not silence the grousing, which went on all the time I was in London, as did the blackout—profound, terrifying, impenetrable. The girl at Paddington police station who made out my ration card told me that she hadn't been out in the evening in five years. She would rather stay in than face the blackout. I must say, however, that one night several weeks later the blackout yielded some compensation: for once a full moon overcame it and London lay bathed in silver. Looking back at the Palace from St. James's Street, one saw its turrets against the clear sky as they must have looked at night in the unlit centuries. A companion pointed up to the turret where King Charles had spent his last night before his execution. "He complained," my friend said, "that his feet were cold." I could understand how he felt; it was still nippy. But the walk that night was breathtaking; never had I seen London so unimaginably beautiful. The skeletons of buildings filtered the sky, the ubiquitous pools shimmered, the grayness of the London masonry took kindly to this soft light. I realized that this was the first time I had ever really seen London by moonlight.

Back in my room the first night, I rang for the floor waiter. There he was, my old friend James, flourishing a greatly abbreviated dinner card. He was in tails, as always (the waiters are the only ones left in London who dress for dinner), but he had thinned out a bit and his clothes, quite shiny and threadbare, almost hung on him. Still, he wore them with an air, and his smile of welcome was the only thing in London so far that had not changed. There wasn't much on the menu: a no-man's land of mousses and pilaffs, with nothing really definable. I ventured several choices. "I wouldn't have that, sir," James cautioned each time. Finally I ordered a chicken cutlet, which turned out to have a mealy neutrality. It inexorably filled you up, and that was all that could be said for it. I diverted my attention from it by talking to James.

"Well, James," I began, "quite a lot you've gone through in these five years!"

"Bit rough 'ere and there, sir."

"I'm sure it must have been."

"Worst was in the blitz of '40–'41, when I used to have to walk

29

'ome at night to Maida Vale, ducking into areaways every second, dodging shrapnel."

"Why did you have to walk?"

"Well, sir, during the worst of the blitz the buses would just draw up at the curb and stay there all night. Had to walk. Pretty thick it was some nights, coming down so fast. Why, sir, would you believe it, one night it took me an hour and a half to walk one hundred yards from this 'otel!"

I was indignant. "Why," I demanded, "wouldn't they let you sleep here, in the hotel?"

James was shocked. "Oh, sir, I wouldn't sleep in this 'otel."

"Why not, James?"

"Far too 'ot. Don't care for the central 'eating. I'm a countryman—like open air, open windows!"

Feeling terribly effete for having proposed sleeping in Claridge's, I finished my dinner quickly and said good night to James. Then I started to go to bed. While I was undressing, the sirens began—a long ululation rising in piercing crescendo. I sat down with a shoe in one hand. There was a deafening crash. A buzz bomb had fallen, and seemingly dreadfully close. I hadn't been so acutely aware, till that moment, that I was in the South of England. I looked at the thick, drawn curtains. Flying glass couldn't very well get though those. Or could it? I put out the light and quickly got under the covers.

"The next war," said a keen-minded Anglicized Hungarian at a dinner party a few nights later, "will start with someone pressing a push button in some underground electric works in Central Europe, which will send robot bombs to Detroit." It is generally agreed that London escaped complete destruction last summer by only a hair's breadth, that had the invasion not taken place when it did, the enemy installations in France would have sent across twenty-five hundred robots a day. This they were equipped to do. Even allowing for the admitted imprecision of aim, this would have meant the total extinction of the capital. "The robot is a very clever weapon," a distinguished physicist in the British Civil Service told me. "It is, of course, in the early stages of its development, but it has great possibilities." From a Mephistophelean point of view, it has done pretty well already. I arrived after the V-1s had, presumably, done their worst. They were now sporadic but always impending. And when they fell, they and the V-2s, they did something more than show their possibilities. As I was going to dinner one night in Kensington Palace Gardens, the great park flared suddenly into brilliant illumination. The trees became alive with light and dredged from my memory the awful scene in Arthur Machen's novel *The Terror*. For a moment I thought it was a thunderstorm. The air shuddered, as well as the car in which I sat. With the blackness that followed there came the sound of an immense explosion. Then everything was as before, at least where I was. Nothing daunts the London chauffeur. Mine had stopped the car; now he started it again, chuckling to himself. I didn't ask him what he found funny. I arrived at dinner fifteen minutes late. "I thought," said my hostess as she rose to greet me, "that we should have to revise the dinner table." That was the only reference to the explosion. Next day the same chauffeur drove me somewhere else. The London taxi drivers and chauffeurs know everything. Late at night, in some mysterious rendezvous, they check up on every bomb, every explosion. This man was able to give me precise information about last night's bomb. It had killed many people and destroyed or partially demolished several hundred houses.

The nonchalance about bombs is general throughout England. A lady who drives a lorry to blitzed areas told me that she is never in the least frightened, no matter what happens, while she is driving, nor does she flinch no matter what gruesome charges she has to carry. It is only when she is lying in bed at night that she is frightened, and then more at the sirens than at the explosions, because, she imagines, the former are anticipation, the latter *faits accomplis*. If you are alive to hear the explosion, you are all right. On the opening night of John Gielgud's revival of

The Circle, there was an alert during the last act. The bedraggled and bedizened Lady Kitty was sitting down front on a sofa, admonishing the young Elizabeth to profit by her example and not run away with a married man. The sirens began. In front of the footlights a square transparency lit up to reveal the word "ALERT" in huge black letters—quite unnecessarily, it seemed to me, as the sirens were distinctly audible. Lady Kitty had been describing the shabbier social aspects of life in Monte Carlo. I half expected Yvonne Arnaud, playing Lady Kitty, to say, "My dear Elizabeth, go to the nearest shelter at once." But Lady Kitty didn't. She went on fervently imploring Elizabeth to avoid scandal. No one in the audience stirred, except to strain forward a bit to hear Yvonne Arnaud better.

William Wyler, the director of the motion picture *Mrs. Miniver,* once told me that he wants to do a scene in a film of people having lunch or dinner during an alert, with the conversation proceeding completely undeflected by the bombing. (He says that he'll shoot the scene without telling the actors anything about it and add the sound effects afterward.) In the two months I was in England, I encountered this sort of thing five times. To get a change from the inedible food at Claridge's, I used to go out for the inedible food at several little restaurants I knew. One day I was lunching in one of these with Chaim Weizmann and a number of his friends. Everybody was enchanted with the quietly ironic utterances of this extraordinary man. An alert began, screaming in crescendo over the very roof of the restaurant. Weizmann lifted his voice slightly—the only time I have ever known him to lift it. The conversation went on to its end without a reference to the alert. Not long before, a bomb had fallen on a restaurant in this neighborhood during the lunch hour, killing hundreds of people, but no one said a word about the incident. I never discussed an air raid with any one in London except taxi drivers and chauffeurs. No one else will talk about them. Three or four lines in the papers will tell you that several bombs fell the day before in Southern England, but that is all. Beyond the casual remark that was made the day I arrived, the V-2s were never spoken of. Presumably it has been different since Churchill's speech about them.

This nonchalance has affected Americans, too. There is the story the Lunts tell. Alfred Lunt was standing in the wings one night ready to make his entrance in the second act of *There Shall Be No Night*. The sirens sounded, and a bomb exploded quite close. Lynn Fontanne, who was onstage, turned to address the young man playing her son and found him not there. He had obeyed a conditioned reflex and run off the stage to the doubtful shelter of his dressing room. Disregarding this, Lunt made his entrance. His first line was to Miss Fontanne: "Darling, are you all right?" The audience applauded when she said she was all right. "Do you know," Lunt told me, "what Lynn's first remark to me was when we left the stage after the curtain was down? She turned on me accusingly and said, 'That's the first time, Alfred —that's the first time in the years we've been doing this play— that's the very first time you ever read it properly!'" I remarked that I had always suspected that the only really effective director for Lunt was Himmler. This consoled Miss Fontanne.

The country's absorption in the war is complete, but the peculiar anomalies of English life and English character, political and otherwise, persist. The taxi driver who took me to see Harold Laski knew about him. "Oh, yes, Professor Laski," he said possessively. "I am Labour and I think we'll get in at the next election. Clever man, Professor Laski. Churchill likes him." Laski was amused by this when I told him, as well as by another remark I quoted to him, made by an American when the New York *Times* carried a story that the Laski home had been blitzed during the night. Laski, the *Times* related, had been knocked out of bed, had fallen down several flights of stairs, and waked up. "He must be a light sleeper," said the American.

Then, on a four-hour trip to Cardiff, on a train on which there was no food, no heat, no seats, I stood in a corridor talking to a young instructor in the Home Defense. He was full of gruesome details of the work performed in London by his Home Defense volunteers, one of them a man well over seventy. "Unsparing," he said. "They work sometimes for days with no sleep at all." The most unbearable part of his work, he said, was finding the bodies of children. Only the week before, he had pulled out of the wreckage of a bombed building the body of a little girl about the same age as his own, who was, he thanked God, evacuated to Gloucester and whom he was now on his way to visit. "It isn't all unrelieved gloom, though," he said. "Sometimes funny things happen." I encouraged him to tell me a funny thing. "Well," he said, "one day we were clearing out a badly blitzed house. We found a decapitated man. We looked and looked for his head but couldn't find it. Finally we gave up. As we were carrying the torso through what used to be the garden into the van, we heard a chicken clucking. Hello, I thought, what's that chicken clucking about? There's certainly nothing left for him in the garden. We went back and followed the clucking till we found the chicken. It wasn't in the garden at all but in part of the rubble and it was clucking at the missing head." I was happy to find that there was a lighter side to this man's work.

At the station in Cardiff I was met by Jack Jones, the novelist and playwright and the biographer of Lloyd George. Cardiff, I had been told in London, was hell even in peacetime. Jones took me to a sing in a local tabernacle. The banker in the town had organized a series of Sunday-night sings for service men. The place was packed, the mood warm and informal, and the singing, in Welsh and English, magnificent. The phenomenon of a great crowd spending the evening just singing struck me as extraordinary; in America it wouldn't occur to people to sing en masse without being paid for it. Jones walked me back to my hotel afterward. It was obvious, once we were on the street, that only a few of the American service men in the vicinity had gone to the tabernacle. The rest appeared to be walking the streets with girls, many of them almost children. The atmosphere was high-pitched, like an American college town on a football night. In the few blocks between the tabernacle and the hotel I must have seen twenty pickups. "The girls like the American approach," said Jones. "Your boys dispense with preliminaries. Result: high illegitimacy." It was obvious that the blackout was a help. Long after I went to bed, I could hear the boys and girls tramping the streets, laughing and singing. I heard a boy teaching a Welsh girl "I Can't Give You Anything but Love, Baby." She seemed apt. I was eavesdropping on the active permutation of cultures; I could almost feel the graph of illegitimacy soaring. The process sounded gay.

During a trip to the Valleys, as the mining areas in Wales are called, Jones and I stopped at Merthyr Tydfil, his birthplace and the cradle of the Industrial Revolution. Jones showed me the hut in which he was born. It was one of a whole block of identical huts. He pointed out, at the corner, the privy which served the entire block. Fifty yards from these dwellings is a bronze plaque commemorating the fact that from here the world's first steam locomotive made a run of twenty-seven miles. In the middle of the nineteenth century, Jones told me, Merthyr Tydfil was one of the busiest industrial cities in the world; the products of the surrounding valleys went to every part of the globe. All one can say is that the Industrial Revolution hasn't done well by its birthplace—the eroded hills, the rows of boarded-up buildings the squalid artifacts left by succeeding generations make one wonder who got the benefits of all this. A few London mansions occupied by absentee mine owners could scarcely compensate for the scars, topographical and human, on the landscape. These hovels are the shelters of the Industrial Revolution and they are not much better than those of the current one; they're aboveground, and that's about all you can say for them. We went through village after village with shops boarded up, their districts all mined out. The inhabitants go by bus to work in war plants some distance away. What they will do after the war Jones didn't

35

know. It was through one of these villages that the Duke of Windsor made a tour when he was King. As the vistas of misery opened up before him, he muttered, "Something has to be done about this." For this mutter the people are grateful to this day. The Duke is popular in the district. " 'E was done in by the 'igher-ups," a taxi driver in Cardiff said to me. There is a decided impression, even in other parts of England, that it was not so much Mrs. Simpson as a program of social improvement, forming slowly in the Duke's conscience, that cost him his crown.

Having been in London's shelters, I can see readily why most people—at least those who have some alternative—will take their chance on being hit rather than go into them. There are three main types: surface shelters, which look like enlarged Nissen huts; shallow shelters, which vary in size and depth and are only fairly safe; and the deep shelters, of which there are five in London. Each of the last can accommodate eight thousand people. Then, of course, there are the subways, which are still favored by many. On the concrete platforms of the stations are built tiers of steel shelves somewhat like the ones used in American railway stations for checking baggage. On them you see men, women, and small children asleep with their clothes on. As a concession to light sleepers, the trains do not run after eleven-thirty at night, but no alarm clock is needed in the early morning. One morning, while I was waiting in a station for a train, I saw a little boy rather younger than my own, who is seven, lying asleep, his arm curved up over his eyes as if to shield them from the light. The train roared in. Just as I was caught in the crowd that sucked me aboard, quite in the New York fashion, I looked back at this child. The noise of the milling crowd must have penetrated the planes of sleep; he turned abruptly, huddling himself and his blanket against the glazed brick wall behind his bunk.

When I asked why people used the subways when they could use the regular shelters, which at least didn't have trains rushing through them, I was told that the subways appeal to many simply because of their safety; several of the regular shelters—that is, the surface and shallow ones—have been hit and their occupants killed. What I found most trying in all the shelters, though for the habitués it is probably a solace, was the constant blaring, through loudspeakers, of ancient records of American popular tunes: "Whispering," "Avalon," "Blue Skies." These nostalgic idyls, dinned out in incessant fortissimo, impart an atmosphere of phantasmagoria to scenes that might otherwise be merely abysmally depressing. This public music is a wartime phenomenon; the railway stations, too, have acquired the habit of playing American, or mainly American, jazz records to speed the departing trains. The raucous evocation of the melodies of the seven fat years makes the prevailing dreariness macabre; the orchestrations of "This Side of Paradise" somehow fail in their efforts to diminish the electrified gloom of the urban foxholes.

There are children who have never known any homes but shelters. A pretty young woman sat in one of them beside her baby, which was in a pram. I asked her whether she couldn't be evacuated. She said she had been but hadn't liked the place where they had sent her. "It was the noise," she said. "The place was near a bomber command and I couldn't stand the racket of the bombers making off for France." An apple-cheeked old lady smiled cheerfully at the young woman and me. Someone asked her whether she had had dinner. "Yes," she said, "I went home and cooked it in my own kitchen." "But weren't you bombed out?" "Oh, yes," she said. "The rest of the house is gone, but Jerry didn't get the kitchen." Obviously she was proud of having put one over on Jerry.

The deep shelters are amazing. They are cities hundreds of feet underground. A companion and I timed the descent to one in the lift; it took several minutes. It is planned, after the war, to use them for stations in a projected express subway system. The interminable, brightly lit corridors curving beside the endless shelves of bunks have the antiseptic horror of the German film Metropolis. These shelters are really safe. The one we

37

visited has a long bar-canteen which serves cocoa, milk, and sandwiches at nominal prices. There is a fully equipped hospital with nurses and doctors in attendance. We walked miles on concrete platforms while the loudspeakers blared "Dardanella" and "Tea for Two." We went to a lower level and visited the power room, which might serve as a sizzling, violet-lit shrine to the God Dynamo. The girl in charge manipulated switches; the immense electric bulb in the heart of an intestinal coil of lighted glass tubing changed its complexion from violet to magenta to lemon. We went to the telephone control. The operator there told us that she could instantly get in communication with the four other deep shelters.

We went up again and walked around the corridors. A good-looking, very neatly dressed man of forty was sitting on a bunk beside a boy who must have been his son, about twelve and also nicely dressed. The boy's hair was brushed smooth and he looked as if he had got himself up to visit a rich aunt. I talked to the man. He said he had lost every possession he had in the world except the clothes he and his son were wearing. They had been living in this shelter for eight months. In the morning he went to work and the boy went to school. The problem in the shelter was to get up early enough, before six-thirty, because after that hour lift service, except for the aged and crippled, stopped and there were seven hundred stairs.

We finally left the deep shelter. My companion wanted me to see still another type of shelter. I begged off. I simply couldn't stand one more. I was aware that the people in them had been standing them for over five years.

"Perhaps," an Englishwoman in the Civil Service said to me of the shelter residents, "you would have been less shocked by what you have seen if you were familiar with the peacetime homes of these people." This, of course, is a devastating comment on the civilization which the war is implacably destroying.

The transfer of great populations underground has been accomplished, but its accomplishment divides your feelings when you walk the surface of the city. At the end of their day's work, the miners in Wales, emerging with blackened faces, have their cottages to look forward to for the evening, far though they may be from the idyllic interiors of the film version of *How Green Was My Valley*. The Londoners submerge.

The Londoners submerge and sit and listen to the loudspeakers and huddle around the stoves and are patient. Their patience is rather appalling. Nor are they vindictive. They are humorous about "the Jerries." I had been told that the robot raids had changed all that, but I saw nothing to prove it. They have got used to the robots, too. The people I saw do not seem to comprehend that human beings have done this to them. They take it as they might a flood or an earthquake. The bitterness against the Germans is almost entirely confined to the articulate classes, and even among them many think that Vansittart is a crank with a "fixed idea." Compared to the English, we Americans are a very violent people indeed.

It is somehow a misstatement to say that the British are indomitable. It is rather that capitulation is a concept with which they are not equipped. Perhaps it is precisely because they depersonalize the enemy that the idea of a negotiated peace is also foreign to them. After all, you can't negotiate with a flood or an earthquake. The conditions of their life are stringent to an extent which we cannot imagine. For more than five years they have been underfed, underclothed, moving in a darkness lit only by bomb flashes and the venomous streaks of robot bombs. An American congressman from a western state made a hasty trip to England. He stayed four days. He clamored to go to France, where he stayed four more. He went back to New York, bearing the nimbus of one who has stood his ground within the sound of the guns. Upon his return, he gave a statement to the press in which he said that the English were well off, that the shop windows were full of things. One wonders what would have satisfied this congressman, exactly what deprivations he would have liked to see. For myself, I can only say that a case might be made for sending over to England our civilians instead of our soldiers. The war would last longer, but so might the peace.

IT'S
COLD AT
LADY
WINDERMERE'S

1947

ON THE FIRST LEG OF A FLIGHT
I made to England in 1946, I
exchanged consolations with the
rather sardonic Englishman who
sat next to me on the plane which
at midnight lifted us off La-
Guardia Field. I tried to comfort
him for having been unable to get
on the *Queen Elizabeth,* and he
tried to comfort me for having
been unable to wait for the *America,* which was held up by a strike.
The flaps in the backs of the

41

seats in front of us were stuffed with literature provided by American Overseas Airlines. A booklet with fancifully humorous colored sketches set forth the delights of travel on flagships. (I have yet to travel on a plane that is not a flagship.) Every phase of air travel, according to this booklet, provides a vista of delight. Even the sudden dips into air pockets, which cause some passengers to hold on tight to the arms of their seats in spasms of self-preservation, were described in this booklet as agreeable variations in the smoothness of journeys that might otherwise be tinged with monotony. The hypersensitives who are affected by these dips were put in their place. "So you mind these dips! Boo-hoo!" it said, making you feel contemptible and lily-livered. A plane is never referred to as what it is in such literature; it is always called a ship, if not a flagship, a euphemism calculated, I suppose, to convey the suggestion that the aircraft has the solidity and comfort and safety of an ocean liner. The incredibly pretty and smartly uniformed hostess came along and instructed us in putting on the gear we were to use in case the flagship foundered. She told us where to noose our heads, and just how to buckle and unbuckle, and where. "When you leave the ship . . ." she said parenthetically, making it all sound as if such a departure would, of course, be entirely voluntary and as agreeable as a stroll on deck on another, old-time kind of ship. Such is the necromancy of words and so naturally did the phrase slip off her lips that you forgot for a moment that even if you got the chance, in an emergency, to make use of this gear, "leaving the ship" would still have a certain insistence about it. The Englishman and I smiled over that as soon as the hostess had passed on to instruct other potential strollers and we had had a moment to think about it.

We exchanged a few more desultory remarks, but after that we didn't talk much. I notice that people don't converse a great deal on planes. Each passenger—except the incurably air-minded, who zestfully jump on a plane carrying newspapers with screaming headlines on the disaster of the day before—is insulated in his private concentration on the next stop. Ours was in Gander, in Newfoundland, at four o'clock in the morning. It is very cold in Gander, in Newfoundland, at four o'clock in the morning. We huddled in the newly built, neon-lit terminal—I wonder why the airplane companies don't call it a dock—and had coffee and cold sandwiches. At five, in a steely dawn, we mariners boarded the ship again and were soon looking down at the swamps and fens of Newfoundland. These changed into cloud formations, through an occasional rift in which we caught a glimpse of the Atlantic. For the next twelve and a half hours, we passed over cloud formations, and I submit that after five minutes of it, nothing is more dull and inhuman than a cloud formation. A certain reserve formed between the Englishman and myself, caused, I believe, by nothing more specific than that we were shipmates. We kept getting bulletins from the pilothouse—that we were so-and-so many feet higher or lower, that we were slowing up because of headwinds, or perhaps tail winds. Anyway, we were going to be late getting into Shannon, in Ireland. It was also announced that, owing to weather conditions in London, we were to spend the night in Ireland, in an inn at which accommodations were to be provided by the company.

As we approached Shannon, at around 9 P.M., my neighbor brightened perceptibly and we resumed the cordial relations of the night before. "I advise you," he said, "to feed well in Ireland. Stoke up, because you'll get nothing to eat in England." He paused for a moment and then as an afterthought gave me another piece of advice: "Take plenty of matches from the plane. The hostess will give them to you. They'll come in handy in London, where they're next to impossible to get." He paused for another moment and added, by way of explanation, "You see, we won the war." This phrase, "We won the war," uttered with various degrees of ironic intonation, was one that I was to hear repeatedly, like a refrain in Poe, for the three months of my stay in England. It was said to me by hotel clerks, porters, taxidrivers, doctors, businessmen, stage stars, Members of Parliament, economists, novelists, editors. One of the times I heard it was at Claridge's, where I stayed while I was in London. I had been told that though you could not get fruit or eggs or bacon for breakfast in England, you could get kippers. My first morning there, I ordered kippers. They looked like kippers, but they tasted funny. I asked the waiter about it. He explained to me wearily (he must have done it often before) that kippers are no longer smoked. Smoking kippers takes fuel and there is no fuel for smoking kippers. These had therefore been dipped in a chemical that gave them the appearance of having been smoked. "You see," he said, "we won the war."

A well-known English woman novelist came to lunch with me at the hotel. She ate my lunch as well as her own, which I was very happy to let her do; the quality of the food was such that forgoing it was a negligible sacrifice. She told me about the improvisations of housekeeping in Britain at present. She has to baste her meat—when she gets any—with mineral oil, which formerly she had used to cure her dog of constipation. She gibed at me. "What do they know of England who only Claridge's know?" she said. As she is an extremely good friend of mine, she did not feel that she had to moderate her feeling about Americans, to whom, under less abnormal conditions, she is devoted. "We would almost rather have cut our throats," she said, "than have accepted the loan. But we had to accept it. And the effrontery of your politicians in telling us what to do in the Middle East about complications of which they know nothing!" She is one of the fairest and kindest and most acute and best-informed people I know, but now, perhaps because she was overtired and hungry, she was bitter. During the war she had worked incessantly, going out on small boats in mined waters to get material for articles for the British Ministry of Information. The Manchester *Guardian,* which before the war used to pay her twenty-five pounds for an article, now pays her two. Her reward, she felt, as well as the reward of England, is mineral oil at home and being misunderstood by overfed Americans. "You see," she said, finally, "we won the war."

After lunch with a friend in his house at Hampstead Heath, where the talk was warm and brilliant but the atmosphere was distinctly cold, I got back to my hotel with a chill and a fever. I had been aware for some time that I was inadequately dressed for the British climate. Instead of a dinner jacket, I should have brought heavy underwear. Unless you have been in England two months, you can't get a ration book, and I hadn't been there that long, so I couldn't buy any underwear, or even a handkerchief. The hotel doctor put me to bed and left me a prescription. "Can't you prescribe some heavy underwear for me instead of these medicines?" I asked him. "I do not issue that sort of prescription," he said, somewhat loftily. But a moment later, as he picked up his kit and started to leave, he softened a little. "I quite appreciate your difficulty," he said. "You see, we won the war."

In the Caledonian Hotel, in Edinburgh, when I got into an ice-cold room after an appalling journey from Blackpool on three unheated trains on a blizzardy day, I rang for the porter and asked him if I couldn't have a fire in the grate. "Sorry, sir," he said. "No coal." And as he left the room, he turned to give me the reiterated explanation: "You see, we won the war."

Another day at Claridge's, breakfast and lunch having been unsatisfactory, I ordered tea and pastry. I bit confidently into a little pastry skiff, which unexpectedly revealed the quality of a dreadnought, with the result that I broke a tooth on her. When I explained to the dentist what had happened, he made a hearty joke about the sturdiness of the Claridge confectionery, and as he braced himself with his pliers to extract what remained of my tooth, he let me have the theme song.

At the Shannon Airport restaurant, where all the passengers from our ship herded together at one table, we had a hearty enough dinner. My prime objection to airplane travel for long journeys is the absence of privacy. It is like being on the subway for thirty hours, except that there is nothing to hang on to when you feel like getting up to stretch your legs. Even at our airport dinner, the maritime powers who ran this particular excursion were determined not to let any of us slip off by ourselves. And now, in obedience to some further caprice of theirs, we could not go to our inn—the Dunraven Arms, in Adare, twenty-five miles away—until long after midnight, because there was no immediate transportation, but we could not leave the airport, either, because the bus that was to take us to Adare was expected at any minute.

When, finally, the bus came, I sat next to the young driver, with whom I got into conversation. I wanted some information about the lady called "the Countess," who is the proprietor of the Dunraven Arms and about whom I had heard many stories during the war. But this Irishman had an extraordinary (perhaps an ordinary) idiosyncrasy: he knew "the Countess" and started to tell me about her, but after a sentence or two he managed to lose her in a general denunciation of England. His agility in this respect was astonishing. No matter what I tried him on—his working hours, unionization in Ireland, unemployment, which movies he preferred—it all came to the same thing: what England had done to Ireland, as far back as the sixteenth century. I got him off on Mayor O'Dwyer for a minute, but even Mayor O'Dwyer, at the mention of whose name his eyes lit up, somehow led right into the Battle of the Boyne. I had the feeling that on a longer journey this young man might develop into a bore. We reached the Dunraven Arms at 1:30 A.M. I was assigned a room with two other passengers, and as we got between the icy sheets, the room was filled with humorous expletives from the pampered Americans. We were awakened at six and trundled back to Shannon, where a terrific breakfast awaited us—porridge and heavy cream and eggs. So fortified, we got aboard our ship again.

Over London, there was a thick mist. The pilot circled the airport for about half an hour; he seemed to be changing his mind all the time—another of those breaks in the monotony provided gratis by the company. During this prolonged vacillation, the hostess approached me—a new hostess but of the same immaculately handsome type that seems to have been evolved for this purpose. "We are going to land by instrument," she said quietly. Whether I was expected to derive comfort or apprehension from this faintly Caesarean prophecy, I did not know, but ten minutes later I had landed by instrument. I remembered my English friend's advice of the night before and, from a tray offered by the hostess, stuffed my pockets with match books that blazoned a picture of a flagship. Then I stepped out into the cold drizzle of Heathrow.

The driver who taxied me to my hotel was, like his opposite number in New York, willing to talk, and he began without preamble. "Except for the blackout and the bombing, we're worse off than we were during the war," he said. "No housing, no food you can eat, and nothing to buy with what you're paid." I said that somebody must be satisfied, because the Government was winning all the by-elections. He chose to ignore this interruption and went on to inventory his grievances. He spoke scornfully of the industrial exhibition then current at the Victoria and Albert Museum and of its slogan, "Britain Can Make It." "Yes," he said, "Britain can make it, but Britain can't buy it." He was the first person to make this stock remark to me, as well as to quote to me a doggerel that, he claimed, was framed above the empty display bottles in his favorite pub:

No beer, no ale, no stout.
You got 'em in, now you get 'em out.

Fair-minded Conservatives, when I pinned them down to it, told me that Churchill couldn't have done much better than Attlee, except, possibly, to be less pedantic about petty restrictions, but this driver, a Labourite, was quite intolerant. At least, I thought he was. I was warned later to discount the grumblings against the Government that I might hear from waiters, taxicab drivers, and hotel valets. I was told that they grumble so vociferously because they think their capitalist customers like to hear it, just as, during the Roosevelt election campaigns in the United States, taxidrivers would assure their presumably Republican patrons that they were voting for Willkie or Dewey. But on this first day in England I naïvely took my driver at his many words. While he droned on pessimistically, I looked out through the drizzle at the city I hadn't seen since 1944, when the V-2s were falling. The bombed-out parts looked about as before, boarded up, with rank grass growing in them. The oblong tanks that were then full of water for use during incendiary raids were still there, but now they were empty, and looked like swimming pools on estates in the wintertime. Grosvenor Square, which was the heartland of the late American occupation and which is where the controversial statue of F.D.R. is to stand, was quite changed; the American jeeps and war gear were no longer there. I asked the driver to go out of his way a bit and drive me by Piccadilly Circus. I wanted to see if the winged and beckoning Eros, who had disappeared when I was there in 1944, was back on his pedestal. He was still not there; the pedestal on which he had stood, in an attitude of taking off, as if on a mission to shed his special commodity over a world famished for lack of it, was still topped, rather lamely, by an octagonal wooden shed. One knows that this essential boy is safely poised somewhere else, but the illusion that he is inside the octagon, beating his wings painfully against it to be free, is inescapable. In the cleverest of the London revues, called *Sweetest and Lowest,* there is an entertaining skit on the nostalgia evoked by the absence of the god. The scene shows Piccadilly Circus with an assortment of characters strolling about—bobbies, ladies of the town, flower girls, and nursemaids. A sailor, back from overseas, comes looking for a stenographer with whom he had been in love before he left. He finds his girl and they begin where they left off, but something is lacking. It suddenly strikes them that it is the sympathetic Eros; all the others, even the ladies of the town, feel that a key inspiration is lacking. They sing:

Let's have Eros
Near us,
Just to cheer us,
In the center of the center of the world.

At the end of the skit, the mass wish-dream produces results; the wooden box flies open and the most fetching blonde in the show pops out. The actors (and the audience) accept this apparition—despite the change of sex—as the real thing, and almost instantaneously the moonstruck sailor is able to make a satisfactory adjustment with his girl. As the cab went down Regent Street, I realized that my driver, unaware that he had not held my attention, was still droning on about his deprivations. "Well," he said by way of summary as we drew up in front of the hotel, "you know, we won the war."

At LaGuardia Field, I had paid a hundred and twenty dollars' excess fare because I was carrying a good bit of canned food— orange juice, sardines, salmon, and so on. I thought that the least I could do for the kind Londoner who had invited me to share his apartment, in a hotel where it is very difficult to get a room, was to put this cache of food on his desk before settling down. My host, not to be outdone, asked me if I wouldn't dine in the apartment with him. There was to be an ex-Cabinet member and the attractive daughter of an ex-Prime Minister. I thanked him but declined. Landing by instrument had exhausted me and I was fit only for bed. The next morning, I asked the waiter for some of my orange juice. He retired to the apartment's "fridge" and came back to report that there was no orange juice. In fact, all my canned food had disappeared. The exes and the other guests had taken it away the night before. "I knew that if you had seen their expressions when they saw this heap of food," my host said, "you would have said to them, 'Take it away.' That is what I said." And yet, in this famished country, a strong and

49

steady protest is being made that not enough food is being sent from England to the starving people in Germany and Central Europe.

There is a popular superstition in America that English people don't mind the cold. Of course, their climate, which is of such consistent inclemency that it staggers metaphor, has inured them to rigors that would (and do) knock Americans out. As for the present fuel crisis, the Labour Government gambled on the weather and lost. To gamble on the weather in England represents a high degree of optimism. Although the English are tougher than we are and can stand what we can't, they have nevertheless suffered acutely from the cold this winter. A play I'd written was going to be put on in London, and the leading light comedian of England, who was going to appear in it, rang me up to make a lunch date. "I can't invite you to my flat," he said, "because I have no heat. I can't invite you to my club, because it is unheated too. Where shall we lunch?" I asked him to the hotel. He came into my rooms and made at once, beaming, for the electric heater. Bending over to rub his hands in front of it, he said, "This is luxury. There is no other room in England as warm as this." By American standards, the room wasn't warm at all. In fact, you had to keep pretty close to the heater not to shiver. In my bedroom, there was a thing called panel heating. One rather slender wall panel, behind which were alleged hot-water pipes, was supposed to heat the room. It sounded like Niagara all night, but it didn't do much else. (My host walked in on me one afternoon to find me sitting with my shoes off and the soles of my feet pressed against the tepid wall. "What on earth are you doing?" he asked. "I am trying to keep my feet warm," I said with dignity.) The light comedian and I had a jolly lunch, and after it was over, he said, "I am going to ask you something and I hope you will be frank with me and tell me plainly if I am asking too much." He wanted to know if I would mind if he just sat there for a couple of hours. He smiled

50

ironically. "My house has authentic Georgian panelling," he said, "but it is bitter cold." When he finally left, several hours later, he had the air of one who is checking out of Elysium.

Another superstition among Americans concerns the London fog. They regard it as an agreeable pastel, softening ugly contours—a subject for popular songs and romantic plays. One of George Gershwin's last songs, "A Foggy Day in London Town," had Fred Astaire wandering dreamily through one, swinging a stick and confiding his melancholy to its cozy swathings. In one of the most popular plays of my youth, an English importation by Hubert Henry Davies called *Outcast,* there was, as I remember it, a nasty fog outside the set. Out of its amber depths, it yielded a glamorous lady of the night, Elsie Ferguson. For many years, I thought of the London fog as a warmly enveloping medium in which you strolled in an Inverness cape and from which, with passable luck, you might emerge with Elsie Ferguson. Actually, the London fog is paralyzing and murderous. At its mildest, it merely keeps people away from home all night who have been unlucky enough to start out in its early stages. One evening, I invited a lady to dinner. She was late, and explained that the fog had forced her taxi to go very slowly. The lights of London, ordinarily visible from the hotel windows, had disappeared; a thick-textured, almost tangible substance pressed against them, obscuring everything. At midnight, my friend suggested that perhaps she had better go. I went to the telephone and called down to the hall porter and asked for a taxi. He laughed at me. "No taxis tonight, sir," he said. "People who have left the hotel for the evening can't get back." An hour later, my guest went to the telephone herself to call a private driver who, she said, never let her down. I heard this loyal driver's apology over the telephone: "Sorry, Madam, it is too dangerous tonight for passenger and driver." The difficulty was ended, at 2 A.M., by my calling downstairs for a room. As my guest was known to the hotel people, they stretched a point and consented to let her have a room belonging to a guest who was stranded somewhere

51

else. A few formalities ensued: the porter came up with the elaborate form that has to be filled out by all hotel guests; when he asked for baggage, my friend ceremoniously offered him her handbag.

The next day, the papers reported assorted incidents. There had been a motor block all night near a bridge. It was not discovered until morning that the car at the head of the block had no driver. Deciding that it was useless to try to go on, he had abandoned his car and ventured off afoot to find some place to spend the night. In another instance, a man and his wife had driven from their place in the country to Southampton to meet some friends arriving from India. By the time the passengers had disembarked, the fog was thick, but the reunion took place. The newly arrived passengers got into the car. The driver started off, trusting to instinct, since his headlights availed him nothing. He drove his car off the dock. Everyone in it was drowned.

The fog penetrates into hotel lobbies, museums, theatres. Mary Martin, who is playing in Noel Coward's South Seas operetta, *Pacific 1860,* told me what it was like to stand in the great, windy spaces of the stage of the Drury Lane, singing tropical ditties on a foggy London night. "You sing not at an audience but into a haze," she said. "You shiver and sing." Rather desperately, I gathered. But the fog is only a modest hazard compared to the more exacting cold. As the consequence of having to walk on blithely every night in a summer dress, swinging a sunshade, against a background of Miss Gladys Calthrop's gracefully bending palm trees, another actress in Miss Martin's company suffered from frostbite on one leg. Can this be the first case of the kind on record? Some girls in the same company had attacks of nausea —a surprising reaction to cold. The audiences are better off than the actors, because they are able to take their eiderdowns off their beds and bring them to the theatres. Couples snuggle up together in their quilts to watch the play, somewhat the way their ancestors who colonized Massachusetts Bay bundled up on winter nights and settled down for less detached diversions.

52

To rehearse a play this winter in England requires a hardihood our actors are never called upon to display. The first rehearsal of my play took place in the Haymarket, one of the loveliest and most distinguished theatres in Europe. *Lady Windermere's Fan* has been playing there for more than a year. In the gold and ivory and crimson damask of Lady Windermere's drawing room sat my company, muffled to the ears, mittened and hatted and booted, looking as if it were engaged in a performance of *Icebound,* Owen Davis's dour play about New England. But the agony of rehearsing in cold theatres is nothing compared to the ordeal of the actual performances. At the rehearsals, the actors can wrap themselves up any way they like; at the performances, they must dress and behave to create the illusion that whatever unresolved problems they may be wrestling with do not concern fuel. Every night, in *Lady Windermere's Fan,* Mrs. Erlynne protects her daughter, but not from the cold!

Against the star of my own play, Miss Yvonne Arnaud, I committed the unintentional sadism of requiring her, in Act II, to appear in formal evening dress. Women in the stalls no longer wear evening dress, but I was told by everybody that the English audiences love to see such clothes on the stage, because it is for them simultaneously a reminder of an amenity that is gone and an augury that it may come again. We opened on New Year's Eve in Blackpool, an indescribable year-round pleasure resort in the north of England. As I watched the folk from Liverpool and Manchester being ushered into their unheated hotel rooms on the last day of the old year, I wondered that any one should subject himself to this kind of holiday of his own volition. When I went into Miss Arnaud's dressing room after the opening performance, the first thing she said to me was "I cannot tell you what it was to go out on that stage with my shoulders bare. I thought the audience would see them shaking." For subsequent performances, a casual scarf was provided for Miss Arnaud, but I never watched her make that entrance again—in Blackpool, in Edinburgh, or in London—without suffering a twinge of remorse.

While we were in Edinburgh, a fascinatingly beautiful, black city, I dropped in, without being invited especially, at John Knox's house. It is the oldest still-inhabited (though only by the caretaker) house in Scotland. I was rewarded for my courtesy. I climbed up the ancient but firm stairs to John Knox's study, an unbelievably tiny room—no bigger than a good-sized closet—whose leaded windows look down on the High Street, from which the rebels fired up three times at him. I could see how wise the eminent divine had been to make this room his study; with his mantling beard and his books, he must have been fairly warm in it. But now it had an electric heater besides, the only one in the house, and the room was so comfortably warm that I felt like remaining there myself to study.

The new London theatre hours, which were made necessary by the blackout emergency during the war, when audiences had to be on the way home before it was too dark to find the curb, have apparently come to stay. Evening performances of plays begin at six-fifteen, six-thirty, or at seven. On Saturday, many theatres have their matinées at four or four-thirty, so the evening performances start very soon after the curtain has fallen on the matinée; the actors say they feel like the drudges of the old five-a-day vaudeville houses. The managers are in favor of keeping these hours, because through them they have tapped an entirely new theatre public. It is an upper-bracket working and white-collar public for the stalls, a graded-down one for the balconies. Less and less do the theatres depend on the smart, formerly rich upper classes, who now have all they can do to keep their country places going. The new theatregoers have a cup of tea, or a sandwich, when they leave their offices or shops, make the theatre handily, and then go home by Underground or suburban train for supper and the good night's sleep that the nine-o'clock final curtain permits them.

Not only are the upper classes no longer depended upon to buy theatre tickets; they are no longer called upon for leadership.

54

It is the general belief that the Conservative Party is not likely to return to power, and that if it should, the change will amount to a counter-revolution—a counter-revolution, to paraphrase Harold Laski's familiar phrase, by dissent. The Government is determined quietly to tax the upper classes out of existence, and the process is going along swiftly. There are a great many people who still live on their country places in something of the old style, but they do it by selling other country places, or parts of the ones they're on, or pictures. There is no capital-gains tax in England, which has given some businessmen a certain leeway, but I was told that it is coming. The proprietor of an estate which his family has owned for a hundred years, and on which he provides cottages for young writers and other needy, was able to get some belated repairs done on his house only because, in addition to making them, he proposed to build some flats to house workers on the estate. This proprietor, a brilliant Oxonian and a war hero, descanted mournfully on the role of the country house in English history and English life. Rather sadly, he quoted Walter Bagehot, who said, "Toryism is enjoyment." Presumably, and paradoxically, it is the ambition of the Labour Government to make Toryism, under this definition, more pervasive.

A large number of the upper-class English want to emigrate. They suffer from an accumulated claustrophobia which started during the war. This group may be divided into two categories: those who want to get away willy-nilly and are thinking constantly of means to effect their escape, and those who want to go and could manage it but won't think of doing so until things begin to look up for England. The coherence of the mighty, unified effort, and the gaiety and gallantry in ever-present danger, that were characteristic of wartime England have largely vanished. "We knew the war would have to end one day," a lift man said to me. "We don't know when this will end." Many of the English apologize to you for the disappearance of their traditional politeness, but if they have become impolite, it is by their standards, not by ours. The service on the *Queen Elizabeth* is still impeccable. (A New Yorker who returned to the United States on the *America* told me that he knew he was back in the Land of the Free when he and his wife boarded the ship at Southampton. In a corridor, along which they were wandering in an effort to find their cabin, his wife asked a steward where M-44 was. The steward jerked his thumb toward a diagram on the wall and said flatteringly, "You can read, can't you?") It is nevertheless true that a certain good feeling has gone out of English life. There is resentment, envy, and even hatred between the classes. In the East End of London, there is hatred of the West End. The Conservatives say that the Labour Government has deliberately fostered this interclass animosity. The upper classes find that the servant class is no longer as reliable as it used to be. "I cannot tell you the effort it takes to give even a small dinner party for six people," said a normally hospitable London hostess. "I have to prepare for it weeks in advance. For one thing, my cook refuses to stand in the queue for the rations, so I have to do it myself." In a certain hotel patronized by Americans, the waiters are frankly resentful because the guests are in a position to press buttons to summon them. Many years ago, when I was crossing on an English ship, the purser energetically defended the caste system to me. "I believe in being governed by my betters," he said. The belief in "betters" seems no longer to exist, a fact that leaves the mass of the people free to denounce not only the defeated Conservatives but their own victorious leaders. Leadership itself is suspect.

There is even—and this I had never heard before in England —open grumbling against the King and Queen. In a crowded compartment of the *Flying Scotsman,* going from Edinburgh to London, six of us sat around in overcoats, gloves, and mufflers. In the corridor stood several airmen who had got on at Newcastle and were complaining because they had bought first-class tickets and there were not enough seats for all of them. One of them, smiling and saying wryly, "Democracy!" tossed a copy of an illustrated weekly magazine to a companion who had been lucky enough to squeeze into our compartment. The magazine was opened to a double-page layout of colored photographs of the train that was to transport the King and his family through South Africa. The airman in our compartment studied the pictures—the Queen's robin's-egg-blue bedroom, the King's study—and handed the magazine around, making humorous comparisons with the conditions on our train. It is, however, also true that when the Queen, a woman of immense charm and friendliness, attends a matinée, the streets around the theatre are badly congested with admirers who want to watch her come out. Nevertheless, when the King and Queen visited Oxford recently to attend a quadricentennial celebration at one of the colleges, there were audible murmurs of disapproval in the streets when they passed through in procession. It was particularly striking that this could have taken place in Oxford; had it happened in a proletarian town, like Glasgow, it would have been less surprising.

It is frightening to think that the amenities of civilization require for their sustenance certain margins of surplus, not only in material goods and money but in vital energy and sense of security. In England, all these margins have been noticeably narrowed, but, fundamentally, kindliness and gentleness and the sense of the inviolability of basic human rights are so imbedded in custom and national memory that one still feels that these rights are safer in England than they are anywhere else in the world. In America, violence always seems nearer the surface; there is the tendency to settle an argument with fists, or even with a gun or a rope. While the American visitor is conscious of an inter-class exacerbation in England, he cannot but reflect upon how much more intense this exacerbation would be in the United States if the margins had been pared down as far as they have in England. In our "Brother, Can You Spare a Dime?" era, the majority of our people were still getting along pretty well, and yet jagged and ugly intolerances and hatred jutted up through the thin crust of our good manners. In England, the impoverishment

57

affects everybody. "To come from New York to London now," an Englishman said to me, "is, as far as the standard of living is concerned, like going from London to Belgrade before the first World War." This is true, and yet one feels, as surely as ever, that the traditional decency and fairness and orderliness among the ordinary people of England make unthinkable some of the excesses that are commonplaces in this country, even at a moment when our own prosperity is relatively overwhelming.

In spite of the grumbling, the anger, the indignation against the Labour Government, in spite of the charges of inefficiency and a congenital incapacity to plan among the planners, there is a solid basis for the continuing victories of the Labour Party in the by-elections. The great mass of the people feels that it is better off than it ever was before. The people love, for example, the prefabricated houses provided by the Government. A Conservative who had told me, the last time I was in England, that the workers would never accept these prefabs now cheerfully admits that he was wrong. The housewives are enthusiastic about the gadgets in these structures; they reduce housework. The houses are, of course, cramped, but they are cozy and they are easy to warm. Opponents of the Government call this bribing the masses; the masses accept the bribes unashamedly. The Conservatives, like my defeatist taxidriver, say also that the increased wages in the lower brackets are illusory, because there is nothing to buy with the money; the recipients are content with the illusion. Milk, which is practically unobtainable in the hotels and restaurants, is practically unobtainable because the children of the poor are getting it. The children of the poor get half a pint of free milk at school every day. With the illusory extra wages these same people buy oranges and grapes and even pineapples. I am told that the diet of this group has been enriched by things they never knew before the war. They are aware, also, that the Government's long-range plans (whether they will ever materialize or not) are concerned with the general amelioration of their

58

lot. They can hope, for example, that their children will attend the great public schools—Eton, Harrow, and Winchester—because the Government is planning to convert these closed preserves into schools that may be entered by competition. Altogether, the evidence is unmistakable that the mass of the people knows on which side its bread is buttered.

The upper classes feel themselves sliding toward the abyss and the middle classes grouse, but there is a high enthusiasm for England's destiny among the young and rebellious Parliamentarians. They see an England that, almost alone in the world between the coverging colossi of Russian Communism and American Capitalism, will keep alive the free, inquiring, individual, humanistic spirit. They are not the least bit interested in preserving the British Empire; in fact, they are intent on liquidating it. And when you talk to them, you see that they are animated by a belief that there is imminent a new and liberating renaissance for the creative impulse in man, as heady as the winds that blew on Shakespeare and Milton. They see, without being in the least pompous about it, an England emerging from a series of temporary crises, an England that will never succumb to a totalitarianism of either the Right or the Left and that will perpetuate its best traditions.

Meanwhile, to visit England now is like going to stay with honorable, incorruptible, highly cultivated, extremely poor relations. I have heard critics of Churchill say that he is responsible for England's plight because he tried constantly to pull, and somewhat grandiosely succeeded, more than England's weight in the war—a criticism that would sound strange in the ears of an American chauvinist of the "England expects every American" school. These critics say that Churchill acted on the assumption that England was a first-class power, whereas she wasn't, and they also criticize Bevin for acting on the same premise and keeping abroad British soldiers who could be home mining coal. Others, considering poverty, as Bernard Shaw does, the ultimate sin, say flatly that England should have fought neither of the

German wars. Still others rail at the patience of the English people. The English will stand for anything, they say, and out of stubbornness won't complain. Often this anger of Englishmen at English docility has a partisan tinge: the complainers cannot endure patience with government regulations they themselves are weary of. What is extraordinary, amid all these bewildering crosscurrents, is the continuing and pervading preoccupation of the people of England with music, the theatre, and art. A prime example was the great exhibition of the King's pictures recently held at Burlington House. It was a glorious collection of more than five hundred paintings that have belonged to the Crown since the fifteenth century. The attendance at this exhibition was enormous. It is inconceivable that Americans would come in such crowds, day after day and month after month, to look at pictures in a building as frigid as Burlington House was. One shuddered for the nymphs. The love of the British for the theatre, too, must be an emotion more intense than ours. Bundled in their overcoats and eiderdowns, they sit with their feet on hot-water bottles and watch *King Lear, The Alchemist, Antony and Cleopatra,* the complete *Back to Methuselah,* and *The Master Builder.* The concert halls and opera houses and ballet theatres are equally crowded, and equally cold. I went to a concert in Usher Hall, in Edinburgh. A Russian pianist sat down to play a concerto. Never had I seen a pianist massage his hands for so preternaturally long a time before beginning. I looked around me at the audience during this extended interval, and many of its members were doing the same thing.

On the night before I left London for America, I attended a dress rehearsal of my play. The theatre was so cold and my fingers so stiff that I couldn't use a pencil to make notes until I put on mittens, which didn't help the legibility of my writing. When I came out of the theatre, the blizzard that was to initiate the winter's great fuel crisis had started. The next morning, I drove to Waterloo Station through rising snowdrifts. London, which I

60

had never seen under snow before, looked singularly beautiful; the soft gray masonry became impalpable through the haze of the gently falling, lethal flakes. Soundlessly, gently, they ushered in the Second Battle of Britain, outmaneuvering the Government in its gamble on the weather. At Waterloo Station, the loud-speaker announced that, owing to a frozen engine, the boat train would be delayed. It was held up nearly three hours. My companions and I stood about, stamping our feet, then went into the waiting room and drank a tepid liquid humorously called coffee. The train was unheated. We walked about in it to keep our circulation going. We ordered Scotch and soda. The soda came frozen solid in the bottle. Some children laughed at our efforts to shake out a few drops. But, as everything ends, this journey ended, too, and presently we were on the *Elizabeth,* her decks drifted with snow. I got into my tiny inside cabin, mercifully no bigger than John Knox's study. It was warm. An electric heater was going great guns. In ecstatic relief, I sat down before the fire and took off my shoes.

. . . .
. . . .
. . . .
. . . .

Characters

. . . .
. . . .

. . . .
. . . .
. . . .
. . . .
. . . .
. . . .
. . . .
. . . .
. . . .
. . . .
. . . .

"LET
HER
BRING ME
YES!"

Gabriel Pascal and Bernard Shaw

1965, 1943

THE APOCRYPHA OF THE FIRST
encounter between Gabriel Pascal
and George Bernard Shaw are as
various as the accounts of other
miracles. They are practically in-
finite, even the modulations admitted in varying moods by Pascal
himself. And yet, from the whirl-
ing sediment of rumor, there appears to settle a fairly safe precipi-
tate of fact. For thirty years Shaw

had been beseiged for the film rights to his plays. To one of the Hollywood bigwigs who sent Shaw an interminable, exquisitely composed, telegram describing his qualifications to put Shaw on the screen, the successor to Voltaire replied by cable: "Your telegram is too literary. It is obvious that your aspirations would conflict with mine. I am the literary man. Besides, the costly and unnecessary length of your cable convinces me that you are a poor businessman and I want a good businessman." These caustic flirtations went on for years. The classic one, probably, is the famous meeting with Goldwyn which is reported to have ended on a psychological impasse, Shaw observing: "The trouble is, Mr. Goldwyn, you are interested in art, whereas I am interested in money."

But where the world failed, Pascal succeeded. The explanations for Shaw's capitulation to Pascal eddy dizzily between outright hypnosis to the implication that Shaw, in his old age, had gone mystic and was subject to spells and incantations. Shaw's later letters, especially on the subject of money, belie any such softening. Allowing for jealous detraction and for the opalescent imagination of Pascal himself, it is possible to collate a synthesis about as follows: In the summer of 1925 Pascal found himself at Cap d'Antibes on the French Riviera, opulently established there, in his own chaste description, "with a great harem." He was married at the time to the Italian film star Maria Carmi, who was, evidently, tolerant. A child of nature, Pascal preferred bathing in the nude, and in order not to titillate unduly the sensibilities of more prudish visitors, he took his swims at dawn. One morning, cleaving the waters beside him, he beheld a white beard belonging to a more celebrated nudist. The following conversation took place:

PASCAL: Very pleased to meet you, Mr. Shaw. You and I are the only ones who understand bathing natural.
GBS: Who are you?
PASCAL: I am Gabriel Pascal and I make films.
GBS: That doesn't interest me.

PASCAL: But I am the Tsar of the Italian Film Industry and married to the leading Italian film star.

GBS: These are not occupations for a man of talent. One day you will be hard up. Come to see me.

With that the older nudist swam away, leaving Pascal alone to fulfill the prophecy. This took quite a little while, rather more than the seven lean years allotted by Joseph. The great harem, the film star wife, the Italian career itself, evanesced with the suddenness of earthly glory. Pascal approached France, not tentatively, but with the expansive and headlong optimism which was perhaps his most engaging characteristic. In France there were great doings. There was talk of pyramidal deals soaring into millions of francs. But it never got beyond talk. And though you may accomplish many things without money, the making of films is not one of them. Undaunted, Pascal shed the radiance of his personality, which gleamed like a great, black opal, over Sweden. In Stockholm, with his advent, there occurred that agitation and flurry, that heady sense of the momentous impending, which Pascal managed to generate wherever he found himself. But again there was no money. Pascal went to Holland, summoned by the agents of the Munitions King, Sir Basil Zaharoff.

In Amsterdam things went rather better, at least on paper. Sir Basil wanted to send Pascal to make idealistic films in China. This appealed to Gabby but, as a side-chore, Sir Basil's agents wanted him to circumvent the machinations in China of Generals Seeckt and von List, two formidable men. The Generals, they felt, would be pie for Pascal. But, Pascal told them: "If I want be adventurer I go for myself adventure." A lone eagle, he did not cherish other people's adventures. He refused to make films in China. The sinister Zaharoffites kept him a prisoner in his hotel, practically starving—an experience to which Pascal was not unaccustomed, even without Zaharoffites. He began to suspect the motives of these agents: "They would have masacrated me," he said nostalgically. When they saw that he was adamant

67

about China, they made him a counteroffer: They would put millions at his disposal to make films in Spain. "Fine," said Pascal, "I go." But here, too, there was a catch! While he was making the Spanish films would he also undertake to reconcile the King and Queen of Spain, who were on the outs? Pascal, who was just emerging from the pain of his own domestic difficulties with Maria Carmi, did not want to get embroiled with other couples. He refused again and, in the dead of night, escaped from his hotel. As one got to know Pascal, one became aware that there were few hotels from which he had not escaped.

He escaped to London. There he sketched ambitious projects, manipulated, all cheerfully, radiantly, with no sense of hurry or desperation. The film world knows when a man is broke, but Pascal, though the self-appointed genius of the film world, did not appear to suspect it himself. In this respect he was like the traditional cuckold living behind the strong moat of his own ignorance. This faculty of his was remarkable. One day Pascal came to lunch with me in my hotel room in New York. He deprecated the food, the service, the mise en scène. "This is not place for you," he admonished. "Tomorrow I take you to lunch with the President of Sherry-Netherland. *That* is hotel for you! I introduce you to the President and the President he will fix you up." The next day the lunch took place. The President, it turned out, was a classmate of mine at college. We had a nice reunion. The President was seemingly on the coziest terms with Pascal and I moved to the Sherry-Netherland so that Pascal would be more comfortable when he came to see me. But vague queries formed in my mind. Why did not Pascal himself, the President's so-close friend, take advantage of these superior luxuries? It took only a surface inquiry to reveal that Pascal had indeed lived there and that the hotel was even now holding his trunks. But Pascal, who was extremely generous when in the money, was even more generous when out of it. Dining in the Oak Room at the Plaza with a writer whose fortune he was undertaking to stratosphere to undreamed of heights and whose guest he was, he beheld the shambling figure of an outmoded theatrical director sitting vacantly in the corridor waiting for something to turn up. Pascal's host murmured something commiseratory about the luckless director. "Let him not worry," said Pascal, whose concern was more practical, "I produce him a very rich man. In the meanwhile do you mind if I bring him over for a cup of coffee?"

One day Pascal had an illumination. He remembered his meeting with a fellow nudist in the blue waters of the Mediterranean and he decided to go to see him. He astonished the next friend he met by asking for a loan of five pounds, a sum too microscopic for the vision of a man who looks at life through great Maecenian lenses. The man gave Pascal the five pound note and walked away with an indescribable sense of having pulled off a wonderful deal. Pascal took the five pounds, went to the Savoy barber shop for a shave, took a room, had a bath and his suit pressed, hailed a taxi and royally ordered the cabby to Number Four Whitehall Court, then the most famous address in Europe after Ten Downing Street.

Could Shaw have had a sense in the Mediterranean that Pascal was his man? Whatever may have been in Shaw's mind then, he must have reached a decision when he saw Pascal with his clothes on. Pascal told Shaw he wanted the exclusive screen rights to his plays, that he was the one man in the world who best understood them, that he was the only man in the world who would put them on the screen without vulgarizing them. In detail and in panorama, he sketched for Shaw the story of his life: his early days as a cadet in Hungary; his desire then to act, a failing shared by Shakespeare, (this appealed to a man who was very sensitive to Shakespeare's failings); his career as a hussar and as a Captain of Cavalry. Which version of himself he gave Shaw at this meeting one does not know, but they are all fascinating and it is not difficult to understand that Shaw, who was a collector of originals, was enchanted.

The mesmeric Pascal was short, thick-set, swarthy, with great dark eyes that remained solemn while recounting the most fabulous adventures. Shaw, in a letter reproaching Pascal for being impressed with a speech by Anthony Eden, says sarcastically that "it would take a Magyar militarist aristocrat like you to be taken in by a speech like that." Actually Pascal did not suggest the Magyar militarist aristocrat, nor the Cavalry officer nor the hussar. He may have been all of these things but what he looked like and talked like and lived like was a gypsy. A lady of his acquaintance said of him: "You feel sure that his ears must be pierced for rings."

Pascal had immense geniality and genuine good will, toward himself and toward the world. His belief in his own legend was child-like and engaging. From the magic carpet of his past he was fond of recounting what he called "lovely episodes." With which did he regale Shaw? Did he tell him, in his incomparable English, how he became one of the legendary heroes of the cavalry in Russia where he was on patrol duty in the first World War? He was adored, he admits, by the Russian population. Did he tell the peer of Shakespeare the "lovely episode" of how he took a great batch of prisoners and charmed their sulkiness into worship by giving them a wonderful dinner? They, in gratitude, made for him songs, wonderful gypsy songs. Or did he tell how, as a young boy, he came to the Burg Theater in Vienna and, not to encourage the management unduly, told them that he only came to study. He would not remain permanent because, he told them flatly: "I don't give a damn for masquerade." Yet, as an actor he described himself as a "dark blue flame, very beautiful— very great intensity." By underplaying in a theatre which was accustomed to overplaying, he made a great effect. In the long run, though, he had too much self-control. He had wanted to play Othello and Lear but was handicapped by being only a little boy—very elegant—very good figure—grand allure—very chic— great fencer—but still only a little boy.

Pascal and Shaw switched to the subject of live hormones, in which Shaw took a lively interest. Here Pascal came in very handy as the only living man who had perfected a technique for applying live hormones to himself. Exactly what this process was, whether the live hormones were applied as leeches used to be, Pascal never said. But Shaw went at this discussion with gusto. The old Egyptians, he said, lived on hormones. It is possible to imagine that the conversation had scope and vitality. It ended by Shaw's telling Pascal that he felt that he was the man to whom he would entrust the filming of his plays, provided . . .

The proviso hung on the question of capital. Where fiscal matters were concerned Shaw did not allow himself to be swept away by the pleasures of the senses. "How," he inquired, "are you fixed for money? What is your capital?"

Here Pascal's instinct placed him among the historic masters of intuition. He reached into his pocket, took out the few shillings left from the five pound note and threw them dramatically on the desk in front of Shaw.

"Here, GBS," he said, "is my capital. It is not enough to pay taxi fare back to my hotel."

In the film world, the demand for a thing is in inverse ratio to its availability. When Pascal walked out of Shaw's apartment that day he had the first entree to what would have been considered, before he went in, the most desirable assortment of picture-properties in the world. There wasn't a studio in the world that wouldn't have given its gold teeth for the rights to Shaw's plays. But now that he had them, Pascal found it seemingly impossible to get the money to screen them. Pascal took his contract with Shaw to Hollywood, where every big studio turned him down. It was characteristic of Hollywood in its imperial days that once you offered them what they had so ravenously wanted, they were suddenly unsure whether they wanted it. Had Pascal been willing to accept an advisory job (which would have meant that he could have offered his ideas to the studios for rejection), he might have made a deal. But he had a possessive passion for the Shaw plays and he couldn't bear the thought of having anyone but himself tampering with them.

He was always on the verge of making big deals with the studios, but somehow they never materialized.

For three years Pascal walked about the streets of London trying to raise the money to produce *Pygmalion*. The late Rudolf Kommer used to tell how, during this period, he would meet Pascal about once a year, looking shabbier and shabbier and would ask him: "Well, when do you go into production?" The answer, invariably cheerful, was always the same: "Next week I start. I go now see the old man to talk cast."

This phrase: "I go now see the old man" was Pascal's shibboleth, his program, his theme song. He would be sitting with you at the Plaza or in the bar of the Beverly Wilshire in California and he would get up, apologize and say: "I go now see the old man," as if GBS were just around the corner. And he went. Wars were no deterrent to his movements. During World War II he made at least six trips to England by ship and by plane, his pockets stuffed with priorities signed by important officials.

Pascal had wished to film *The Devil's Disciple* first; Shaw thought *Pygmalion* would be better as a starter. But the starter had great difficulty getting started. Still, in these suspenseful years, Shaw must have enjoyed splashing about in the iridescent surf of Pascal's kaleidoscopic plans. Pascal finally got together £90,000 and felt he could make the film within that budget. He got Leslie Howard to agree to play Higgins. According to Pascal, he also "discovered" Wendy Hiller to play Liza. Production started. But costs were greater than anticipated, remakes had to be taken, and the £90,000 was gone. Pascal raised five more. For this extra £5,000 he had to give away some of the shares reserved for himself. The picture finally cost £125,000. Each additional £5,000 was harder to raise and more expensive. The last investors are always the most usurious; to get end money is always more costly. Pascal had to give up more and more of his share of the film. After three years of money-raising, Pascal found himself with a tremendously successful picture of which he owned nothing at all. During this period of frantic financing he cabled from London to a friend in New York living in The Ambassador Hotel: "Can you get ——— to invest three hundred thousand pounds in my new film company. Wonderful opportunity. Please do not mention my whereabouts to The Ambassador as I owe them some money. Pascal."

But the great day came; the dream became reality. *Pygmalion* was finished and at the press-showing Pascal found himself sitting in the front row with Mr. and Mrs. Shaw, holding Mrs. Shaw's hand. He was full of trepidation: "Hannen Swaffer had predicted me that Shaw would never accept the ending and I shivered in my whole boots." He sat there, trembling, clutching Mrs. Shaw's hand. When it was over, Charlotte Shaw turned to him:

"This is the finest presentation of my husband's work."

"You said it, mother," said GBS.

Blanche Patch, Shaw's secretary, in her book *Thirty Years with GBS,* has a chapter headed "What Gabby Did." Somewhat incredulously, as if she couldn't believe it while she was seeing it, she describes how Pascal got Shaw to write new scenes for *Pygmalion.* For example, he wrote "The Rain in Spain Stays Mainly in the Plain" scene without suspecting for a moment that he was writing a tango for *My Fair Lady.* "Gabby," says Miss Patch, holding her breath, "now had GBS well under control." She also makes the flat statement that: "GBS never met a human being who entertained him more."

The film of *Pygmalion,* considered by many people one of the best pictures ever made, was a great success, but Pascal got nothing from it except prestige. Nevertheless, to make his insolvency secure, to give it a status of permanence, he plunged into producing his second film, *Major Barbara.* As it did not have the success of *Pygmalion,* his bankruptcy rather decreased in proportion. Possibly because he did not feel that Barbara was the natural film-subject *Pygmalion* is, he induced Shaw to bolster up *Major Barbara* by acting in a short to precede it. Shaw put up a token resistance. "Why," he protested, "if I appear it will ruin the regular actors. I can't do that to Rex Harrison!" But he overcame his scruples. "If the picture is a failure with me on the bill, you can go out in a redingote and a sandwich-board with the legend: 'That Irishman ruined me!' Any Englishman will give you a shilling!"

Shaw appeared, not only in the short which preceded *Major Barbara,* with Pascal's connivance, but once again entirely without Pascal's knowledge. He could not resist edging in among the extras in the revival meeting scenes at the Albert Hall and, in spite of seventy-five years of agnosticism, appearing to be carried away by religious fervor. Rather shamefacedly, Shaw wrote to Pascal afterwards to apologize for appearing in this scene without being asked and for dancing too exuberantly and singing too loudly. "I suddenly felt myself twenty years younger," he explained.

Shaw's impersonation of himself in the short preceding *Major Barbara* is superb. Dorothy Parker said at the time that for sheer sex appeal Shaw surpassed any leading man extant, so that it appears that Shaw did impinge somewhat on the domain of Rex Harrison. It is no wonder that Shaw's performance is so captivating, as he played all his parts in all his plays at rehearsal for his actors. The whole thing is a masterpiece of high-comedy; that is to say, it is gay, gallant, profound, and very moving. It represents, in a sense, like the famous last speech in *Too True to be Good,* Shaw's valedictory to the world. It gives the essence of his credo and of his personality and of his style. You hear the crunch of his brogans on the gravel walk at Ayot-St.-Lawrence before he appears wearing a Norfolk jacket and knickerbockers. Shaw proceeds then to summarize his life work. When he was a child, he says (Shaw was born in 1856), he could remember a daily column in a Dublin paper headed: "The American Civil War." One day he read that the war was over and that the black man had been emancipated. That job having been satisfactorily completed by the Americans he decided to devote *his* life to the

74

emancipation of the white man. He thanks us, the Americans, for the old destroyers and offers to send us in exchange his old plays. Lecturers on Shaw, when they get to The Last Phase, should only have to run this short. It tells all. While it was being rehearsed there was a sudden air raid alarm and the droning of enemy planes. Pascal leaped forward. "It was on my backbone," he recounts, "the cold shiver." But Shaw was imperturbable. "We'll keep it in the picture," he said. And he did: while he is chatting to the audience in the film, you hear the droning of airplanes. Shaw looks up, then smiles at the audience reassuringly. "Let me get this word in before it happens," he says. He peers at the audience. "Do I discern an expression of hope at the possibility?"

One thing is certain: Shaw accepted Pascal as a genius. He has set it down, in his own hand, as a kind of To-whom-it-may-concern letter:

Gabriel Pascal is one of those extraordinary men who turn up occasionally—say once in a century—and may be called Godsends in the arts to which they are devoted. Pascal is doing for the films what Diaghileff did for the Russian Ballet. Until he descended on me out of the clouds, I found nobody who wanted to do anything with my plays on the screen but mutilate them, murder them, give their cadavers to the nearest scrivener without a notion of how to tell the simplest story in dramatic action and instructed that there must be a new picture every ten seconds and that the duration of the whole feature must be 45 minutes at the extreme outside. The result was to be presented to the public with my name attached and an assurance that nobody need fear that it had any Shavian quality whatever, and was real genuine Hollywood. Under such conditions I of course would not let my plays be filmed at all, though I quite realized their possibilities in that medium.

When Gabriel appeared out of the blue I just looked at him and handed him Pygmalion *to experiment with. His studio was immediately infested with script writers and he thought that everything they did was wrong and that everything I did was right. Naturally, I agreed with him.* Pygmalion *was an enormous success. When he tackled* Barbara, *there was not a script writer left in the studio, and when he wanted a new "sequence," he very simply asked me for it and got it. He shocks me by his utter indifference to the cost; but the result justifies him; and Hollywood, which always values a director in proportion to the money he throws away, is now at his feet; for he throws it away like water.*

The man is a genius: that is all I have to say about him.

In a postscript to a letter to Pascal, Shaw says: "My film future depends on you. Ought I have your life insured?" Charlotte Shaw said that since Pascal began working with her husband he had become twenty-five years younger. That is easy to understand; Pascal had extraordinary vitality and radiated a sense that things had been wonderful but limited, and that momentarily they were going to be wonderful without limit. He did not ask you to believe in him literally, only in essence. The creator of Dubedat must have found very appealing a character who told you, when you asked him if he had a family: "I made a boy to a little girl—and I adopted him." Or who would seriously try to prove that he was strongly domesticated, a homebody, by recounting how, in his opulent and unregenerate days, he kept apartments in all the capitals of Europe, presided over by different ladies, so that wherever he found himself he would not have to go out, but could spend a quiet evening at home.

It is obvious from Shaw's letters to Pascal, which are voluminous and characteristic, from the elaborate notes on the films in production, and from his visions of the future that Shaw had great fun working with Pascal. Here are some of Shaw's random notes on the musical side of *Major Barbara:*

Here is a champion effort, the musical part of which will probably cost at least £3,000 and involve the cooperation of Toscanini. The name of the Quartette from Mose in Egitto is

"Dal Tro Stellata Soglio." I shall not compose the new words for it until I hear your reaction and his.

I left undone an important bit of Barbara: *the words for the Rossini Quartette. I have now done them and will send you a fair copy when Blanche [Blanche Patch, Shaw's secretary] types it. It has been a horrid job. Nothing would have been easier than to write a few pretty verses, but to fit them to Rossini's notes and accents, and to provide open vowels for the big, recurring portamento was the very devil; and the result is queer but singable. I almost drove my wife mad bellowing it over and over on Sunday night.*

The flourish for the brass is in B flat; so the conductor told me. Ask him to try the effect of a single trombone sounding G flat quite quietly after the others have stopped. Undershaft pretending to play it. It ought to have the effect of a question. It must not be harsh or ugly. The band is first-rate and should not be asked to do anything inartistic or comic. The more you have of it the better. The Prologue stills are all right; but do not let Cusins make a mess of his drumming. On the contrary show him heading the band with all the élan and panache of a first-rate drum major, and Barbara applauding delightedly. The army must not be made ridiculous. Neither must Cusins. The army bands are never incompetent and sometimes very good. Any toleration of a comically inefficient drummer would be impossible and would offend the Salvationists mortally.

Pascal was guileless, loved the greatest artists, and would do anything to enlist them. He was essentially indifferent to money. Not so his adored collaborator. Shaw's commercial sense was as keen as his artistic one. In a letter to a famous actress with whom he was considering a film venture he writes:

I notice that you ask for ten percent of the profits. Do you notice that I ask for ten percent of the receipts? There may be no profits but there are always receipts and sometimes it may take ten lawsuits to determine what the profits are but you can always determine the receipts.

He writes to Pascal in a similar vein:

Let me remind you that I need make no further concession to the financiers. They have now ventured so far in that they must go on to completion or else lose what they have already advanced. If they could stop and get their money back we should be at their mercy; but as they cannot they are at yours. Their real hold on you is that unless you treat them fairly and bring them in a good profit, nobody will find capital for you next time; but on the other hand if they demand too much and the film is a success you will easily find capital elsewhere next time. This should keep both parties on their best behaviour; but the point to remember now is that they must go on; you can receive any threat to cut off supplies with the thumb to your nose. Only, the more you spend, the less will be left for everybody except the author, who being a ruthless shark, takes care to come in on the receipts and not on the profits.

Another time he advises:

The more outrageously expensive you make the film the easier it will be to get the money. On the other hand all the new scenes can be discarded and the film restricted to the printed text. But it will pay to out-do Korda in extravagance.

When the question of casting Liza Doolittle in *Pygmalion* first came up, Shaw's advice to Pascal was to walk out blindfolded on Piccadilly, reach out and touch the first prostitute he came across and there would be his Liza. Even for Pascal this casting method seemed too haphazard. Leaning on more conventional formulae, Pascal picked Wendy Hiller. For once Shaw admitted that Pascal's conservatism was justified. He wrote on a post card:

The stills are magnificent. She will be the film sensation of the next five years. There is a fortune in her.

Another figure, less well-known than GBS, but, in Pascal's estimation, almost equally powerful in the shaping of his destiny, was an Egyptian palmist and dabbler in the occult named Cheiro.

On Cheiro's divinations Pascal depended utterly. "Cheiro predicted me a car accident and I had car accident just when he predicted. He predicted me *Pygmalion* contract and I got when he predicted—at 4 o'clock Friday the 13th. Cheiro was," Gabby told me, "old school aristocrat, amateur yogi, and son of the Governor of India. He was great friend to Kitchener. He predicted Kitchener that Wednesday, 4 o'clock, he would go down at sea. Kitchener say, 'I know, Cheiro, whatever you say is right, but I never change my route once I decide on it!'" For this inflexibility, Kitchener paid by going down at sea at 4 o'clock on Wednesday. When Cheiro passed on, Pascal engaged another prophet, named Sorell, who in the press of his other duties, found the time to write a formal essay: "An Analysis of Gabriel Pascal." At the end of this analysis Sorell says:

What his fellowmen may call success or already great achievement in his art, it does not interest him. He may have attained certain peaks in his career, but he climbed right down to go the way once more and to conquer another mountain. At the end of his forties he will have to destroy the old world in him for the last time. The beginning of his fifties (52 to 54) will find him on his final ascent. In those years he will see himself on the way of fulfillment. And between his 52nd and 62nd year of age we shall harvest the fruits of Gabriel Pascal's lifelong struggle with himself.

Pascal himself was the most fascinated observer of his struggle; he was consumed with curiosity about its outcome.

I have had to deal often with charlatans and megalomaniacs. Sometimes they are united in the same person, as they were in Gabriel Pascal. They fascinate me. To what extent does the charlatan know that he *is* a charlatan? I am inclined to think not at all. The megalomaniac saves the charlatan from self-awareness. I am sure that Pascal simply knew he was a genius. He was also convinced that he was a great director—better than anybody. This delusion of Pascal's proved ultimately to be tragic for him. Sir Alexander Korda, a fellow Hungarian, and willing to be a friend of Pascal's, once told me that this mania of Pascal's to shine as a director had ruined him. Had he been content merely to produce Shaw's plays and to engage competent people to direct them, he would have become a very rich man, Korda said, and attained a respected position in the British film world. In any case, Pascal was upheld in his opinion of himself as a director by the "Sweet Irish Pope" himself. Still, by his insistence on directing the films, Pascal threw shooting schedules way out of kilter. As a result, costs were astronomical. Shaw didn't mind this in the least, but for Pascal himself these costs proved ruinous.

The truth was that I found Gabby irresistible. Except occasionally, when he was rude to waiters, I greatly enjoyed his company. He wasted months of my time. He caused me endless inconvenience, but it was all somehow worth it. What was so engaging about Gabby was that he never made the least effort to give his inventions the vulgar gloss of consistency. Not long after I first met him we were walking together to a restaurant for lunch. Gabby confided in me: "You know, Som, have I told you I am illegitimate descendant Talleyrand?" I found this very interesting. A few weeks later we were walking to the same restaurant. Gabby was reminiscing over the past: "Som, did I tell you? I am illegitimate descendant Metternich." Evidently, whatever superficial differences agitated the Congress of Vienna, it was united on at least one objective: to have some share, however remote, in Pascal's paternity. On another occasion I had a somewhat acrimonious dialogue with Pascal. He was miffed. He got up abruptly from the table. "I must go see Rex Harrison," he said. Rex Harrison was, I happened to know, in England. Pascal turned to me and made an astonishing remark: "I persuade him," he said, "to play in London your *No Time For Comedy*." He said it reproachfully, as if to convey that, although I had offended him, he bore no grudge and would return good for evil. It was essential Pascal. Since I had written *No Time For Comedy,* anyone else would assume that I knew something about Rex Harrison's part in it, but Pascal soared in an empyrean of fantasy that was far above such petty considerations. It was this sublime and God-like superiority to prosaic fact that had, from the beginning, endeared him to me.

On Pascal's next visit to New York he was to cause me considerable trouble. His objective was to film *Candida* with Katharine Cornell, whose revival of the play that spring was an enormous success. Shaw cabled to his lawyer in New York: "Never mind about advance to me. Get advance for Gabby so he won't ruin himself as he did over the first two pictures." For months and months there were immense goings-on over the production of *Candida* with Miss Cornell. One day Pascal came to me, his fluorescent smile lighting up the entire room: "How you like do *Candida* with Katharine Cornell for Metro-Goldwyn-Mayer? You work in New York. When is finished we go see old man." It was indeed a seductive proposal, and I accepted it. But not long after that I had dinner with Miss Cornell and found that she was very far from settled in her mind about this proposal. I told Pascal the distressing news. He waved it aside. "Let her bring me yes," he shouted, "and we go ahead. Now call Louis B. Mayer."

I found myself suddenly a kind of agent for Pascal in this venture. But Pascal was hypnotic, and I did call Louis B. Mayer to assure him that both Miss Cornell and *Candida* were at his disposal. Mr. Mayer was far from enthusiastic. He had indeed heard of *Candida,* but nothing about her so seductive that he wished to screen her. All of this took a lot of my time—and without profit. I finally told Pascal that his scheme for getting *Candida* on the screen was vaporous. Pascal was imperturbable. "I go see the old man," he said. And twelve hours later he departed by clipper for London.

Pascal had been married twice and twice divorced. His first wife was the Italian film star and his second later became Mrs. Paul Gallico. Pascal and the Gallicos were great friends and he saw a lot of them when he was in New York. Until he established connections with the British financier, Joseph Rank, he lived in the New York Athletic Club. After he made his deal with Rank, he moved to the Plaza. People who knew him from pre-war Europe said that there wasn't a good restaurant on the Continent which he didn't know, no matter how obscure. Out of his losses on the Shaw plays he managed to buy himself an English country place which once belonged to Simon de Montfort. He was a British subject and in Simon de Montfort's village he was known as "The Squire of Chalfonte St. Peter." He loved this place and was fond of showing pictures of his livestock there. Altogether, rain or shine, his manner was democratically imperial. He arrived for a weekend at the Kurt Weill's in New City, above Nyack, with the demand: "Are there horses?"

His approach to writers whom he wanted to work for him was ample. Maxwell Anderson was lunching with a friend one day in a restaurant. Pascal came up to him: "We go to Saratoga," he said. "I take corner suite so we get air. I am convinced you will have the most enjoyment of your life and that the work we do will give you great happiness. You will have great happiness with me." Anderson said he'd love to come but as Pascal went off at once to another table in the restaurant, he never did find out what he was expected to do in Saratoga. Of an actress with whom he didn't hit it off Pascal said: "She had the duty to be consequent and put herself in my hands." As she wasn't consequent, she lost out. Pascal saw himself as a Cagliostro working beneficence: "I tell you lovely episode—I am Cagliostro to Shaw—I keep him alive fifteen years more." Whether by applying live hormones or not he did not say. He was constantly pulling out of his pockets cables from Shaw and from Eastern potentates like the Governor of New Delhi. There was a strong mystic strain in Pascal. He was always talking about new souls and old souls. He himself was an old soul. He believed firmly in reincarnation. In one of his earlier incarnations, he recalled, "I was young Assyrian King." As he looked back on that happy time, he was saddened by nostalgia.

His own telegrams to his friends were less voluminous than Ziegfeld's, but more apocalyptic. I got one such while I was working in Hollywood in 1942 on a cruder assignment than *Candida*. "Arrive next week. Have big plans for you." Arrive Pascal did, during an air raid alarm in the Thalberg Building at the Metro-Goldwyn-Mayer Studio in Culver City. In those days there were constant rumors of Japanese attack on some part of the California coast. The air raid alarms were taken very seriously—but not by Pascal. Pascal barred the way to the shelter: "Do not disturb yourself. I have been through bomb-bing in London. This is not real bomb-bing. Let us have lunch. I take chef's salad." The studio warden stuck his head in the door with a peremptory final warning to clear out—it was the real thing this time—strange planes had been sighted off San Pedro. "We'd better go, Gabby," I said. Pascal settled himself on the sofa. "I cannot go to shelter," he said. "I do not like see Greer Garson, my nearly wife," he explained. "It would upset me for the week. If not meatless I have steak. Well, I see the old man. He embrace me. He kiss me on the front. I tell you lovely episode. Once I meet the old man in the park. We kiss on the front. A young girl watches us. GBS chuckles. He say: 'What that girl think of us, eh, Gabby?' We make *Saint Joan*. How you like make *St. Joan* with Garbo, eh, my friend?"

The town buzzed with the rumor that Pascal had arrived to get Greta Garbo, who was suffering from chronic maladjustment at Metro-Goldwyn-Mayer, to appear in the film version of Shaw's *Saint Joan*. A letter from Shaw to Pascal at this time reveals that both Katherine Hepburn and Elizabeth Bergner were eager to play the Saint, but Pascal preferred Garbo. Two weeks later Pascal popped in at the studio to say goodbye. His aspect was that of a man whose dearest hopes have been crowned. He had it in black and white. Miss Garbo was signed. He was off to see the old man. This time he took Maxwell Anderson with him. He was also going to produce Anderson's play, *The Eve of St. Mark*, in London.

Arrived in London with a signed contract with Miss Garbo in his pocket and $2,500 which he had borrowed from Anderson, Pascal went to see the old man and, directly thereafter, to meet Joseph Rank, the British financier. In England, Rank was Metro, Paramount, 20th-Century-Fox all rolled into one. Hugh Dalton, the President of the Board of Trade, had him up in Parliament for monopoly. Rank was not a film man, having made his great fortune in the flour business. He had been the major investor in Pascal's first two productions. With Garbo in his pocket, Pascal's tone was now slightly more peremptory. He wanted an independent film company, lavishly financed, with himself at its head. He needed money to start operations and asked, to give himself time to breathe, an immediate down-payment of £15,000. Rank sent the money, which Pascal deposited in his bank. He was now head of his own company, Pascal Films, Ltd. The next day he saw Rank again.

"Mr. Rank," he said, "I now have money, £15,000 in bank minus $2,500 I return Mr. Anderson his loan. Now Mr. Rank I can talk business with you." Rank, impressed with Pascal's new-found wealth, consented to talk business. The company was formed. The initial venture was to be *Saint Joan* by George Bernard Shaw with Greta Garbo. "I take you now," said Pascal to Rank, "to see the old man."

Pascal's account of this interview makes one wish one had been there: Shaw didn't believe in rich men. He didn't believe in their reality. His millionaire Magnin in *Heartbreak House* doesn't really have any money; he is merely the possessor of vast quantities of papers in vaults representing the fortunes of other rich men which he manipulates. When Pascal brought Rank in, Shaw inquired: "Are you really a rich man, Mr. Rank, or only a bluffer? If you are, tell us so frankly. Once you confess your poverty and we know that you are poor like Pascal and myself we will treat you like one of us!" As Rank knew himself to be one of the richest men in England, he was unable to confess. And since Shaw himself was said to be worth four million pounds at

84

the time, Pascal might have felt himself a bit lonely in this trio.

Marvelously launched at last, Pascal ran at once into a snag. The British Government did not want *St. Joan* filmed till after the war. Pascal went from government bureau to government bureau. He got the consent of de Gaulle, but this was hazardous because Pascal said de Gaulle wanted to play the Saint himself! There was a quick proposal to make two other Shaw plays, *The Devil's Disciple* and *Caesar and Cleopatra*. GBS blocked that. He wrote on a postcard: "I cannot afford to have two films running simultaneously!" One day Pascal stepped off the boat in New York. "We make *Caesar and Cleopatra*," (Cleo-patra he pronounced it) he announced triumphantly. "John Gielgud is Caesar. Vivien Leigh is Cleo-patra. Wonderful, no? Ralph Richardson is Brittanus." As for Saint Joan, he departed at once for Hollywood to bring Miss Garbo no—at least Not Yet.

"WE
GO SEE
OLD
MAN"

Bernard Shaw and Gabriel Pascal

1965, 1943

IN SEPTEMBER OF 1944 I WAS IN
London. So was Gabriel Pascal,
filming *Caesar and Cleopatra* at
the studio in Denham. London
was abuzz with the V2's and, at
least the theatrical portion of it,
with scurrilous jokes about the
length of time it was taking
Pascal to finish the costly venture.
Pascal was indeed obeying Shaw's
plea to "outdo Korda in extrava-

87

gance." At its annual conference the Cinema Technicians' Association charged that Pascal had spent $4,000,000—more than the film could earn in Britain—deprived other studios of space and slowed down the schedule by insisting on bigger plaster pillars than were used in *Henry V*. Pascal, in retaliation, wished to "remind the Association I was the only man who had the guts to carry on at Denham during the blitz. There was plenty of studio space then. Nobody seemed to want it." Shaw came to Pascal's defense. He said that the picture was costing three million and not four and that "if the Association saw money coming in they would change their minds." I remembered that David O. Selznick was similarly criticized in Hollywood for the amount of money he was spending on the filming of *Gone With the Wind*. But when the money began to come in all was forgiven. Sadly, in the case of *Caesar and Cleopatra,* the money didn't come in.

On a Saturday, Pascal invited me to spend the night with him at Simon de Montfort's erstwhile residence in Buckinghamshire, and on Sunday, "go see the old man." Before I left, I paid a call on Harold Laski. I told him I was going to see Shaw. He asked me to take his regards. He had just reviewed Shaw's book, *Everybody's Political What's What*. It was sound on education and politics, Laski said, but nonsensical about science and medicine. (I had recently been treated, as it happened, by Dr. Stewart Hensman, Shaw's doctor. I asked Dr. Hensman whether Shaw was really a total vegetarian. "He cheats," said Dr. Hensman. "I see to it.")

Laski told me that Shaw's memory must be lapsing, because he recalled in this book that when, in his early days, he had delivered a lecture on the nationalization of land, the Cambridge philosopher, Henry Sidgwick, had gotten so angry that he stalked out of the room in dudgeon. Laski said he had looked up Sidgwick's memoirs and found *his* account of the lecture. Sidgwick describes the occasion very favorably; he had been greatly impressed by Shaw's brilliance. I asked Laski whether he would mind my bringing this up with Shaw and Laski said he wouldn't mind a bit. In order to be ready for Shaw, I looked up Sidgwick's memoirs for myself. Laski was certainly right. Sidgwick's diary accounted Shaw's lecture admirable. . . "Altogether a note-worthy performance."

Then I referred to Shaw's account in *Everybody's Political What's What.*

". . . When I assumed the necessity of land nationalization . . . Henry Sidgwick, a professor of political economy and ethics who had never before been known to lose his temper or raise his voice, sprang up and cried out that advocacy of land nationaliza-tion was advocacy of crime and he would not countenance it by his presence. Thereupon he not only left the platform but actually slammed the door behind him violently."

On the drive to the house in Buckinghamshire, Pascal was in a state of euphoria. He was happy about the way the film was going and about Shaw's delight in it. He showed me a postcard from Shaw. In it Shaw complained that when he went on the set for one of the night scenes in *Caesar and Cleopatra,* he noticed that the stars in the film-heaven were all equidistant. This killed the reality of the scene for him. He implored Pascal to read up on astro-physics and recommended a series of books on the subject to him, beginning with Sir James Jeans. I wondered. Surely, I thought, Shaw must know that Pascal was not a reader. I knew it. Pascal was not addicted to reading even simple books. As I read the long list of books on an abstruse subject which Shaw had carefully written out for Pascal's attention, it was hard for me not to believe that these communications were written, not to edify Pascal, but to amuse Shaw himself. Shaw was, in any case, incapable of sitting still without writing *something.* On the way to Chalfonte, Pascal stopped at his studio in Denham to show me the sets. We saw Caesar's council-chambers, august and splendiferous, much more so than Forbes-Robertson's when he first brought the play to America. When I was sixteen I went by street-car from Worcester to Boston to see that production at the old Park Street Theatre. It had seduced me to the theatre. I thought it would be agreeable to write plays like that.

Toward the end of the ride Pascal suddenly confided to me that he was getting married. The bride was, even then, awaiting him at Chalfonte St. Peter. I asked him when the happy event was to take place. He grinned widely. "I ask it the bride," he said, "when we get Chalfonte." We got Chalfonte. Simon de Montfort's house, considering its antiquity, proved very comfortable—at least Pascal had made it so. It was a pleasant, dowdy, rambling country house. I met the bride, whom I had admired over the years for her brilliant performances in many plays. Pascal left us together while he went to change into the habiliments of a country squire; he emerged in a long tweed coat and high boots. He still looked very much like himself, the Assyrian King, though no longer in the first flush of youth. He beamed at me. "Come! I show you farm," he said. We went out and wandered around. Standing in a field, a little up the road, I saw a bizarre, strangely shaped, gaily painted wooden vehicle with a tin stovepipe sticking out of its roof. It was flamboyantly painted like a Sicilian cart, only much bigger. It looked like a circus-wagon in a street parade. I stared at it; in the gentle English countryside it seemed outlandish.

Pascal took pleasure in my astonishment. Finally he ventured an explanation.

"Gypsy caravan," he said. "Some day I run away in this. Come. I show you."

We walked over to it and I peered inside. There was an iron stove in it with a tin pipe leading through the hole in the roof and a narrow cot bed. It looked very cozy.

"Let's go now," I said.

Gabby was pleased.

"Cannot go now," he said, "because tomorrow we go see old man."

I reflected that his impending wedding might also have been a deterrent but I decided not to bring that up.

The next afternoon, still in squire costume, Pascal drove me to Ayot-St.-Lawrence. We were received in the former vicarage by Shaw's secretary, Miss Patch. She was friendly, spinsterish, faintly astringent. She teased Pascal about his costume. As a countryman, she did not find her dear Gabby persuasive. Gabby laughed, sharing her opinion. "GBS," she said, "is in his studio." Pascal piloted me across the lawn to the world-famous heliotropic studio. Shaw had put it on a swivel so that it could turn with the sun. It was a tiny shack. We peered through the window; we saw the typewriter with a half-covered sheet of manuscript paper in it, books and papers scattered around, but no Shaw. The room was so small that although *it* might turn around, it was difficult to see how its occupant could.

"We find him," Gabby said and walked me down a path behind the studio. Presently we came upon Shaw, busily raking leaves. He was wearing a Norfolk jacket, knickerbockers, and a peaked cloth helmet with a green visor on it, presumably to protect his eyes from the sun. But there was no sun. It was quite nippy, and the tip of his nose was reddened from the cold. His skin was clear and healthy and his blue eyes keen and direct. His manner, on introduction, was exquisitely courteous. He abandoned his rake and we started to walk back to the house. Pascal and Shaw plunged at once into shop-talk about the film. Just as we reached the door of the vicarage, Shaw stopped.

"Have you killed Ftatateeta yet?"

"Killed her yesterday," said Pascal, with satisfaction.

"How did you manage her death-scream?"

"Like this," said Pascal and began to scream at the top of his voice.

"Too high," said Shaw. "Lower. Like this."

And he started to scream in a lower register. The two of them stood there for a moment, counter-bellowing.

Shaw was too excited about the proper scream to go into the house. He turned from Pascal to explain to me. He had had a leg injury and when the doctor came to remove the bandage, he

91

heard himself screaming before he felt the pain. "That's the scream I want for Ftatateeta."

We finally got inside the little parlor and Miss Patch joined us for tea, brought in by a maid. I told GBS that I had seen Forbes-Robertson and Gertrude Elliott in Boston when I was sixteen. Shaw was still on the scream. He remembered when he was rehearsing the Forbes-Robertson company what trouble he'd had with the off-stage screamers. He had exhausted them after one performance and replacements cost the management half a crown a night.

He winked at me.

"Films, you know, are a strange business. You can get in, but you can't get out." He looked at Pascal. I thought I saw an odd expression in his eyes; affectionate interest and also a certain puzzlement at finding himself so closely involved with this man.

Over tea I brought up Laski's reference to Sidgwick.

Shaw retorted quickly, but without asperity.

"I was there, you know, and Laski wasn't."

Then I told him about the passage in Sidgwick's memoirs.

"When a man makes a fool of himself he is not apt to recall it in his memoirs." He went on as if that settled that. "I don't see why Sidgwick was so shocked at the idea of land-nationalization. The idea was old. Voltaire wrote a pamphlet on the subject." He quoted the name of the pamphlet in French.

The talk turned to Pascal's impending marriage. Both Miss Patch and Shaw appeared to take great interest in it. I said:

"I don't know what she sees in Gabby, do you?"

"I don't care *what* she sees in Gabby," Shaw said, "what I am worried about is that he will see in her a leading-lady for *all* my films!"

He flung his arms wide in a gesture of despair. Miss Patch asked, as I had asked, when the wedding was to take place. Pascal said very soon; he was, in fact, going to discuss it with his bride tonight.

"You are going back to London tonight?" said Shaw.

"No," said Pascal, "she is at Chalfonte."

The moment he said it, Pascal, in the prim silence which followed, realized that he had made a mistake. I realized it too. Ayot-St.-Lawrence, before Shaw bought it, had been a vicarage. It became a vicarage again. There was a censorious reverberation over the tea-table that was almost audible. It was obvious that for Miss Patch and Shaw both, it was an impropriety for the bride to be lodged prematurely in Pascal's residence.

"Wouldn't it have been advisable to lodge her in a hotel until the wedding?" Shaw asked, more in sorrow than in anger. There was an awkward pause. Pascal finally blurted out a belated alibi:

"She goes back tomorrow to hotel in London!" There was another silence. "With Som," he added limply.

By adding this postscript Pascal converted me suddenly into a professional chaperone, under whose vigilant eye nothing untoward could happen. With this assurance the subject was mercifully dropped. GBS asked me whether I had a play going. I told him I had one on in New York, *Jacobowsky and the Colonel*.

"That's an amusing title," said Shaw and Miss Patch murmured agreement. I said that I was pleased to hear this because everyone involved with the production had objected to the title and that it had remained only through inertia. I told them a story of Louis Calhern's, the actor who played the Colonel. He was coming into the theatre for a matinee and saw two East Side Jews with beards staring up at the billboards. He overheard one of them say:

"Jacobowsky and WHAT?"

This appeared to amuse them. Pascal laughed immoderately, happy to be rid at last of the uncomfortable subject of the housing of his bride.

Miss Patch asked whether I had been present when Shaw spoke at the Metropolitan Opera House during his one-day visit to New York on his world tour. I said I had heard it on the radio.

"I was introduced," Shaw said, "by a Morgan partner. The

place was full of big industrialists. I didn't know it till afterwards. I believe I had a go at them."

Shaw's speech on that occasion was actually a disappointment but his opening sentence got a big laugh. I asked Shaw whether he remembered it.

"I remember nothing of that evening," he said rather curtly. I had the feeling that he knew he hadn't been at his best.

Miss Patch asked me to repeat the opening sentence and I did:

"Ladies and gentlemen: before this distinguished audience and in this magnificent Opera House, I feel an irresistible desire—*to sing*."

Pascal and Miss Patch were amused, but Shaw seemed suddenly morose.

The tea party came to an end. Shaw walked us out to Pascal's car. When Pascal was installed behind the wheel, Shaw asked him a few questions about the next day's shooting. Pascal said he would report by telephone. Shaw stood submissive while Pascal took his hand and kissed it repeatedly. As the car moved away, Shaw raised his arms in a mock-Fascist salute and waved us off shouting farewell. I looked back as the car moved down the driveway. The frail old man was still standing there, waving and waving.

For the first part of the journey back Pascal drove in silence. I could see that he was brooding over the gaffe he had made in the vicarage. His face worked. Finally he burst out in hurt indignation: "Did you ever see in life," he said, "such *innocent* people?"

ZION
COMES TO
CULVER
CITY

Chaim Weizmann

1944

ON A JUNE MORNING IN 1941 I
was immured in an office in the
Thalberg Building on the Metro-
Goldwyn-Mayer lot in Culver
City, California, contriving dis-
asters to bring about the final
doom of Miss Greta Garbo.
Things were bad enough with her
already: the chronic misunderstanding with her husband had
become opaque, the fever chart of

her little boy was alarmingly angular, the man on whom, with a kind of deliberate impulsiveness, she had set her hopes for salvation was becoming, in their intimacies, increasingly absent-minded. Yes, things were bad enough, but since the emoluments deriving from Miss Garbo's sufferings are in direct ratio to their duration, I couldn't polish her off yet. But what more could I do to her? How much longer could I delay the inevitable? What further agonies could I invent through which she had not already passed, what refinements of torture that would also be *photo-génique?* Through the Venetian blinds the California sun lay in bars across my desk, across the inventory of dolors on which I was laboring. I felt myself shiver slightly, whether from sympathy or fatigue or the air-conditioning I could not tell. What should I do to her next? I did not know. There were still two reels to go. It was not as simple as for the author of the Book of Job who did not have to think of the camera. She must suffer, yes, but exquisitely. She must endure, yes, but with an enhanced visibility. She must die, yes, but unravaged by mortality.

I got up, pulled up the blinds, and looked down at the court-yard below blazing in sunlight: executives in pongees, stars in slacks. At the corner was a mean little building with a sign almost as large as itself bearing the legend: *morticians.* Terminal also, but not Miss Garbo's. Could it be that this dingy little hut was concerned with the same phenomenon toward which, with a faltering sadism, I was slowly maneuvering Miss Garbo? That was depressing. Mausoleum for Miss Garbo! Apotheosis for Miss Garbo! I turned away from the window and sat on the green cloth sofa. I was at an impasse. I needed a break. What to do? How to kill this high-paid time? Lying on the sofa was a Los Angeles paper. I picked it up, staring at it with the unseeing focus which is reserved for quite no other form of writing. I followed the black headlines from page to page as one stares down at a river from the deck of a boat without seeing the banks. But a name forced itself through my inattention. Chaim Weizmann. I learned that he was addressing a meeting at eight-thirty that night at the Biltmore Hotel in Los Angeles.

I had met Weizmann twice. The first time was at a small luncheon party in New York to which I was invited by a friend. What did I know of Weizmann then? Really very little: that he was a chemist with a fascinating personality who had the knack of alluring prime ministers. Also, he had some kind of lateral obsession with a thing called Zionism. What did I know of Zionism? Even less. As I rode in my taxi to the restaurant a memory swarmed into my consciousness from early childhood, a quite vivid and panoplied memory, evoked by the name of this man. From the mist of the forgotten resolved a clearing. I awoke in my parents' flat in Worcester, Massachusetts, and looked out on a Providence Street gay and beflagged. I remember wondering whether I was still in a dream. Was it the Fourth of July? Was it Memorial Day? It was neither. And yet these dreary double-decker tenements spouted color. When I looked more closely I saw that beside the American flags were others, strange, blue and white. I asked my father. He explained it. A man named Nahum Sokolow was coming to Worcester to speak. Who was Nahum Sokolow? A Zionist leader. If my father explained to me what that meant I do not remember what his explanation was. I remembered too in almost every Providence Street living room, together with prints of *Washington Crossing the Delaware* and horses by Rosa Bonheur champing futilely at jagged streaks of lightning, photographs of a very handsome, somber-eyed, black-bearded man, with his arms folded prohibitively across his frock-coated chest. That was Theodor Herzl. He was also a Zionist leader. And that was all I knew about Zionism.

It was little enough preparation, but perhaps none was necessary. I can only say that from the moment I met him, I found something in Weizmann tremendously moving. He was impressive, of course, but I had met people who were impressive without conveying the other quality. I was aware of the beauty of his head, massive and sculptural. I remembered the photographs of

97

the head of dignitaries in Latin textbooks in high school. The set of the eyes especially reminded me of them—immemorial, unchanging, timeless in time. But his eyes, unlike those sightless Roman eyes, speak to you, and it is their expression, I think, that gives Weizmann his special quality when you meet him and talk to him: a yearning, touched with an intimation of futility, to cross the limitless areas that insulate in loneliness even those most desirous of communication. We sat down to lunch. I sat between Mrs. Weizmann and a lady who asked Dr. Weizmann about his first meeting with King Feisal. Weizmann told her. He speaks very quietly, with almost no inflection. He makes no effort to dramatize the dramatic. He understates it. This is characteristic.

We made with Weizmann the journey to meet Feisal. In the last days of World War I he was in Palestine and had arranged to meet the Emir Feisal in Transjordania. Under normal circumstances the journey would not have taken more than five hours. But at that time the Turkish front still bit into Palestinian territory, and in order to make his way to the Emir he had to make a long detour and go southward toward Egypt, then cross the Red Sea and come up again to Transjordania. Twelve days he traveled on his mission, five days through the burning desert past Sinai and then across the waters of the Red Sea. North again through the land of Moab, and word was sent to the Emir that Weizmann was approaching. And there were sent out to greet him a number of the Emir's servants bearing gifts and bread and salt.

With a kind of Biblical simplicity Weizmann conveyed to us something of the marvelous sense that suffused him of the wonder of his journey. Like Abraham of old he was approaching the land which God had promised. And like him he was coming through the lands of Moab, as it were, to take possession. There rolled away from him two thousand, three thousand, four thousand years. The sense of ancestral continuity became close and immediate: he felt as if it were only yesterday that his forefathers had been living there; as if it were only yesterday that his grandparent Abraham, some generations removed, had gone forth on the errand of his people under the guidance of God and with His blessing. And he was overcome by a deep emotion of recognition and return: not all the years of exile, not all the lands he had dwelt in, neither the persecutions nor the indignities, nor the sufferings—none of these mattered any more. For the gulf had been bridged: this was home; this was the promise and the fulfillment; this was certainty.

The meeting took place, and the friendship began that had such far-reaching results and was to be terminated only by the untimely death of the King. When he described the actual meeting Weizmann dropped the note of Biblical inspiration: he told it in terms of contemporary social comedy. "He gave me," said Weizmann, "one of his blooded Arabian horses, and this embarrassed me because I hate gifts that eat."

While this horizontal drama unfolded I said to myself: "Whatever else, this man is a great artist." After all, science is only another one of the arts, as is statesmanship. But these are categories. From Weizmann, from his voice, from his speech, from his eyes and hands, from his mastery of words and from his humor I felt the reach of a man who has at once the gift of panorama and the gift of intimacy which characterize the most winning artists.

I sat with the Los Angeles paper in my lap on the green baize sofa, thinking of this strange journey of Weizmann's. "Through the land of Moab." I did not really know where Moab was, but some of my people, a hundred generations removed, must have known. What was there about the rhythm of that phrase that was so moving, so poignantly evocative? What was I doing in the Thalberg Building? Why wasn't I in Moab? How did this displacement come about? I looked at the script on my desk and my heart sank. Miss Garbo wasn't any worse off than when I came in several hours before. It was almost noon, I hadn't invented a single fresh disaster. The producer was coming for lunch to gloat over Miss G's new tribulations. But there were no new ones. I must get to work. Instead, I remembered my second meeting with Chaim Weizmann.

That time he told the story of Fritz Haber. On a visit to Berlin before the advent of Hitler he was shown through the Kaiser Wilhelm Institute, the leading scientific establishment in Germany, by its head, Fritz Haber. Haber was a converted Jew, like Walter Rathenau more German than the Germans, a Nobel Prize winner and acknowledged as one of the two or three foremost chemists in the world. Later the Nazis were to claim that they lost the first World War through Jewish betrayal; actually it was a Jew, Fritz Haber, who made it possible for them to fight as long as they did. When the supply of nitrates from Chile, indispensable for the making of gunpowder, was shut off from Germany by the blockade, Haber employed a method of making nitrates from the air which he had discovered and gave Germany's armaments industry a new lease on life.* This service to the fatherland was acknowledged. It won for Haber the personal friendship of the Kaiser. He was the other Jewish friend of the Kaiser, the first being Albert Ballin, the steamship man. When the Kaiser fled Germany, Ballin committed suicide in the despair of grief. Haber turned in all his money to buy bonds for the Third Reich and was given, by a grateful nation, the headship of the Kaiser Wilhelm Institute so that he could continue his researches. He was probably one of the half-dozen most important and venerated individuals in Germany.

Haber showed Weizmann through the Institute. In all the faculties two or three of the leading positions were held by Jews. When the inspection was over, Weizmann conveyed to Haber a sense he had of malaise, of a growing insecurity in Germany, of an impending storm which might engulf Haber himself and his Jewish colleagues.

* It is not impossible to make an analogy, fraught with irony, between the service that Haber did for Germany in World War I and that performed by Weizmann for England.

Haber was indignant. He resented the classification as arbitrary.

"We are not Jews," he said. "We are Germans."

"That," said Weizmann, "is an opinion the Germans may not share."

Haber scoffed at this. The idea of giving out positions on a theory of racial percentages appeared ridiculous to him. That any German government would ever indulge in such sportive fractions in the realm of pure science was an idea so vulgarly remote that Haber was irritated. And yet Weizmann insisted it could be so; he smelled it. The situation in the Kaiser Wilhelm Institute was not healthy; he felt a foreboding about it. He broached to Haber the subject of his visit, which was to invite him to come to Palestine to teach at the Hebrew University.

The idea did not appeal to Haber at all. It was like offering a great prima donna a role in a provincial stock company. Why leave the greatest scientific institution in a country, inevitably to be again the greatest, for an obscure chemical laboratory on a hilltop in Jerusalem? The impulse towards Palestine that had thrilled through Weizmann from his earliest boyhood in a Russian village was foreign to Haber. He was a German of the Germans. What he had to give he would give to Germany. Why yield what he had now for the caprice of a man, however gifted, who was after all an *Ost-Jude?* Weizmann went away empty-handed. But in 1933 he heard from Haber! Weizmann offered him asylum in London. When Haber arrived, bewildered and broken, Weizmann met him at the station. He had secured for him a position in Cambridge.

At Cambridge, Haber was received with great distinction, but the adjustment was not easy for him. He did not know the language. He suffered from chronic asthma and the climate was unfavorable. He went to Switzerland for his health. There, while Weizmann was taking his own holiday, he went to dinner with Haber. They talked on general subjects when suddenly Haber

101

said: "Dr. Weizmann, is the offer you made me in Berlin still open?"

It was the first time either man had made any reference to the conversation years before in the director's office at the Kaiser Wilhelm Institute. Weizmann said it was indeed open. But didn't he want to return to Cambridge where the atmosphere was so friendly to him?

"I want," said Haber, "to go to Palestine. I want to end my days teaching there."

Weizmann made the arrangements. Haber started for Palestine. On the way there, at Basle, he had a severe attack and died. When his will was opened it was found that he had left his library and papers to the Research Institute in Rehovoth, of which Chaim Weizmann is the honorary director. They are housed there now in a special room called the Haber Library.

I believe that in the course of this narrative Weizmann told how, in 1935, he had called on a Stuttgart lawyer, who was then farming in Palestine. This man said: "I am very glad to meet you, Dr. Weizmann. I've been interested in Zionism for thirty years." Weizmann expressed surprise; somehow this reformed agriculturalist didn't, to his practiced eye, show the stigmata of a Zionist. "Oh, yes," said the pioneer. "thirty years: twenty-eight against—two for!"

But Haber's conversion was on a plane more heroic. I sat there, dawdling away Metro's time, while I contemplated this extraordinary hegira. What a scenario! Why was I writing for Miss G. when there was Haber—a genius who had dealt subtly and securely with the infinitesimal, fleeing the insanity of other human beings to a land that was always his without his knowing, forced suddenly to select, in the immense cross reference of biology and of history, the one all-but-extinguished clue that could unite him to his blacked-out past, that might restore to him his faculty and his skill and his home? What a journey— Berlin to Rehovoth—1935! Shaw once said that films bored him because they showed you interminably people getting in and out of limousines, trains, buses. He found himself less interested in how people got to different places than in what they did when they got there. But here was a transit in the grand manner, intimate as well as epic, lit by the sparks from the great voltages of historic forces, holding in solution all the elements of our contemporary tragedy. At the same time very simple, greatly simple—a man going home. The death in Basle; the Promised Land shut off. Clip forward a century with a dissolve: flash into the future: some student in the library taking down one of Haber's books, coming upon a marginal note illuminating some dilemma of his own. He looks up at the bust of Haber in the wall niche. Was this Haber? What sort of man was he? Must look him up. . . .

I was startled out of this meditation by the cheery voice of my producer.

"Well, Sam, have you got anything? Oh! I see you're thinking!"

There is genuine respect in Hollywood for a writer's thoughts, since they are so highly paid.

His voice came back again, friendly, wistful.

"Want to see me? Got anything?"

"Not really."

"Oh, well, take your time. What about tonight? What about a conference tonight?"

"If you don't mind," I heard myself saying, "I'd rather think tonight as well."

Eight-thirty that evening found me in the vast lobby of the Biltmore Hotel, inquiring for the Weizmann dinner. I was directed to the Grand Ballroom. I looked in. The place was full of diners, thousands of them, but at the festooned speakers' table there was no Weizmann. I lingered outside; evidently Weizmann was dining elsewhere. Perhaps he was something of an epicure. I went to the coffee bar for something to eat and then sat in the corridor leading to the Ballroom, watching the

103

phenomena of the Grand Hotel: salesmen waiting for girls, girls waiting for salesmen, or salesmen just sitting. Presently I saw Dr. and Mrs. Weizmann and their friends walking down the corridor. I went up to them.

It must have been more than a year since I had seen Weizmann and he was surprised, but his quiet greeting and his smile of welcome made me happy I had come. He arranged a seat for me at one of the tables, and I went inside.

This was the first meeting of the kind I had ever attended. Soon after the speaking began I realized that it wasn't primarily a Zionist meeting at all. It was the culminating effort of several drives to raise funds for worthy objectives; only a fraction of the money was to go to Palestine. Moreover, there soon developed a kind of fiscal controversy between town and gown, a keen rivalry of generosities. The leading businessman of Los Angeles insisted that his colleagues—"the merchants of this great city"—had in the past contributed to these funds out of all proportion to that contributed by the arts, represented by Hollywood. At this the next speaker, a top executive from one of the famous studios in Hollywood, naturally took umbrage. He denied this disproportion. There was one, but it was the other way round. He matched the businessman statistic for statistic. Things, I thought, were rather tense. A rabbi arose (not the sort of rabbi I had known in my boyhood in Providence Street, patriarchal, learned, and patient, but another type altogether, streamlined, quite indistinguishable from the businessman who had preceded him). Over these lacerations the rabbi sprayed thickly the heavy oil of platitude—fortissimo.

I looked at Weizmann. What was he doing *dans cette galère?* His face was impassive. He looked like a wise Tibetan lama, unseeing and unhearing, as if he were absorbed in some close and intricate inner speculation of his own. The rabbi's voice thundered on. He praised both sides. They were both wonderful —in moderation. He expected them, however, to be more wonderful still. He depicted the plight of people in far places and appealed for more help than had ever been given before. But if the rabbi meant to be ameliorative he did not succeed. Another Montague arose, exhorted, and asseverated, and another Capulet. The atmosphere was shrill. Weizmann arose.

The great crowd got up to greet him, then settled back to listen. The room became very quiet, serene. Weizmann reassured them. Even if the contributions exceeded the wildest expectations, it was a drop in the bucket compared to the need. The portion that would be allotted for Palestine would be at best infinitesimal. He had raised more, he said, from poverty-stricken Whitechapel Jews. They were not to worry about money. Money was not important. The important thing was growth, spiritual growth, spiritual regeneration, spiritual security. If the Nazis won the war there would no longer be a Jewish problem. The Nazis would have settled it in their own way. But he was sure they would not win it, that England would win it. (England was then fighting the German war alone.) Even so; what would be the position of those millions of Jews—what would be left of them—living now in a limbo that was neither death nor life?

Weizmann had been described by the generous chairman as a statesman: he was a statesman without an army, without a police force, without the power to tax. And yet in Palestine itself a miracle had been effected. He told of the work of the halutzim, or pioneers, how they had fought an intractable soil neglected for two thousand years and had made it blossom. He told of a little band of men who had gone to make a settlement in the North. They made a start, they built huts and barns and started an irrigation project. There was an Arab foray, and during the night what these halutzim had built was destroyed. They built again. It was again destroyed. The colonists built again but this time behind a stockade. The community is now one of the most flourishing in the region.

It was rather a miracle. The miracle was also in that hall. Here were three thousand people sitting at midnight, five thousand miles away from Palestine, and they were absorbed in the development of a country most of them would never see and for which, moreover, they were expected to pay! Weizmann made visible what was being done there: the extraordinary and succeeding effort to build up a country which had been waste for two thousand years with a people which had been waste for two thousand years, and at a moment when a great portion of them, perhaps the best portion, had been decimated in one of the most terrible persecutions in history. It was being done. Weizmann told how triumphantly it was being done.

"We are reproached by the whole world. We are told that we are dealers in old clothes and junk. We are perhaps the sons of dealers in old clothes, but we are the grandsons of prophets. Think of the grandsons and not of the sons. . . ."

As the quiet, matter-of-fact voice permeated the room, I got a sense of perhaps the most distinguishing and inspiring of human manifestations: the spectacle of a dedicated man, to whose passion and vision the impossible was merely an invitation. In a kind of trance the audience listened to the last sentence:

"For if you root a tree deep in the soil and water it with love and devotion, it will grow and it will flourish, and its branches will reach to Heaven."

There was a lit response from the audience—an emotional upsurge in which I shared. It was not clamorous—as stage people say, we "took the speaker's tone"—and there is nothing clamorous in Weizmann's oratorical method. But everyone was unexpectedly stirred, the common denominator notched up; a glow of some sort of release suffused everyone. The applause was long, murmurous, and intense. Town and gown came together for once; each forgot what the other hadn't given. There was a consciousness of an objective higher even than the most laudable of drives. I made for the dais and found Mrs. Weizmann. Her husband was surrounded. Finally, through a gap in the shifting crowd he saw me and made a sign to me. I joined him for a moment.

"I see that tonight will be no good," he said. "Will you join

106

me Saturday in Arrowhead? The hotel will be closed except for us. There will be no one there. You can dine and spend the night if you like."

I promised.

On the longish drive home to Beverly Hills I tried to analyze the emotion I had felt in the hall, the spell of which abided still. This crusade of Weizmann's had, of course, the excitement and the gallantry of any contest against impossible odds—David alone in a Goliath world of apathy and hostility. Here was this man, with a brilliant scientific career behind him and ahead of him, who could spend his leisure agreeably with his intellectual equals, splitting his life in two, traveling to the ends of the earth, incessantly in contact with people who could not specially interest him, in order to ignite them with his ardor, meeting opposition, indifference, misunderstanding. Only tonight a man I knew well, an executive sitting at my table, who had met Weizmann a few days before at a private dinner, said to me: "Yes, he is a fascinating man, but why is he here? Why isn't he in Palestine?" I refrained from saying what I wanted to say: "Probably he would prefer infinitely to be in Palestine to being in Hollywood talking to you."

For half a century Weizmann had spent his life in this eroding dualism, because obviously for him the summons was imperious. But was it imperious for me? I was aware that this whole Zionist concept was ambushed by hecklers. Wells and Shaw, Mrs. Weizmann once told me, were uninterested. They were above the claims of "small nationalities." The radicals of the left, of course, sloughed it off in a familiar patter. What the world suffered from now was a superfluity of nationalisms. Why add to their number? But among many of these was manifest a tendency to ignore the fate of living people—they planned interminably for the unborn, but they were rather callous to the sufferings of those who had already made the hazardous commitment. After all, there were 550,000 Jews already living in Palestine who might not be there but for this dream, and Palestine might offer

107

a haven for millions more who might otherwise be tortured and killed. But Weizmann was not concerned, except incidentally, with asylum; he was concerned with recognition. For this artist-dreamer the essence was here.

Weizmann's soul lived in Palestine. But mine didn't. What was it I felt then? What was the source of the tug? This was his reality. Was it mine? His childhood had been spent in a Russian village under the Tsars. Beyond the hill was the eternal specter of the pogrom. But across the city from me, beyond the hill up which ran Providence Street, there was no pogrom. In fact, on the other side of town from me lived no Tsarist official but Robert Benchley, who, I was to find out many years later, was as wistful on his side as I was on mine. I remembered Herzl, whose conversion to Zionism began in Paris when he heard the cry of Frenchmen—watching the proudly disgraced figure of Dreyfus, parading his dishonor before squads of soldiers: "*Mort aux Juifs.*" But I had not heard these cries. Of course since 1933 the complexion of things had altered. The Nazis had considerably widened the potential of human malevolence; but again Weizmann was not concerned with escape—his longing was for recovery, for home. But was I? In the dissolving planes of social and economic revolution would not these racial atavisms be dissipated in the astringent ozone of a New Order, filtered through panaceas? This nostalgia might be a reality for Weizmann. Was it for me?

And yet there was something. There was something. I thought back. Wasn't there, from earliest childhood, a sense of not belonging with the unconsciousness of the others, an anxiety, a distress, a feeling here and there of tentativeness, a sensation like the sudden fall of an elevator, a sense altogether, even anticipating any outward slight, of the penumbral, the unresolved? There was. Well, what if there was? Would this dream of Weizmann's, even if it were realized, make the essential difference? And yet, I could not deny it, there was something terribly intimate in the pull of all this. But was this emotion vicarious, borrowed? Was I yielding merely to the immense persuasion of Weizmann's personality?

I must be on my guard!

It was out of season, and, except for the Weizmanns' cottage, the Arrowhead Springs Hotel was closed. I had known the head-waiter, Tony, for years. I always thought he was Italian, but he turned out to be a Zionist from Palermo, who had once attended a Weizmann meeting in Rome, and having his idol and Mrs. Weizmann all to himself in the small dining room put him into an ecstasy of service. Weizmann was in a mellow mood, and told some very funny Jewish stories. He roamed over his past; told of his teaching days at the University of Manchester; of his friend-ship with C. P. Scott, the famous editor of the *Guardian,* whom he adored; of Rutherford, who was then on the faculty; of Schuster, the physicist, who had a sharp wit. Marie Stopes, who later became a leader in the movement for birth control, was there at the time doing research on botany. She was full of exuberance and expressed definitive opinions on many subjects. Professor Schuster was more circumscribed. One day he inquired of Miss Stopes how she was getting on in her work, and she answered: "Oh wonderfully! I make a new discovery every day!" Professor Schuster's inquiry was statistical: "Tell me, Dr. Stopes, if you discover on Tuesday that your discovery of Monday was all wrong, do you count that as one discovery or as two?"

Weizmann told of going to see Baron Edmond de Rothschild, the greatest individual benefactor of Palestine in its earliest days, to ask him for five million additional pounds for colonization. He presented it as an investment: the colonies would pay him till his capital was refunded. But the Baron said: "Dr. Weiz-mann, do you know what a rich man is? He is a man who lives on the interest of his interest. By that definition, if I make this investment I should no longer be a rich man." Weizmann desisted from his effort to impoverish the Baron, but he com-mented drily: "The irony is that if Rothschild had taken the chance, the colonies would have remained in the family after everything else had been taken away by the Nazis." He told of going to see the great Ehrlich to interest him in the Hebrew University in Jerusalem. Ehrlich knew of Weizmann's scientific work and assumed that his visit was about that. Weizmann allowed Ehrlich to show him his experiments, wondering all the while how he could switch the conversation to the University. At last he took his courage in his hands and told Ehrlich that he had come at the suggestion of Baron Edmond de Rothschild of Paris on the subject of the Hebrew University in Jerusalem. Ehrlich listened for a few minutes and exclaimed: "But why Jerusalem?" Weizmann told him. Ehrlich listened. After a time he pulled out his watch. He was rather frantic.

"Do you realize," he said, "you have kept me nearly an hour? Do you know that out there in the corridor there are counts, princes, and cabinet ministers who will be happy if I give them ten minutes?"

Weizmann answered: "Yes, Professor Ehrlich, but the difference between me and your professional visitors is this. They come to get an injection from you. I come to give you one!"

Interspersed through Weizmann's conversation was a series of sharp, swift portraits of great personalities Weizmann had known in the Zionist movement and outside it: General Smuts, for whom he has a special affection; Lloyd George, Churchill, Zangwill, Herzl, the founder of modern Zionism, Ruppin, with whom he first went to Palestine in 1907 and who successfully introduced mixed farming in the difficult terrain there; Ahad Ha'am, pen name of the brilliant Hebrew writer Asher Ginzberg, and Shmarya Levin. When he spoke of the latter his eyes lit up: "There was a marvelous man. I wish you could have known him." He talked a lot about Levin, of his eloquence, his devotion, his learning, and his wit. Of an august American jurist who discovered Zionism late in life, Levin had remarked: "He became *bar mitzvah* at sixty!"

After dinner we sat in the living room of the Weizmann

110

bungalow. I had occupied a similiar maisonette some years before on a weekend visit with George Gershwin not long before he died, the last time but one I was to see him alive. Then the resort was teeming with people. Now it was deserted save for us. On the way out Gershwin sang for me what were to be his last melodies, with that transparent eagerness to please which was one of the most engaging of his qualities.

Now, again, it was a lovely evening. I looked outside at the same view, at the same snow-capped, uncaring mountains, rosy against the setting summer sun, so indifferent to the identity of the people who came season after season to stare at them. I sat talking to Mrs. Weizmann and to the others in the room. Mrs. Weizmann told me of their travels. They had come across the country, they had been to Toronto, to Montreal, to Ottawa, and had finally reached here by way of San Francisco. I stole a glance at Weizmann. He looked tired. I didn't wonder. To how much, in these many cities, rabbinical oratory had he listened, to how many exhortations, on how many assembly lines of cliché had he been trundled! What distances had he not had to travel to cross the areas of complacency and combative arrogance! And yet he was used to the stillness of laboratories. He was inured to the pursuit of a secret which, however elusive, was mercifully silent. I remembered a story someone had told me about him. Lord Peel, who was chairman of the Palestine Royal Commission of 1936, coming into the Weizmann laboratory in Rehovoth found him bent over a test tube.

"What are you doing, Dr. Weizmann?" asked Lord Peel.

"I am creating absorptive capacity," said Weizmann.

I had read about Herzl that when he went to Russia to see the notorious von Plehve, Russia's bitterly anti-Semitic Minister of the Interior, the Jews of the villages ran out kissing his hands as if Messiah had come. From his official biography I learned that Herzl had several times erred by treating his hopes

111

in terms of promises. But here was a Messiah who knew the costs, who knew the dangers, who knew the penalties. Here was a Messiah with a genius for measurement. Whatever inner exaltation his dream fed him must be filtered, in his public utterances, through a close mesh of understatement. To be Messianic without flamboyance couldn't be easy. On the one hand, to deny the bread of ready promise to the hungry—on the other, to deflate the complacency of the overfed—this was a hard life.

Several times in his brief career Herzl felt that he had the materialization of his dream within his grasp: a Jewish state in Palestine under German protection. True Palestine then was a part of the Ottoman Empire, but the Sultan, after the Armenian massacres, had only one friend in Europe—the Kaiser. The Kaiser's word with the Sultan, Herzl was assured by the Kaiser's own advisers, would go a long way. Herzl asked for an audience with the Kaiser. It was granted him; not in Berlin where Herzl wanted it, but in Palestine where the Kaiser was going to dedicate a church on one of his grandiose junkets.

Perhaps nothing could more vividly epitomize the difference between two leaders and two countries than the contrast between this meeting and another which took place eight years later between Weizmann and Arthur Balfour in Manchester and was to result eventually in the Balfour Declaration.

In 1898, after a long approach and much encouragement from von Bülow and Eulenberg, the German ambassador at Vienna, Herzl was granted two interviews with the Kaiser, first in Constantinople, then in Palestine. As a result of the encouragement he received from the Kaiser's representatives, Herzl's hopes ran high. But the actual audiences described in Herzl's official biography are the most insulting and degrading interviews between two representative men I have ever read. The Kaiser, von Bülow, and Hohenlohe talk like three Kleagles, wondering whether to postpone a lynching.

"There are among your people," says the Kaiser, "certain

112

elements whom it would be a good thing to move to Palestine. I am thinking, for instance, of the usurers of Hesse. . . ."

When Herzl tells them that he can raise the money to irrigate Palestine, you can see the Kaiser's and von Bülow's mouths water:

"Well," says the Kaiser, "you certainly have enough money —more than all of us."

And von Bülow: "Yes, when it comes to money, which is such a problem for us, you certainly don't suffer from a shortage."

Here are made audible the authentic voices of the men whose descendants were to offer to barter five hundred thousand Jewish lives in Hungary for a price. The German negotiations, of course, beyond giving the Kaiser a grandiloquent moment, came to nothing. They merely dashed Herzl's hopes and the hopes of the poor millions who depended on him. The poor Jews of Europe who were already packing for the emigration the belongings they did not have, had to unpack again. Unlike Herzl, Weizmann's orientation was always toward England.

During the conversation on that Saturday night Mrs. Weizmann said: "Chaim, tell Mr. Behrman about that letter you got after the Balfour Declaration from your old Hebrew teacher." With a wry smile Weizmann told it. He was born in a village near Pinsk. (Reflex memory: Pinsk—knew it well from constant jokes about it in vaudeville shows at Poli's in Worcester. Pinsk —terminal for travelers from Minsk.) When he was ten years old, Weizmann made the journey from his village, Motol, to the, for him, bewildering metropolis of Pinsk. Nearly forty years later, after the Balfour Declaration was issued, Weizmann received a letter with an enclosure from the man who had taught him Hebrew when he was ten or eleven. In this letter, the teacher congratulated Weizmann and said that he was very proud of his pupil and especially of his having written the enclosed letter, the contents of which he considered prophetic. Evidently the teacher had written to Weizmann when he had made the dangerous leap from Motol to Pinsk, enjoining him in the blandishments of the great city (population of Pinsk in those days, 35,000) not to forget his origins. The ten-year-old boy wrote back reassurances, and this was the letter the teacher had kept all these years. It was written in copperplate Hebrew and still clearly legible. The boy thanked the teacher for his good wishes. He promised that he would never forget that he was a Jew and then branched off into a kind of fantasy of Zionism, which did not exist then except in the enthusiasm of a little group called the Choveve Zion, or lovers of Zion. In this fantasy he said that the only thing for the Jews was Palestine, that he would dream always of the return to Palestine. At the end of the letter he said that the Jews would have to accomplish this restoration by themselves, that they could not rely on anybody but that if assistance ever did come from anywhere it would come from England.

From there it came. Early in 1906 a general election took place in England, and Balfour was chosen to contest the Clayton division of North Manchester. Charles Dreyfus, who was managing director of the Clayton Aniline Works and chairman of the Manchester Zionist Society, was also a member of the Manchester Home Council and a prominent Conservative. In the middle of the hullabaloo of the campaign, at Dreyfus' suggestion, Balfour consented to receive Weizmann. He was interested in meeting one of the Jews who had fought against the acceptance of the Uganda offer made by his government. Dreyfus was anxious for Balfour to persuade Weizmann that he had made a mistake in opposing the offer. Weizmann described the scene: he was brought up to see Balfour in a room in the old-fashioned hotel which was the Conservative headquarters. The corridors were crowded with people waiting to see the candidate. Balfour granted fifteen minutes for the interview "simply to break the monotony of his routine," Dreyfus explained.

Weizmann had been less than two years in the country, and

114

his English was none too good. He describes Balfour sitting in his usual pose, his long legs stretched out in front of him, his expression imperturbable. He went at once to the heart of the interview: he wanted to know why some of the Zionists were so violently opposed to the Uganda offer. The British government was really anxious to do something to relieve the misery of the Jews, and the problem was a practical one calling for a practical approach. Weizmann told him. He dwelt on the spiritual side of Zionism, on the immense tug of the scattered Jewish people for the return to Palestine and to nowhere else on earth. He said that if Moses had wandered into the Sixth Zionist Congress when it was adopting the resolution in favor of the Commission for Uganda, he would surely have broken the tablets once again. He felt sure that the Jewish people would never produce either the money or the energy needed in order to build up a wasteland and make it habitable unless that land was Palestine. For the Jews Palestine had this inescapable appeal that was at once magical and romantic. Jewish history had been what it was because it had never let go its grip on Palestine: it was an imbedded racial memory. They would never—no matter what the difficulties—forsake it.

Weizmann said he looked at Balfour. Had he lost him? He was sweating blood. Was Balfour's expression of interest and courtesy the mask of boredom? He was ready to bow himself out of the room, but Balfour held him back and began to question him about the growth of the movement. Weizmann answered his questions when suddenly he heard himself saying: "Mr. Balfour, supposing I were to offer you Paris instead of London, would you take it?"

Balfour sat up a bit and looked at him. He said: "But, Dr. Weizmann, we have London."

"That is true," said Weizmann. "But we had Jerusalem when London was a marsh."

Balfour leaned back and continued to stare. Weizmann remembers vividly two things Balfour said. The first was: "Are there many Jews who think as you do?"

Weizmann answered: "I believe I speak the mind of millions of Jews whom you will never see and who cannot speak for themselves but with whom I could pave the streets of the country I come from."

Balfour said: "It is curious. The Jews I meet are quite different."

"Mr. Balfour," said Weizmann, "you meet the wrong kind of Jews."

During that Saturday evening, because I told my host that my knowledge was so scrappy that I had not even a basis for dissent, Weizmann gave me a whole purview of the Zionist movement. He described his childhood days in Russia. His father was in the lumber business. In the summer as a boy he used to travel on the lumber rafts with the logs on the Pina River and through a canal which connected the Pina with Brest Litovsk on the Bug, the main tributary of the Vistula, which empties into the Baltic Sea at the port of Danzig.

He told of the effect of the advent of Theodor Herzl, how the nascent, vague, mystical feeling for the Return was given body by Herzl's epoch-making pamphlet, *Der Judenstaat,* though Herzl actually didn't mention Palestine in it. He remembered that when Herzl called the First Zionist Congress at Basle in 1897, he first heard the news in Moscow where he had gone to negotiate for a small chemical patent. He left Moscow at once and went to Brest Litovsk, which was the train junction for Warsaw, Berlin, and Basle. There he met his father, who was a poor man. He brought out a passport and ten rubles and said: "I know you want to go to Basle. Go ahead. If you start now you will arrive on the third day of the Congress." Weizmann couldn't bear to take the ten rubles and didn't go. Instead, he went to work to mobilize for Zionism in Russia. He and his

116

friends traveled from city to city, from town to town, on boats and in canoes, through the swamps and marshes, to all the ghettos they could reach. They preached to the Jews that a great time had come—a Congress was taking place where for the first time in two thousand years the Jews as a national entity were to do something about their own destiny. The foundation was to be laid for a Jewish State. They spoke to them in a vein, partly romantic, partly Messianic, partly realistic, and as the people to whom they spoke were all young and oppressed they were exalted and believed and were ready for a miracle. "Because," said Weizmann, "when you are young and oppressed you believe in miracles!"

I was certainly not young but, as the tapestry unfolded, I began to believe in a miracle, too. I saw the dream approach its fulfillment: on this millennially deserted Mediterranean coast cities and flourishing colonies, scientific institutions and libraries, the Hebrew University on Mount Scopus, theatres and concert halls. When Toscanini came to conduct the Palestine Orchestra and walked out on the veranda of the Weizmann house in Rehovoth and saw before him the efflorescence and the clear vista of the Promised Land, he wept.

By the time Weizmann finished his précis it was very late. I felt sorry for him. After all, he was under no obligation to conduct a special seminar for my benefit. Mrs. Weizmann ordered coffee and drinks. We sat around talking. Somebody turned on the radio. It was Saturday night, June 22, 1941. The radio blurted its news. Germany had attacked Russia! Already the Germans were on the march. I looked at Weizmann. His eyes were grave. "It's the second time," he said. He recalled that when World War I came, two years after his father's death, his mother was still in Pinsk and had to flee then from the German invasion. From Pinsk she fled to Warsaw, from Warsaw to Moscow. She was then sixty years old and endured the storm of the Revolution and the Civil War. It was not until 1921 that Weizmann suc-

117

ceeded in getting her and his brother out. He built a house for her in Haifa where she lived until her death at the age of eighty-seven.

"But now they're coming again—the Germans. What will become of all these people?"

In his eyes I saw the tragic premonition of what actually did happen to them. There was silence in the room.

"Yes," he said, "for our people there, millions of them, it will be terrible."

But after a moment his eyes brightened. He leaned forward.

"But in the long run—and this is the important thing—it will be good for England," he added.

The next morning I said good-by to my hosts and started back to Hollywood. On the way in, in the car, I heard Churchill's speech in which he promised all-out aid to Russia. The next morning I was back in my room in the Thalberg Building. I summoned will power. I had to get this thing done. But I was suffused with the impression of Weizmann. He was obviously one in that rare category of men who make you feel like throwing everything over and following them, who make you feel that in following them you can do no wrong, only be expressing more intensely the best impulses in yourself. What was the extraordinary synthesis of personality that gave certain individuals this power? Perhaps the chief element was an incandescence of self-dedication in the leader himself. Fuse this with enormous personal charm, and the combination is irresistible. I was sunk. I was—as the ultramodern musicologists have it—I was "sent."

As I bent over my desk, taut, determined willy-nilly to operate on Miss Garbo, I saw between me and the page the image of a young man, his face set, paddling a canoe through a dark and lonely Russian swamp, his objective one of those villages that were to figure in the news in the next years—a hundred occupied places taken—a hundred occupied places retaken; there unrolled before me a great and tumultuous and scarred procession of which this young man was one.

What a film it would make! What a story! What a relief it would be, for once to work on that instead of toiling toward dissolution, to be caught up in a dream whose end was affirmation!

Meantime, I dug my scalpel into Miss Garbo.

HYPER
OR HYPO?

Dr. Emanuel Libman

1939

ON HIS SIXTIETH BIRTHDAY, IN
1932, the "pupils, friends, and colleagues" of Dr. Emanuel Libman
undertook to pay him a tribute.
There was a dinner party at the
Waldorf with speeches, but the
occasion elicited from Dr. Libman's friends a more enduring
memorial than the pleasantries of
after-dinner congratulations. Eminent doctors all over the world

who had either been pupils of Dr. Libman or had been influenced by him or admired him were asked to contribute articles in their respective fields to be presented to Dr. Libman on his birthday and to be known as the *Libman Anniversary Volumes*. The editorial committee, in its introduction to the books that resulted from this invitation, apologizes that "material limitations rendered it impossible to publish the contributions of all who desired to voice in this way their admiration and friendship." Nevertheless, enough got in to fill three closely and beautifully printed volumes. Scientists from England and America, from France and Germany, from Italy and Norway, from Japan and Sweden put their best foot forward: 147 savants cover 1,284 pages with alembicated thoughts on their specialties. The authors listed in the table of contents constitute a scientific *Almanach de Gotha:* Alexis Carrel and Albert Einstein, Lord Horder and William H. Welch, Harlow Brooks and Alfred E. Cohn, the Mayo brothers and Östen Holsti. Ryokichi Inada has written about "The Disturbances of the Circulatory System in Beriberi," Pierre Lecomte du Nouÿ on "The Biological Problem," Jonas S. Friedenwald on "The Pathogenesis of Albuminuric Retinitis," Cesare Pezzi on "The Radioscopic Sign of the 'Hilum Dance,'" F. J. Poynton on "The Dawn of Heart Disease in Childhood," Professor Achard on "La Maladie des Cardiaques Noirs." The late Dr. William H. Welch, probably the greatest figure in American medicine of his time, in his introduction to the anniversary volumes said that they reflect "in a most impressive manner the character and variety of the fields of medical science and art cultivated by Libman, his international reputation, and the wide extent of his professional and human contacts and influence."

The subject of the *Libman Anniversary Volumes* is a bachelor. Since 1889 he has lived in a narrow four-story brownstone house at 180 East Sixty-fourth Street. The Doctor is proud of the antiquity of his house; he will seize you by the arm, take you to the front windows on the fourth floor, and make you look back through the hall and his study to the windows facing on the garden. The line is not true. The house curves somewhere along its middle, and this architectural eccentricity Dr. Libman cherishes. With him live his sister and two nephews. The nephews are twins and so alike in appearance that you can hardly tell them apart. Both did well at Johns Hopkins and have lately been appointed to interneships at Mt. Sinai. Dr. Libman has very Spartan ideas about the bringing up of these young men. When other people are there, he will pass his nephews in the hall of his house, without greeting them, and none of his friends have met them. While they were at Johns Hopkins hardly anyone knew of their relationship to Dr. Libman, but although he never speaks of them, he is probably proud of the fact that they have come along entirely on their own. "Young people," he says, "should work in the dark." For their sakes, he does not want people to think that they have traded on his position.

The waiting rooms and consultation offices on the ground floor have the sobriety and the steel engravings of porticoed ruins and bearded dignitaries characteristic of most doctors' offices. You get perhaps the first hint of the Doctor's unorthodoxy when you discover that he has added to the gallery of distinguished medical men that line the walls of his inner sanctum the portraits of several distinguished patients. Hanging with Koch and Pasteur, with Welch and Janeway, are Sarah Bernhardt and Albert Einstein. The dramatic portrait of the Divine One, whom Dr. Libman attended in her last illness and whom he adored, has a florid and affectionate inscription in French; the one on Professor Einstein's reads in German: "To the noble-minded Dr. Libman with the secret-divining eyes."

Professor Ludwig Aschoff, generally considered the world's leading pathologist, who contributed "Uber den Enterokokkus Libman" (the streptococcus named after Libman, its discoverer) to the anniversary volumes, tells how much he was impressed by Libman's "infallible physician's eyes" when he first met him at Mt. Sinai. It is undeniable that Dr. Libman is one of those individuals who convey instantaneously a suggestion of genius, and it is probably chiefly due to his eyes. They are gray, clear, and penetrating. He is a small man, about the size of Toscanini or Napoleon, with both of whom he has elements in common: authority, great mobility, and colossal memory. His skin is dead white and his flatly brushed hair is silver. His gray mustache is neatly trimmed. His fingers are long, youthfully supple, and active. He fixes you with a falconlike, darting look—a mercurial ghost. The diagnostic sixth sense, the ability to sniff disease, the accurate, swift generalization are facets of a temperamental inability to do anything slowly, a highly charged and incessant volatility. Those who disbelieve the Libman legend derogate this quickness, as the temperamentally slow inevitably suspect the temperamentally fast, and the epithets "superficial," "guesswork," "flamboyant" have often been applied to Libman's lightning diagnostic method. But those in a position to know will tell you that Dr. Libman's knowledge in every field of medicine is encyclopedic and his memory phenomenal. He has read everything and remembers everything. He will see a patient whose father he treated thirty years before and tell the son details of the father's illness which the son had forgotten or never knew. He is the last of the old clinicians like Janeway and Delafield, who were consultants before the human body had been zoned and subdivided by the departmental specialists. He is equally at home with the bacteriologist, the clinician, and the pathologist. This universality in Libman's knowledge is stressed by his partisans. These, indignant at the imputation of superficiality, say that Libman is one of the few men who check the references printed at the end of each scientific paper to see whether they are accurately quoted. Such papers are sent to Dr. Libman by the hundred from all over the world. Dr. Carrel once said, "In the same manner as Claude Bernard personified physiology, Libman is medicine itself."

Libman has a tremendous admiration for Dr. Carrel and sees him occasionally but, as he says, sparingly, because he considers

Dr. Carrel's work too important to be interrupted and feels that his energy should be saved for his research rather than dissipated in social amenities. Once in a while Libman also visits Dr. Einstein in Princeton. Among Libman's limited list of friends are some who are also patients, such as the Eugene Meyers and the George Backers. They all call him Libby.

Once Dr. Libman was invited to a dinner attended by President Harding. The story goes that the following morning Libman called up Eugene Meyer and said, "Who is Vice-President?" When Meyer expressed surprise over this sudden interest of the Doctor in minor officialdom, Libman explained, "Because whoever he is, within six months he will be President. The President has a disease of the coronary arteries." And so it came to pass.

Dr. Libman is supposed to have an uncanny instinct that tells him whether a patient will survive an illness. In examining a patient, he pays close attention to symptoms likely to escape the superficial observer: color and expression of the face, posture, odor, pigmentation, the breathing, the speech, clubbing of the fingers, tenderness over the sternum, and other manifestations. It is said that once on entering a hospital ward he sniffed and said, "I smell typhoid here." It turned out that a patient just brought in was in the early stages of that disease. Another time he "smelled" a case of gas-bacillus infection. His uncanny instinct for color and smell in disease leads him often to impromptu diagnoses when he is off duty. As when he peered at a mother-and-child painting by an old master in the drawing room of a millionaire friend and proclaimed, "Rickets!" On another occasion, so the tale runs, he came up close to a tall Van Dyke and declared that the bearded immortal hanging there undeniably suffered from subacute bacterial endocarditis, a disease which it remained for Osler and Libman to discover some centuries later. Often, at a movie, Dr. Libman will dim somewhat the irradiation from a glamour girl by telling you that she is working up to pernicious anemia. One day, while he was lunching with Belle

125

Greene of the Morgan Library, the waiter became maddeningly inept, misplacing dishes and forgetting orders. Miss Greene was irritated. Dr. Libman mollified her. He explained to her that the waiter was suffering from an obscure disease that made him momentarily unable to coördinate—he would be all right by the dessert. He was.

Very early, Dr. Libman became known as a remarkable diagnostician. A paper of his on the dread disease subacute bacterial endocarditis has become a classic. Doctors will tell you that if he had done nothing else in his long career, this paper alone would assure him of immortality. The disease, observed and described by many, was first firmly established as an entity by him and is therefore also known as Libman's disease. Though many bacteria may be the cause, streptococcus viridans is the most common. It took tremendous patience to prove that this bacteria invade the endocardium, the lining of the heart, where they cause irreparable damage. To make a positive diagnosis of this disease is generally possible only when the bacteria are found in the blood stream, but it is said that Libman can do it without such evidence and that in many cases post-mortem findings proved him to be correct.

In later years, working almost entirely as a diagnostician, he has become absorbed by the distinction between patients who are under- and over-sensitive to pain. For this, he has devised the Libman test: he presses or pokes the patients (most often without warning) with the thumb just under the ear, in the mastoid region, and from the response he grades the patients as normals, or as hypo- or hyper-sensitives. In his paper "Observations on Individual Sensitiveness to Pain," he has some interesting things to say about the courage of Indians, for example, who are usually not very sensitive to pain. He had a study made of leading pugilists and found that 97 per cent were hypo-sensitive. "The pugilist," he wrote, "suffers from shock, usually not from pain."

The Eugene Meyer chauffeur, a middle-aged stalwart of Irish

126

extraction, was astonished one day, while he was holding the door for Dr. Libman, when he was suddenly given the Libman test behind the ear. "If it wasn't that I knew he was a great friend of yours, Mrs. Meyer," he said later, "I'd have let him have it." The chauffeur, it seems, was hyper-sensitive.

To the patient who happens to be "hyper," the introduction to the Libman test may be disconcerting. Oscar Levant, who is no respecter of persons, wished to have Libman look him over and was introduced by one of the Doctor's patients. Levant entered the room, and before he could get across it to shake the Doctor's hand, Libman whispered to the intermediary who had arranged the meeting, "Enlarged gall bladder." The introductions over, Dr. Libman promptly poked the unprepared patient behind the ear. As Levant happens to be "hyper," he fell into a chair, speechless. When he got his breath, he looked up at Libman and said, "Professor, you and I are through!" This arrangement was entirely satisfactory to Dr. Libman, who is really interested only in difficult cases, and he permitted the conversation to drift to general topics. This did not finally satisfy Levant, who, recovering from his shock, pleaded with Dr. Libman to resume his examination. "Give me," he begged, "some of that famous sixth sense of yours." Dr. Libman preferred to go on chatting about this and that. The meeting ended pleasantly enough with Levant taking Dr. Libman off to Lindy's, a restaurant not hitherto patronized by the author of the classical paper on subacute bacterial endocarditis.

Libman tells endless stories of his medical practice. There was the woman to whom he was forced to say that her child had syphilis and who cried out ecstatically, "Thank God! I thought it was measles!" Another is about the East Side colleague who sent him a heart case. Dr. Libman examined this patient and saw that he was hopelessly ill. He dismissed him and instructed his wife to take him home at once and put him to bed. He would telephone the family physician later. The patient departed. Dr.

Libman telephoned the man's physician at the end of the day. It was a time when the standard of medical education was much lower than it is now. "Your patient," said Dr. Libman, "has coronary thrombosis." "He has vot?" inquired the bewildered doctor. Libman repeated the name of the disease. "He has coronary vot?" Irritated at his confrere's illiteracy, Dr. Libman abandoned the formalities. "Anyhow, he is sick," snapped Dr. Libman. "No, he isn't," came the imperturbable reply. "He's very sick and he's going to die," insisted Dr. Libman. "He vouldn't. He did!" shouted the East Side man.

Then there was the rich though not overliterate patient who called for an appointment and was told that the fee would be ten dollars. He came in and was examined. As his ailment was negligible, the fee of ten dollars appeared staggering to him. Dr. Libman was firm. "Tell me, Doctor," demanded the patient, "are you really such-a-much that you charge ten dollars for nothing?" Dr. Libman admitted that he was. "Since how long are you such-a-much?" "About four months," said the Doctor. "Four months! That's not long enough for ten dollars. Please, Doctor, write yourself a check for seven dollars."

A patient visiting Dr. Libman for the first time is likely to find his method of examination bewildering and incoherent. To go through such an examination is quite worth the price of admission. After he has given you the Libman test, he will jump from one part of the body to another, tapping hard in one place, lightly elsewhere, pulling down eyelids, pressing under ears, running his thumbnail across the chest. His eyes shift everywhere, his movements are jerky, his speech rapid, his questions staccato and continuous, with no time out for answers. It is only when he reaches auscultation (listening through the stethoscope) that his tempo becomes slightly legato. Then, as like as not, the telephone rings. Someone wants Libman's advice about a student who has been sent to Europe with money from the Emanuel Libman Fellowship Fund, set up some years ago in his honor by patients and former pupils. "I cannot," you hear Libman say, "take the responsibility of sending that young man to Istanbul. However, I've been thinking about him. I have a feeling he should go to Vienna." (This was in the good old days.) He returns to the thumbnailed torso, acquiescent on the sofa, taps and pokes, asks a few more questions without waiting for the answers. The telephone rings again. This time Dr. Libman only listens. He returns, picks up a derby, and clasps it on his silver-gray head. "Sorry. Have to go to Brooklyn. Very interesting case—suppuration behind the ear." And he is gone. You get up to put your shirt on, disturbed by the suspicion that without suppuration behind the ear you are an egregious bore.

On another day you may undergo further tests, and if by this time you are lucky enough to have in some degree won Dr. Libman's confidence he will take you upstairs to the third floor of his house and invite you to hear a record. He is very proud of his records and his phonograph and his piano. He will put on a record, start it going, make a remark about its special soul-searing quality, be seized with impatience, stop the record, and put on another. It has yet to be chronicled of any of these impromptu Libman musicales that he has let a record play through to its end. He will put on in fairly rapid succession ten to fifteen records and give you a brief sample of their quality, or at a still more advanced stage of intimacy he will take you down to the second floor, sit at the piano, and tell you that he would like to give you a little selection of his own. He will then play a part of a short piece by Beethoven, stop abruptly, and promise sometime to let you hear a record by Hofmann of this same piece. You return to the examination room. The mail has come in. There is a long envelope, which he opens feverishly. He shakes out a letter and a check. "Just what I've been hoping for," he announces triumphantly, "a check for $10,000. Gift from a patient. Now I can give that medical library some books they need badly." He is at the telephone calling the hungry librarians.

Dr. Libman asks you to go with him to a consultation. You

walk down Sixty-fourth Street. He is smoking a cigar in an amber holder. The holder drops and breaks in two. He is devastated, because the holder, it turns out, was given to him by a priest who came to him with a disease of the coronary arteries. Dr. Libman has long had the idea that there is a relation between this disease and gout. He has noticed that groups that get one get the other. The priest developed a gouty toe and Dr. Libman is enormously grateful to him for this coöperation.

As Dr. Libman is in a hurry to reach his patient, you hail a taxi. This he waves away impatiently. He walks on for several blocks and finally points to a taxi on a corner. "This is the one I want," he says, and gets in. You drive to the Drake Hotel, Dr. Libman talking incessantly about gout. At the Drake, he asks the taxi to wait outside and you to wait in the lobby. Forty minutes pass. Dr. Libman reappears, but the taxi-driver, for the moment, has disappeared. You ask Dr. Libman why he asked the driver to wait in the first place. "He is, as a matter of fact, not very efficient, but he has dizzy spells," Dr. Libman says. "I once took a trip with him and he waited for me an hour. I thought that was nice, so since then I always use him and ask him to wait. Would you like to see a wonderful collection of kidneys?"

Before you can express your delight at this prospect, the ailing taxi-driver has turned up and Dr. Libman has ordered the man to drive to the Academy of Medicine at Fifth Avenue and 103rd Street. It is after midnight. The attendants stiffen and almost salute as he appears. Dr. Libman passes rapidly down the marble corridors. You go into a great room, the walls covered with row upon row of glass cases containing kidneys. Dr. Libman's sharp eyes run down the rows of cases. He raps on one of them. Evidently this particular kidney has some special pathological distinction. He looks at you and you make a feint at sharing his appreciation. "Come, I'll introduce you to Dr. Martland. He's done wonderful work. This exhibition couldn't have been got together without him." He takes you into a room where three doctors are bending over specimens, carefully printing tags for them. Dr. Libman is greeted with the deferential joy that might meet the Duke of Windsor at a Long Island houseparty. Dr. Libman listens to complaints about the inordinate demands from various institutions for space in this exhibition. There is simply no room for all these kidneys and Dr. Martland will have to draw the line someplace, Libman advises. At one-thirty, he tells Dr. Martland to stop working and says goodbye to his colleagues, promising to appear at the opening of the exhibit on Monday. Fifth Avenue, after these humid chambers, is cool and refreshing. The dizzy taxi-driver holds open the door for him. "I've got to go back to the Drake," says Dr. Libman. "Got to see that patient. Nothing to be done for him, but it will make his wife feel good."

Dr. Libman was born in New York City in 1872. His father, Fajbush Libman, was a picture-framer of fairly comfortable means who lived to see his son's rise to prominence. Emanuel was educated in the public schools and got his A.B. degree from the College of the City of New York in 1891. Three years later, he got his doctor's degree from Columbia. Of all his teachers at the medical school, Dr. Delafield, who later became his friend, made the profoundest impression on him. After graduating from Columbia, Libman became an interne at Mt. Sinai. One of the attending physicians was Dr. Janeway, who also was an inspiration in his professional life. At this period Libman fell under the influence of the great Dr. Jacobi and became interested in the study of pediatrics. In 1896, he went abroad for a year of graduate study in Germany and Austria. The matrix of his scientific future took form during a period of three weeks that year, three weeks spent in Graz under Professor Escherich, an outstanding authority in pediatrics. It was here that Libman undertook a bit of experimental research—a study of streptococcus enteritis in infants, the results of which he published in 1897, when bacteriology was a very young science. It was during this period and

131

this work that Libman's interest in blood cultures and the study of streptococci began.

The universality of Dr. Libman's knowledge, clinically, of pathology and bacteriology has its foundation in this preoccupation, which he has pursued for over forty years. An associate points out that Dr. Libman did a great deal of early work on hematology before it became a specialty and that he is still able to give opinions on obscure and baffling blood specimens. His studies of streptococci have resulted in the publication of several other papers which insure a medical immortality, particularly his work on sinus thrombosis, a serious complication of mastoid disease. When he returned to New York in August, 1897, Libman was appointed assistant pathologist at Mt. Sinai Hospital. His father had bought the house on East Sixty-fourth Street some years before, and the young doctor moved in with the family and opened an office on the parlor floor. He carried on a general practice at first, but he was already known to many doctors as a diagnostician and before long he was a successful consultant. Even as a young man he set arbitrary limits on the time he would spend in making money, reserving a good part of the day for his researches. It is probable that he has never earned more than $30,000 or $40,000 in a single year, which is said to be about a fourth of what an ambitious doctor with his reputation could make if he wanted to. Beyond the expense of keeping up the house, which he eventually took over from his father, he has little need for money and is in the habit of giving it away. With his own funds, he established the William Henry Welch lectures at Mt. Sinai and the Noguchi lectures at Johns Hopkins. A diagnostician in his position may, with no compunction at all, charge rich men heavily, but Dr. Libman usually sends bills for less than the rich man expects to be charged, which often moves the patient to contribute to one of the Doctor's various philanthropic schemes. He minimizes his philanthropy, which actually is a major preoccupation. "Most people do nothing," he says, "and so when one does something, most people think he is doing a great deal."

Dr. Libman became associate pathologist at Mt. Sinai not long after he went there as an assistant, and he held that position for twenty-five years. Physicians who worked as internes during that period speak of it as the Golden Age of the hospital. He was tireless in his efforts to make Mt. Sinai a world center for the advancement and diffusion of medical knowledge. He went after rich men to establish fellowships and lectureships, to provide funds for some special line of investigation, or to aid promising young students. The list of men who have been helped and encouraged by him is long and distinguished. The Emanuel Libman Fellowship Fund exists for the purpose of supporting promising young men so they can do research in special fields, and it is Libman's chief hobby. With Dr. Carrel and other celebrated men, he also will help administer the Dazian Fund of over $1,500,000, provided for in the will of the late Henry Dazian, the theatrical costumer, who was a friend and patient of Libman's.

His desk is crowded with books sent to him by his protégés. "I don't write books," says Dr. Libman. "I don't have to. My protégés write them and send them to me—many copies." From the number of books dedicated to the master, you conclude that he has inspired an entire medical literature. People have been trying for years to get him to write a book. They say that if he did so, he might reorient medicine for a long time to come. But though he won't do a book, he does an enormous amount of writing. He has written ninety-one papers, of which it is said he has never had to retract one word. Libman doesn't believe in regular working hours for those who are not suited to it, but in spite of the seeming irregularity of his own life, he obeys some marvellously attuned inner coördination of his own. Actually, those close to him say, he never stops working.

Dr. Libman suffers acutely from sinus trouble and a large

133

part of the time while he is examining a friend or talking or playing a record he keeps imbedded in one nostril a long pencil wrapped in medicated cotton. He shifts the pencil from nostril to nostril; the severe pain in his nose does not impede his movements or the rapidity of his speech. He has been operated on for sinus trouble a number of times and he has suffered intense pain for years, yet he has never permitted this to stop his work. Because the staphylococcus of sinus disease shows golden in the culture, it is called staphylococcus aureus, and Libman says that he will soon celebrate the golden anniversary of his union with this organism. Once he had shingles, an extremely painful ailment, and lay at home in a darkened room for over a month. He refused, he said, to bore people by asking them to come to see him, and pretended to be out of town. He does the same thing when he is working under special pressure; his servants say he is out of town. Sometimes he will answer the telephone himself and say, "Dr. Libman is out of town."

He loves good food. He thinks that certain restaurants are best for certain dishes and he will sometimes have soup or hors-d'œuvre in one, go to another for the roast, and still another for the dessert and coffee. He is fond of boiled potatoes, and will go to a restaurant because it serves good boiled potatoes. Or he will have a run on black pepper and will go to places that use it in their cooking. He has an excellent cook, but he very seldom dines at home. He drinks wine and mild apéritifs, and smokes a good many cigars.

Since the advent of the Hitler regime, he has done an enormous amount of work for expatriated German physicians. He is tireless in his efforts to get exiled German doctors positions in universities and in private practice all over the world. When he succeeds in getting a place for one, his sense of triumph overflows. He takes equal pride in showing you a book by some disciple or in telling you that a specialist from Heidelberg whose chromosomes are not arranged in a pattern suitable to the

Führer has just been placed in Chicago or in the university founded by Kemal Attatürk in Istanbul.

While he is playing a record, he will dart to his bookshelves, pick out a volume, and read you a quotation from a book on gout published in 1846. It is one of his ingratiating qualities that he assumes that you share his concern over the fact that nothing more advanced on gout has been written since 1846. You have an impulse, necessarily frustrated, to write something new about gout. "All the textbooks on internal medicine," he will say, "have to be rewritten." Fortunately, the telephone rings before you can set your mind to this problem.

There are times when Dr. Libman is uncommunicative to his patients about diagnoses. There is one instance of a patient who went to see him almost daily over a period of several weeks. They became friends. The patient heard the beginnings of innumerable records, fascinating stories of brilliant students in whom Dr. Libman is interested, got glimpses into the multifarious concerns of his mind, heard endless anecdotes involving the grotesqueries and macabre humors of a medical practice that started in the East Side and extended to hurried trips to the deathbeds of nabobs and celebrities of all kinds in every part of Europe and America, but got no definite program for his personal physical problem. The relationship, except for this one lapse, was infinitely exciting, informative, unexpectedly and incessantly revealing. A day came, however, when the patient had to depart for the West and he announced this to the Doctor. They were standing on a street corner, the patient having put his clothes back on hurriedly because Libman had just been summoned to a consultation to circumvent death at the Waldorf. Dr. Libman's foot was on the running board of a cab. The patient said he had to leave the next day. "You can't do that," said Dr. Libman. "I haven't given you my diagnosis yet." Nevertheless, the patient left. He didn't see Dr. Libman again for five years. When they met, Dr. Libman said, "It was esophageal diverticulum. What have you done about it?"

OLD
MONOTONOUS

Robert E. Sherwood

1940

MR. ROBERT EMMET SHER-
WOOD speaks very slowly. Between the subject and the predicate of his sentences there ensues
often the charged and prolonged
hiatus that separates the parts of
a mystery serial. With these in-
terstitial silences he holds you like
the Ancient Mariner. There is
no force that can accelerate his
tempo. In simple dissyllables,

where scope for the retard is limited, he puts in an extra hazard —for "tinkling," for example, he will say "tink e ling;" for "dangling," "dang e ling." The extra syllable cushions him against impetuosity. The improvised vowel gives him time and strength to gather his forces for the ultimate commitment of the completed word. Between his words, and even between his syllables, there is plenty of time for personal reverie on the part of his listener. Between subject and predicate you can start, and often finish, a conversation with somebody else, and between his sentences you might read *War and Peace*.

"What is that nine feet of gloom you call your brother?" Noel Coward once inquired of the playwright's sister, Rosamond Sherwood. As a matter of fact, there is nothing in the least gloomy about Mr. Sherwood except his habitual facial expression, which is dour. His silences, like any vast, still thing, are solemn, but they are often punctuated with the musketry of a shrewd wit. No sooner are you relaxed for a comfortable period of attrition than you succumb to a *Blitzkrieg*. At a meeting of the Playwrights' Company,* of which he is a founder and director, one of the members said he was on tenterhooks as to whether he would succeed in procuring the services of a certain actor for a forthcoming production. Another member, with a mania for definition, wanted to know what tenterhooks were. "They are," said Mr. Sherwood, "the up hol stery of the anx i ous seat." Another time, when a foreign manuscript was under discussion in which the author's meaning was cloaked in symbolism and the general tone abstruse, Mr. Sherwood said, "I pre fer the plays of Rob ert Em met Sher wood. He hasn't got much to say but at least he does not try to say any thing else." Again, there was a painful occasion when it devolved upon Sherwood to convey to a director whom he admired and liked that circumstances outside his control made it impossible for the director to continue on

* The Playwrights' Company consists of Mr. Sherwood, Maxwell Anderson, Elmer Rice, and the author of this article.

the play in question. There paraded the room in firm adagio a convoy of inexorable sentences barricading the unfortunate director against humiliation. "I haven't," Mr. Sherwood was heard to pronounce, "the tem per a ment or the ex per i ence to han dle a sit u a tion like this and when it a ris es I do not ask what would Je sus do or what would Abe Lin coln do but I ask what would Gil bert Mill er do and then I can not do it." It is impossible to convey typographically the stately march of a Sherwood sentence and the attempt will be abandoned henceforth. Mr. Sherwood's speech is not, as the spaces may suggest, hesitant. He never hesitates. He never flounders. He waits, as a glacier waits, and then moves.

Simplicity is the keynote of the Sherwood character. Recently, at a night club, where he was sitting with Mrs. Sherwood and some friends, a palmist read his palm. "You are a very disillusioned man," said the palmist. "You don't believe in Cupid and you don't believe in Santa Claus." When the palmist went away and Sherwood was off dancing, Mrs. Sherwood ventured a dissenting opinion. "I don't suppose in the whole world," she said, "would you find anyone who believed so thoroughly in both Cupid and Santa Claus as Sherwood does." In lighter and less familiar gatherings than meetings of the Playwrights' Company, Sherwood is apt to reveal himself as the anxious innocent not quite at ease among the super-sophisticates. He has a reputation as a consistent bore at dinner parties. This is no fluke. He has achieved his reputation honestly, through hard, conscientious labor. He admits that because of his strenuous efforts he has come to personify a figure in the famous cartoon by Charles Dana Gibson—the lonely fellow at the dinner party, making bread pills in isolation because the women on either side of him have resorted to their other partners. At a dinner party on Long Island a few years ago, Sherwood found himself sitting next to Mrs. Preston Davie, an ardent Republican, who was writing daily articles for the *Herald Tribune* denouncing the New Deal, pre-election prose which ticked off the days left in which to save the American way of life. Mrs. Davie turned hopefully to Sherwood and was confronted by a brisk silence. As her partner showed no indication of doing anything about it, she did. "Which," she proposed, "do you think women prefer, Mr. Sherwood—reliable but dull gentlemen or fascinating cads?" This question was right up Sherwood's alley. He marshalled his facts for the reply, scanned minutely the long galleries of his acquaintanceship in both camps, drew careful parallels in his mind, shrewdly picked John Barrymore as the type of fascinating cad, hit on someone who might epitomize the sensible male citizen, and then, feeling himself finally ready, he took careful aim and prepared to return the shot. "Well," he began, and turned to Mrs. Davie, but when his suspensive pause after the "Well" had spent itself, he was horrified to see that Mrs. Davie had gone. She was no longer with him. Lonely, she had edged into the conversation on the other side and Sherwood was left high and dry with his parallels hanging.

In London, at dinner in Adelphi Terrace, Bernard Shaw, the host, was discoursing with wonderful fluency on the main currents of nineteenth-century liberalism. Sherwood ate away abstractedly, happily willing to live and let live. Suddenly, to his horror, he felt the attention of the table focused on him. Shaw had reached the end of his peroration and wanted an opinion from America. He was trying to pin Sherwood down. "Don't you agree, Mr. Sherwood?" Shaw asked point-blank. It was a moment for an epigram, for a riposte, for a neat retort. Nothing occurred to Sherwood but blanket acquiescence. He murmured, "I certainly do," and swallowed some of the food he had been quietly enjoying. No one heard his remark and Sherwood was grateful. But Mr. Shaw was insistent. America must be heard! "What did you say, Mr. Sherwood?" he inquired. Sherwood's first sensation was panic; this was replaced by reassurance. "Thank God, I've got another chance," he thought, saying nothing. With the attention of two dozen of England's sharpest intellectuals converging upon him, he looked once more into his mind and found there nothing more than he had found the first time. At last he spoke. "I said, 'I certainly do.'" Slaked, Mr. Shaw returned to his lucubrations.

Sherwood is one of the greatest literary earners of all time, although, as with any highly paid worker in the present period, there is a vast difference between what he earns and what actually gets into his bank account. The prices his plays have brought from the movies are fabulous: $110,000 for *The Petrified Forest,* $85,000 for *Reunion in Vienna,* $135,000 for *Idiot's Delight,* and $225,000, plus a share in the picture royalties, for *Abe Lincoln in Illinois.* The theatrical producers' and playbroker's share absorbs roughly half of this income, and Sherwood's federal and state taxes in recent years have amounted to around $100,000 annually. The sale of a play like *Abe Lincoln in Illinois* for $225,000 thus means that the playwright receives about $115,000, and, since this sum puts him into the upper-income brackets, he pays roughly $9,000 of the $115,000 to the state and $43,000 more to the federal government. Bernard Shaw and George S. Kaufman, with their long careers of successes, have probably outstripped Sherwood in total earnings, but Sherwood has undoubtedly made more money in any one of the last ten years than Ibsen did in his entire life. He gives a good deal of it away; in the year before the opening of the controversial *There Shall Be No Night,* he had contributed something over $20,000 to various charitable organizations, and all the royalties on the new play thus far have been made over to the American Red Cross and the Finnish relief fund.

The year 1935 was a wonder year for Sherwood. He finished *The Petrified Forest* and left New York for London, where he made the immensely successful adaptation of Jacques Deval's *Tovarich.* He had been divorced from his first wife, the former Mary Brandon, the year before. He went to Budapest to marry his present wife, the former Madeline Hurlock, of Federalsburg, Maryland, who had just been divorced from Marc Connelly in Riga, a Baltic Reno. The happy couple went at once to London, and Sherwood got to work, with René Clair, on the motion picture *The Ghost Goes West*. He followed the perturbed spirit of that pleasant film to New York, where he worked on *Pride and Prejudice* for Max Gordon and wrote *Idiot's Delight* for Alfred Lunt and Lynn Fontanne. The somewhat vertiginous transitions of this period were the outward manifestation of a very profound inner one. He turned his back on the nostalgias of Vienna and St. Petersburg and looked at his own time. Sherwood feels that his career began with *The Petrified Forest*. But though he may believe that the integration between what he is and his work, which was to find completion in *Abe Lincoln in Illinois* and *There Shall Be No Night*, began with *The Petrified Forest*, that integration really began with *Acropolis*, which was produced unsuccessfully in London in 1933. He wrote this play immediately after reading *Mein Kampf* and it was intended to illustrate the incursion of totalitarianism (Sparta) on an intellectually free city-state (Athens). Between these five plays—*Acropolis, The Petrified Forest, Idiot's Delight, Abe Lincoln in Illinois*, and *There Shall Be No Night*—there may be traced a creative blood transfusion. Lines and ideas which Sherwood dropped out of one he used in another, and some of the speeches that were not uttered by Pericles in *Acropolis* appeared in the last letter written by the Finnish Dr. Valkonen to his wife in *There Shall Be No Night*.

Mr. Sherwood's working method is peculiar. He will sometimes carry an idea around in his head for several years, thinking about it, turning it over in his mind, resolving its difficulties, without making a single note. When he reaches a point of cerebral saturation he sits down and writes the play, sometimes in a phenomenally brief time. When he works, he works day and night. He suffers from a terribly painful ailment in the sinus region, charmingly named *tic douloureux*. That sobriquet appears to be an understatement. Doctors say that it is one of the most agonizing afflictions known to man. Sherwood has been all over Europe and America to see doctors for this ailment. The attacks come infrequently, sometimes once a year, but when they come, they are violent; still, if he has an idea for a play, he works through them. His speed is a subject for amused comment among the members of the Playwrights' Company. At the regular Thursday meetings of the group someone will usually ask whether Sherwood wrote a play the night before. At a meeting last winter, Sherwood shamefacedly made an announcement. He was supposed to have been rewriting *Acropolis* for Lunt and Fontanne. He looked guiltily at his colleagues and there filtered from him a confession in slow motion. "I haven't been rewriting *Acropolis* at all. I finished a new play. I got the idea just after Christmas. The scene is in Finland." The meeting at which he made this admission took place on February 1, 1940, which means that he had written the play in five weeks. He had got the idea from a broadcast from Finland on Christmas Day. Maxwell Anderson said, "You are quite right, Bob, not to have told us. Writing is a vice which should be practiced in secret."

This vice Sherwood practices in town. He doesn't go to the country to write. The silence distracts him. He likes the hum and the excitement of the city. He likes night clubs, parties, and social life, and is famous for his solo singing and dancing in the homes of his friends. One specialty is in great demand—his rendition of "When the Red, Red, Robin Comes Bob, Bob, Bobbin' Along." This he sings with a solemn intensity and dances in a style which he calls his impression of Fred Astaire. For this act he puts on an opera hat and uses a smart ebony walking stick.

Sherwood does not feel it necessary to go to a place to write about it. He wrote *The Road to Rome* without ever going to Rome, *Acropolis* though he has never been in Greece, *The Petrified Forest* without seeing Arizona, and *There Shall Be No Night* without a visit to Finland. He travels a great deal, however, and two winters ago spent some time in South America; his friends think he may very well be carrying around in his head an idea or two he picked up there. In his contemporary political plays, he seems to have a knack of ominous prophecy. Two days before *Idiot's Delight* opened in Washington, D. C., in 1936, Hitler occupied the Rhineland, and the weekend before it opened in London in 1938, the Germans walked into Austria. One London paper said, "This play must have been written over the weekend."

In 1927, Sherwood thought out *The Road to Rome,* his first play and a great success, in taxicabs going from one movie to another while he was motion-picture editor of the old *Life.* The actual writing took him three weeks and the first draft was the one that was put into rehearsal and on the stage. In Reno, where, in 1934, he spent the customary six weeks, he took a drive one day with his lawyer, Lester Summerfield. Sherwood was struck by the paradox of the perpetual sluicing through this primeval Nevada valley of the thick, sedimentary stream of decadent urban society. Summerfield also had become aware of this in the course of his practice in Reno, and Sherwood and he talked it over at some length. Sherwood knew instantly that he wanted to write a play about it. He asked Summerfield if he could fix him up with an office. The lawyer could. The next morning Sherwood left the Riverside Hotel, went to the office, and began to write his play. He reached the point at which his hero asks, "Where does this road lead to?" He walked across the street to a gas station, got an automobile road map, and went back to his office and spread it out before him. With his finger, he traced a line on the map from Reno to Truckee, California. At Truckee, on the map, beside a little arrow he saw a notation, "This way to the Petrified Forest." He had his hero's destination and the title to the play. This is how it came to pass that when he was asked once what he did during his six weeks in Reno, Sherwood was able to reply, "Well, I wrote *The Petrified Forest*. I finished

144

it in four weeks and sent it to New York, but the last two weeks were awful boring."

Mr. Sherwood is fond of offices for playwriting. He wrote *Reunion in Vienna* in 1931 in the office building of his publishers, Charles Scribner's Sons, on Fifth Avenue. He had had the idea for the play since 1929. That year he went abroad for the first time after the war. *The Road to Rome* was playing in Vienna and he was invited to see it. He was taken to Sacher's Restaurant and met old lady Sacher herself. She told him of a special room upstairs where she gave parties for broken-down aristocrats. He went up and looked in on one of these parties, and he saw at once the pathos of these discarded and indigent semi-royalties, moving about in a shadow play of vanished grandeur. At the time he was writing his one novel, *The Virtuous Knight*. This was a story of the Third Crusade and was conspicuously unsuccessful. Sherwood found the publication of a novel tame compared with the immediacy and excitement of putting on a play. It was the difference between reading a review on the morning after and a few leisurely paragraphs under the heading "Other Books." He wrote two more plays, *Waterloo Bridge* and *This Is New York,* but all the time he was thinking of that upstairs room in Sacher's. As soon as he finished these plays, he wrote *Reunion in Vienna,* in about three weeks. This was played by Lunt and Fontanne and was an immense success in New York and in London. In the second act of this play, the wife of a prominent psychoanalyst, who had been in love in the old days with the Archduke Rudolf Maximilian, meets him again in the upstairs room at Sacher's. The former Duke, now a taxi-driver in Nice, is febrile and epileptic. He comes to the party and sees his ex-mistress again after many years. He remembers that she has left him to marry a doctor, and as a greeting he slaps her violently in the face. This slap precedes their kiss of passionate reunion. The business of the face-slapping has been attributed to the inspiration of Alfred Lunt, but Mr. Lunt will tell you, with considerable wonder in his voice, that Mr. Sherwood invented it. "That piece of business was in the script," says Mr. Lunt. "Think of his knowing *that*—that shy man!"

Sherwood carried around with him for two years the idea for *Idiot's Delight*. During this time he travelled all over Europe. Once, in Budapest, he went into the Arizona Night Club and saw there an American cabaret troupe. He talked to the leader of the troupe, a hoofer, and got the idea for Harry Van. For the life of him, though, he couldn't see who the woman would be and how he would get her into the play. Finally he visualized her as the phony-Russian mistress of a munitions maker, a girl who had once slept with Van in a hotel in Omaha. Having got that, he was set, and in the apartment in which he was then living in New York he went to work. When he gets started on a play, Sherwood is seized with a spectator's anxiety to find out what is going to happen and his impatience to know drives him sometimes to extraordinary exertions. When he was writing *Idiot's Delight*, he worked one night until one o'clock. Then he went to bed, but he couldn't stand being left in suspense, so he got up at three and finished the second act by dawn. He wrote the entire script in two weeks and handed it to the Lunts.

In 1932, after an extended period in Hollywood, during which he had found himself growing fond of private swimming pools, butlers, and back-yard tennis courts, Sherwood bought a farm at Great Enton, Surrey, England, and determined to spend his summers there, it being six thousand miles from California. The place has no swimming pool, no butler, and no tennis court. Besides a cook and a pair of maids, the servant staff consists of a fearless but ineffectual carpenter whose time is occupied almost entirely in crawling over the roof and hammering at it. It seldom leaks in the same place twice, but it always leaks somewhere. The Sherwoods have gone to Great Enton every summer for some years past, and Mary, Sherwood's daughter by his first marriage, has spent her school vacations with them. This summer the house is occupied by refugee children from London.

Should you, last summer, have revived at Great Enton the

146

day-with-Thomas-Hardy manner, you would have found your host at ten-o'clock breakfast, deep in the *Times*. You would have been left with the *Daily Mail*, which informs you that Sir Stafford Cripps has heckled the Prime Minister keenly the day before about the transfer to Germany of Czech gold. (Remote crisis, June, 1939!) You inquire of your host what is the attitude of the *Times* leader about Sir Stafford. If you do not get a prompt reply to your query, it is not because your host is rude; it is simply because he is not reading about Sir Stafford Cripps but studying the long, scholarly articles in the *Times* on yesterday's races. A good part of Mr. Sherwood's summer is spent in reading about what horses won the day before and in deciding on what horses he is going to bet today. It is quite an elaborate ritual. After he has recovered from yesterday's bad news in the *Times*, he calculates how much he has lost and how much he is prepared to bet today. To place the bets, he has to wait for the midday *Standard*, which comes in just about when he has finished analyzing the *Times'* racing news. The *Standard* helps him decide on his choices, and then he goes to the telephone to place the bets with his brokers. He has two. It is the correct thing in England, when you are what is known as "making investments," to use an assumed name, and Sherwood masquerades under two: Captain Sherwit and Old Savoy.

He comes back from the phone faintly apologetic but already basking in a sense of opulence, happy in the knowledge that he won't know until tomorrow how much he has lost. For a while conversation may become less specialized: the visit of Mr. Strang to Moscow, the royal visit to America (pinwheels of hope, June, 1939!). The guest inquires whether it is his host's habit to do any writing in the morning. "Not here," it is explained to him. "In other places, yes, the morning is fine, but not here." Mrs. Sherwood, who presides over the activities at Great Enton with a kind of acidulated and deflationary charm, generally disdains any part in these sordid race-track speculations, but one day she announced that she had happened by chance to look over the entries in the *Times* and had discovered there a horse whose appeal she found to be irresistible. Sherwood thinks that this was by virtue of her marriage to him; the name of the horse was Old Monotonous. She insisted that her husband bet ten shillings each way on this horse for her. Mr. Sherwood complied. The horse failed to run in the money, but every time he ran, right up to the outbreak of the second World War, Mrs. Sherwood doggedly backed him. In spite of his consistent record of defeat, Mrs. Sherwood's faith in Old Monotonous remained undimmed and he became a kind of family mascot. Mr. Sherwood's daughter, Mary, became infected also by the strange appeal of this steady loser and she followed his career with the fanatical enthusiasm characteristic of the devotees of lost causes. In time, Old Monotonous, the equine Bryan, became more than a mascot. He became a symbol. In their many letters to each other, Mrs. Sherwood and Mary Sherwood have come to refer to their husband and father as Old Monotonous.

By lunchtime the racing news has been assimilated and the Sherwood budget readjusted. Mr. Sherwood then turns to aviation. He repairs to his hangar, a sort of substantial play shed, where the Sherwoods sometimes give amateur theatricals. In even ranks, with chromium wings gleaming in the sun and multicolored bodies beautifully painted, starred and crossed and circled, rests Sherwood's flotilla, waiting for its master to animate it. A new plane has arrived from London. Icarus takes it out of its cardboard crate to assemble it. On its side is painted "Phoebus." "This is a marvellous specimen, one of the best made, and costs six guineas," he says, holding it in his hand. Laboriously Sherwood takes out the sturdy oil-paper wings. He loses a pin, which necessitates a careful search of the floor. He pricks his finger as he finds the pin, but is undaunted. He works till the machine is completed, a shipshape Lilliputian air raider. "Come," says the aviator firmly. You follow him to a height back of the house, where there is a smooth stretch of lawn, and there you are permitted to assist at a maiden flight. There is an interval of tension and the new plane is off, sailing steadily over the pleasant Surrey landscape. The rangy pilot hurries after it, looking up anxiously to follow the trajectory of the "Phoebus." He disappears in a clump of oak trees.

Not far from the Sherwoods' place is the house where George Eliot lived. It is a country which old residents in the neighborhood find greatly changed and faintly suburbanized, but which, in the golden summer weather of June, 1939—a season described by the English as "the sweet of the year"—in that last dreaming interval, the American visitor could still find tranquil and lovely. Possibly the author of *Abe Lincoln in Illinois,* painfully adjusting a strut or a propeller, is assailed by some idea that eventually will be materialized for audiences in New York by Alfred Lunt and Lynn Fontanne, but there is no visible evidence of it. There are letters telling the grosses at the Plymouth Theatre on West Forty-fifth Street and trips to London to see actors for the late Sidney Howard's forthcoming play, which Sherwood is handling as Mr. Howard's executor. During that last summer of 1939, in the intervals between dart-throwing and rummy, the visitors talk discursively of Hitler and wonder how the Russian *rapprochement* with Germany is getting on. By air, Great Enton is about two hours from the Tempelhof airfield in Berlin. Will it happen and when? But the midday *Standard* arrives. Mrs. Sherwood cuts flowers in the sun-filled, droning garden and on the telephone Old Monotonous transmits his latest hunches to his brokers in London.

The Emmett family from which Robert Emmet Sherwood is descended on his mother's side was Protestant but infected fiercely by the cause of Irish freedom, an infection which has obsessed a long line of fervent English Protestants. The first Emmet in America, Thomas Addis Emmet, was an older brother of the Irish martyr Robert Emmet, who managed to utter, before he was executed by the English, the declamatory sentence, "When my country takes her place among the nations of the earth, then and not until then let my epitaph be written."

Thomas Addis Emmet was a considerable personage in his own right. He was exiled to America in 1803, and once here he made a great reputation for himself as a lawyer, in one instance fighting a case against the great Daniel Webster, who said of him after the trial, "The erudition, talents, and eloquence of the Irish bar have made their appearance in America in the person of Thomas Addis Emmet." The intertwinings of the Emmets are baffling to an outsider; members of the family themselves, when asked about the relationships within the clan, get a bewildered and terrified look in their eyes. It is an immensely exfoliated family, studded with celebrated names in medicine, in law, in art, and in science. The playwright's uncle, William LeRoy Emmet, is one of the great engineers of the world. He is an Edison medallist and the successor of Steinmetz in the General Electric Company. At seventy, he was retired on a pension but got restless and is now back in Schenectady, working on a mercury boiler which he thinks will completely outmode the conventional steam boiler. He spends part of his time in Schenectady and the rest with his sister, Robert Sherwood's mother, in her apartment on East Seventy-second Street. In Mrs. Sherwood's dining room are portraits of the original Emmets, one painted by Allan Ramsay, who was a court painter to George III. The resemblance between Robert Sherwood and these

Emmets is striking. They were very tall and had prominent, dark eyebrows. The Emmet girls run to painting and sculpture; for five generations there has been at least one artist among them, down to one of the playwright's nieces, who is a sculptor.

The passion which in the nineteenth century the Emmets felt against England Sherwood now feels against dictatorship and injustice anywhere. He is a fiercely militant liberal. He hates murder, persecution, and censorship, not only when they are committed by Nazis but also when they are committed by Utopians. He is an impassioned New Dealer and a fanatical devotee of Franklin D. Roosevelt, enthusiasms not shared by all the other Sherwoods and Emmets. Recently the film version of *Abe Lincoln in Illinois* was shown at the White House. Arthur Murray Sherwood, Robert's brother, who is a determined Republican, unpleasantly asked Robert to bring him back a souvenir from the White House when he went there to dine. "What would you like?" asked Robert. "His scalp?" At lunch one day in town, Sherwood was approached by a close relative of a former occupant of the White House, a distinguished Republican. The man greeted Sherwood very cordially but got a frigid reception. He hung about for a moment or two, making a few stabs at conversation. There is nothing so lonely as a Sherwood silence. The Republican tried to dent it, to win from Sherwood some ray of human warmth. He failed, and made a lame exit. When he was finally gone it was pointed out to Sherwood that he had not overwhelmed the poor man with cordiality. Sherwood said, with his usual thoughtful deliberation, "I was at a dinner party with him the other night and I didn't like the way he talked about Franklin Roosevelt." Republican candidates for President will have to be very careful what they say in front of Sherwood.

The author of the atlas of plays called *The Road to Rome, Waterloo Bridge, Reunion in Vienna, Idiot's Delight, Abe Lin-*

coln in Illinois, and *There Shall Be No Night* was born in New Rochelle on April 4, 1896. His mother, the former Rosina Emmet, is a distinguished painter whom *Who's Who* lists as a medal-winner in Paris, Chicago, Buffalo, and St. Louis. The Neysa McMein of her day, she was the most popular illustrator in *Harper's Bazaar* and other magazines of the time. When, in 1922, Robert Sherwood married his first wife, Mary Brandon, who came from Indiana, the bride's grandmother was in ecstasy; she said she was so happy that her granddaughter was going to marry the son of the woman who drew all the romantic illustrations in her own youth.

Robert's father, Arthur Murray Sherwood, was a successful investment broker with a craze for the theatre. Though he belonged to the Brook, Century, and Knickerbocker Clubs, his great desire was to get into the Lambs, and he finally made it. He never missed a Gambol and George M. Cohan was his god. Not long ago, after the Yankee-Doodle Boy had been engaged by the Playwrights' Company to star in the late Sidney Howard's last play (a production which was subsequently postponed until next fall), Sherwood ran into Cohan and one of Cohan's friends at the Plaza. Cohan introduced his companion to Sherwood with the remark, "This is Robert Emmet Sherwood, my new boss." Sherwood then told Cohan of his father's adoration of him and said, "How happy he would have been if he could have lived to see the day when you referred to me as your boss!"

The elder Sherwood had played leading rôles in the Hasty Pudding Club shows at Harvard and had founded the Harvard *Lampoon.* In the *Lampoon's* offices today is a gold plaque on which is inscribed, "Presented by Arthur Murray Sherwood, first President." Mr. Sherwood wanted to go on the stage when he left Harvard but was advised not to on account of his height. He was almost as tall as his son is now, which is six feet seven inches.

Sherwood's paternal grandmother, Mary Elizabeth Wilson Sherwood, was a well-known writer. She was the Emily Post of her day. One of her books, called *Here & There & Everywhere: Reminiscences,* a kind of guide to polite society, introduces you to Victor Emmanuel of Italy and Empress Eugénie of France, and tells you about the palaces that kings have built in Bavaria, feudal châteaux on the Loire, and the salons of Bernhardt, Coquelin, Lord Houghton, and the Duc d'Aumale.

As an infant, Sherwood seems to have been a chore. He was secretive and shy, and he had a mind and a code of his own. Once he was discovered in a room in which his bedridden grandmother was ensconced in a wheelchair. The child was manipulating a fishing pole, to the end of which was attached a piece of string neatly tied around a live beetle. With this beetle he was gently caressing his grandmother's face at long range. She was doing her best to dodge and was calling out feebly from time to time, half in laughter and half in fear. To a horrified inquiry about what he was doing, he replied calmly, "I'm tickling up Grandma." He had a strong color sense, inherited supposedly from his painter mother. This color sense sometimes came into sharp conflict with his mother's. One time he painted bright yellow every white object in his mother's dressing room, including her shoes. Once Bobby was sent to stay with his grandfather while his mother and his sister Cynthia went to Germany. His grandfather's house boasted one flush toilet, of which the grandfather was extremely proud. Bobby, sensing this pride and wishing to humble it, dropped the entire contents of his Noah's ark into the bowl. The unhappy grandfather sent for the plumber who had made the installation and raged against him for his inefficiency. The plumber worked for a time and then faced the irate houseowner defiantly. "This is perfectly all right, Mr. Emmet," he said. "It's a good closet, but it won't pass elephants." For months the apoplectic grandfather kept fishing up assorted yaks and rhinoceroses. His days on earth were appreciably shortened by this visit of his grandson. It was also

153

hard on the boy, who remarked, when he got back to his parents, "I'm thoroughly sick of Grandpa."

There is even a record in the playwright's very early days of a fling at arson. To get a rest from him, his mother sent him to Milton Academy. Study didn't interest Bobby very much. He preferred his own interests and on several occasions he was warned that his marks were not too flattering. One day the school building containing these marks burst into flames and Bobby and his elder brother, Phil, worked like heroes to extinguish the fire. They did their work well. When he was congratulated on his exertions by his brother, Bob said casually, "By the way, I started it." No motive could be forced from the secretive child beyond the fact that he wanted a little diversion.

The Sherwoods spent their summers at Lake Champlain. Bobby was a passionate showman and wrote plays for the children around the village to put on. His sister Rosamond complained that after she learned her part in the script, Bobby would take all her good lines and put them in his own part before the performance. He was always enormously optimistic about the attendance at his plays, an optimism which was not justified until very much later. He would have dozens of campstools put up for his entertainments, which were usually attended by his mother and one or two other people from the house.

Like his father, Robert Sherwood went to Harvard. Like him, he also became president of the *Lampoon* and prominent in the Hasty Pudding Club shows. For the Hasty Pudding Club, Sherwood wrote his first play, *Barnum Was Right,* and it was through his editorship of the *Lampoon* that he got his first job in New York. Every year the *Lampoon* put out a burlesque number of some popular magazine, and while Sherwood was editor he produced a parody issue of *Vanity Fair.* This later got him a job on the original. In the meantime, however, America entered the World War and Sherwood quit college, a year before he would have graduated, to go to war. Unable to get into the

American Army or Navy because of his height, he went to Montreal and enlisted in the Canadian Expeditionary Force. He joined a Highland regiment, but didn't know what it was until the kilts were flung at him. It was the Canadian Black Watch Regiment, an affiliate of the famous Scottish organization. In one of his first letters home he wrote to his mother, "By no stress of the imagination can I be called an attractive fellow in kilts, but at least I can say that I am imposing." Mrs. Sherwood has a photograph of him in kilts, taken when he was in New York on furlough. The head is clear, but the legs are shadowy. Mrs. Sherwood complained about this to the photographer, who said, "Yes, it's kind of muddy below, but we found it difficult to focus the whole of him."

Sherwood was gassed in the action at Vimy Ridge and sent to an emergency hospital. On his return to the front, he was shot in both legs. He wrote to his mother that when he looked down and found his hose dyed with New Rochelle's bluest blood, he flung away his gun and ran as fast as his legs could carry him in a direction directly opposite to that prescribed by Marshal Foch. Actually, he was carried off the field unconscious and woke up in a hospital bed in Amiens. His heart was found to be affected and he was in a hospital in England until January, 1919. He kept writing facetious letters home, and the first his parents knew of his true condition was when they got a routine letter from an association which visited hospitals and wrote to parents letting them know how their children were. Sherwood hated the war, the physical discomfort, the filth, and the rats. He was a thoroughly incompetent soldier, and when he found himself in the hospital he prayed that the war might end before he got out.

When he came home, Sherwood's doctors told him that he couldn't live very long, or at least that he couldn't do very much, on account of his heart. He has never had any trouble with it since and pays no attention to it. Faced for the first time in his life with the problem of making a living, Sherwood got a job on

Vanity Fair. He was general handyman around the office. When Ina Claire had to be photographed by Baron de Meyer, Sherwood arranged the appointment. When there was some muddiness in a piece by G. K. Chesterton or an inactive passage in a piece by Grantland Rice on golf, Sherwood fixed it up. During one summer when the regular man was on vacation, he wrote, "What the Best-Dressed Man Will Wear." He filled the column with extraordinary sartorial speculations: "*On dit* that peg-topped pants and cloth-top shoes are coming back; also that the best-dressed man's next year's waistcoats will glitter darkly with cut jade." For the unsuspecting male subscribers he devised costumes that would have startled Vincente Minnelli—all to test his theory that no one ever read the column. No matter how far he went, no one ever protested the fantasies of Sherwood's daydreams until the editor of the column came back from his vacation, fuming. Finally, Dorothy Parker, a member of the staff, was fired for writing unfavorable theatrical reviews and Sherwood and Robert Benchley, another editorial worker, quit in sympathy. They were perhaps the earliest fellow-travellers and wore red discharge chevrons afterward for a while.

Sherwood was now absolutely broke, and could expect little help from his family. His father's business and health had failed a couple of years earlier, and his mother was helping to support the rest of the family by professional portrait painting. While Sherwood was wondering what to do next, he was summoned by the Hasty Pudding Club to Boston to supervise the production of his play, *Barnum Was Right,* which had been called off on account of the war. Every member of the cast had enlisted and many had been killed or wounded. Sherwood lived in Cambridge because he had credit at the clubs. He would eat in one club till he was posted and then go to another till the same thing happened. At this time, Neal O'Hara of the Boston *Post* got him a job as feature writer on that paper. Some educator had tossed off a statement in an interview that in his opinion marriage was more likely to be successful when the participants had had previous sexual experience. The editor thought a feminine point of view on this might be interesting, and Sherwood was sent to probe the Dean of Women at Boston University on this delicate subject. The Dean of Women was curt and noncommittal. What she said was colorless. Sherwood managed, however, to pep it up. Magnanimously he gave the Dean credit for his own views, which were expansive and forward-looking. A Ben Hechtian jazzing up of a serious interview with a well-known female pundit was the last thing the editor expected from the austere Sherwood, and he rushed the heterodox opinion into type. However, before the paper went to press, he was seized by some skeptical intuition and, to make sure, he sent the galleys to the Dean. The Dean was definitely ungrateful for the liberality of outlook imputed to her by the visionary Sherwood and he again found himself suddenly without a job. His journalistic career had lasted two days.

Sherwood came back to New York and got a job on the old *Life* through one of its editors, the late E. S. Martin, who had been a classmate of Sherwood's father at Harvard. *Life* was actually an outgrowth of the *Lampoon*. Robert Benchley joined *Life* and Dorothy Parker became a regular contributor the same week. For ten years, Sherwood, Dorothy Parker, and Robert Benchley worked first for *Vanity Fair* and then on *Life*, arriving and leaving both publications within a few days of each other.

At a dinner a few years ago, George S. Kaufman asked a cryptic question. "Do you realize," he asked, "that there sits at this table the founder of a form of journalism?" He was not referring to Arthur Brisbane but to Sherwood, who in 1920 had started a column of movie criticism in *Life*. He began this job when he was twenty-four years old. By the time he was twenty-seven, he was called the dean of motion-picture critics. He was not only among the first to write critical reviews of pictures; he actually applied to Cecil B. De Mille the term "bore." Sometimes he reviewed one picture five times. He was the regular critic of *Life*, he wrote for a newspaper syndicate, for the New York

Herald, for *Photoplay,* and for *McCall's. McCall's* paid him as much as $250 to $300 for a motion-picture review and the other publications paid fairly well. It was in 1924 that he was made editor of *Life* and he kept writing pieces when he could, yet by 1926 he was $14,000 in debt. It occurred to him to write a play. He wrote *The Road to Rome* in odd moments between editorial and critical duties. He offered it to Gilbert Miller, who rejected it with the remark, "I don't even like *first-rate* Shaw." It was produced by Brady & Wiman. One of the reviewers said, "This play is filled with all the humor which the author has evidently been holding out on the magazines." Starring Jane Cowl and Philip Merivale, it was an enormous success. Not long ago, when Sherwood made a slighting remark about *The Road to Rome,* someone asked him why he was so hard on his first hit. "Because," he answered, "it employs the cheapest sort of device—making historical characters use modern slang."

In spite of the success of this play, Sherwood kept on working on *Life* until he was fired, which came about in 1928 because he refused to treat prohibition or Herbert Hoover with respect in the pages of the magazine. He confesses to an acute antipathy to quitting jobs. This conservatism is in marked contrast to the reaction of success on other people and is somehow curiously characteristic of Sherwood. After *What Price Glory?* Maxwell Anderson went berserk, bought a cane, and walked down Forty-second Street twirling it. Elmer Rice, after his first success, got married. Marc Connelly bought an Inverness cape. Moss Hart went to Cartier's, where he surfeited himself with ingenious gadgets made of gold. But not Sherwood. He bought no canes. He went along monotonously, holding every movie critic's job he possibly could, and besides that taking on the literary editorship of *Scribner's.* His next theatrical effort was the dramatization of Ring Lardner's story "The Love Nest." He made a mess of it and the play failed. Then he wrote *The Queen's Husband* almost immediately. This was not particularly successful on Broadway but it has proved one of the most popular plays on record for little theatres and amateurs. A play may be an immense success on Broadway but have small appeal for amateurs. They have special demands: enough people in the cast to provide everybody in the group a chance, and yet not too many; parts that can give everybody involved the illusion that he is doing pretty well. In fact, the play must be something like the game of golf. *The Queen's Husband* somehow meets these requirements.

Through his friendship with the late Sidney Howard, Sherwood became interested in the theatre in its relation to the community as an element of civic and national culture. Sherwood and Howard met first in the *Life* office. Howard had worked on *Life* and Sherwood got his desk when Howard quit. The friendship between the two men was instantaneous. They were in close contact from the day they met until Howard's death last August. Both men had fought in the World War—Howard as an aviator—and both had their first great public success within a few years of each other. Sherwood always envied Howard his physical courage, because he himself was contemptuous of his own lack of it.

The trend toward active unionism was beginning to infect dramatists and screen writers as early as the middle nineteen-twenties. In New York, the playwrights had banded themselves together and in the nineteen-thirties they began to fight grimly for their grievances against the managers. In 1935, Sidney Howard became the president of the Dramatists' Guild; Sherwood, the secretary. This organization is always engaged in immense and complicated negotiations, which the average member cannot follow and doesn't know much about. One concrete thing which the Dramatists' Guild has accomplished is a more favorable division of money from the sale of plays to the movies. Formerly the playwrights and the managers divided the proceeds equally. Now the playwright gets sixty per cent, the manager forty per cent. This is something that a non-legalistic participant in the Dramatists' Guild meetings can understand, but the Guild is involved constantly in the formation of various "plans," which are sometimes completely worked out in every detail but are never employed. These activities occupy the playwrights when they are not working on plays and exercise their suppressed desires for statesmanship. For instance, there is a plan called the Wharton-Wilk Plan. Mr. Wharton is a well-known lawyer and Mr. Wilk is the representative of Warner Brothers. The Wharton-Wilk Plan is like the Schleswig-Holstein Question, of which it was said that only three people had ever understood it; that one was dead, another insane, and the third had forgotten it. The Wharton-Wilk Plan was fought over bitterly for a long time in the Dramatists' Guild meetings. It has something to do with allowing film companies to finance plays without getting complete control over the film rights. After several years of bitter controversy, the plan was finally adopted by the Guild in its entirety. Having been adopted, it has never been used and no one seems to like it.

Sherwood succeeded Sidney Howard to the privilege of presiding over the Guild's debates. He calls himself the Coolidge among the Dramatists' Guild presidents because he never said anything and never did anything about anything, leaving a Hooverlike heritage for his successor, Elmer Rice. It was on November 23, 1937, that Sherwood presided for the first time at a Dramatists' Guild meeting. There were present George S. Kaufman, Maxwell Anderson, Rachel Crothers, Sidney Howard, Albert Maltz, George Sklar, Leopold Atlas, Melvin Levy, Moss Hart, Elmer Rice, Jules Eckert Goodman, Arthur Richman, George Middleton, Philip Dunning, Owen Davis, and Lillian Hellman. It was a terrible ordeal for Sherwood. Discussion at a Dramatists' Guild meeting never burbles, it rages. At this particular meeting there wasn't much in the ways of results. The Wharton-Wilk Plan was momentarily stymied. It had to wait for a long time yet before it could be perfected so that it would fail to function. After the meeting was over, Sherwood rode down in the elevator with Elmer Rice and Maxwell Anderson. They repaired to a bar for a glass of sherry. It was pure accident that Sherwood happened to ride with these two instead of any of the others. Over their drinks that day the idea of a playwrights' producing company was worked out. Sherwood had tried it once before with Sidney Howard, Maxwell Anderson, Elmer Rice, Philip Barry, and Laurence Stallings, but the idea had foundered at the last moment because just as they were about to make plans for the coming season, Stallings said he was going to Africa and therefore couldn't come to the next meeting. Sherwood now told Anderson and Rice that he had just delivered to his typist the text of a new play and that he was willing to throw in this play as the nucleus of a kitty to which all three men would eventually contribute. That play was *Abe Lincoln in Illinois* and it began the Playwrights' Company's season for 1938–1939.

The formation of the Playwrights' Company Mr. Sherwood considers to be the most important event of his professional life. He had cherished the idea for years. The animus which inspired his great ancestor, Robert Emmet, against the English has, in the case of his descendant, been sublimated into a resentment against the managers. The plan of a playwrights' producing company, so often projected and so universally called chimerical, for the moment seems to be practical. The group has just finished its second season, has produced eight plays by five playwrights, and has in its treasury, with all debts paid, over a quarter of a million dollars. So far the prima-donna differences and the temperamental clashes which it was confidently predicted would wreck any such association between writing men have failed to materialize. Once, in fact, a play which was doing very little business and which the author himself suggested be closed was kept running by his colleagues at great cost on the chance that things might improve. This was not businesslike. The morning after a play by one of its members opens, the playwrights gather, sum up the notices, plan an advertising compaign, and console or congratulate the author, as the case may require. To comfort a colleague for a captious press one morning after an opening, Sherwood quoted by heart a prominent critic who had written of *Reunion in Vienna* that "it is a trifling, inconsequential bit of fluff but far and away the best play Mr. Sherwood has ever written."

Sherwood is also interested in a scheme for bringing the American theatre to the American people whether the American people insist on it or not. The idea is to start a series of companies to do good plays from the contemporary and the classical repertory, to play two weeks in New York and then to tour a circuit all over the United States. This would make possible a run of a hundred weeks. There would have to be enough companies in existence to keep the New York theatre going for a full season. Sherwood is now engaged in the task of raising $300,000 to put the plan into effect.

One night at a dinner party at the George S. Kaufmans', there was a discussion about the failure of the theatre to reflect important and pressing problems of contemporary life. Mrs. George Backer, wife of the publisher of the New York *Post,* remarked that there were vital experiments going on in the life of the city to which no writers paid any attention. Someone said, "For instance?" and Mrs. Backer spoke of B. Charney Vladeck and his municipal housing project, then under way, on Madison and Jackson Streets. Sherwood expressed a desire to meet Vladeck. A day or so later Mrs. Backer took him to a meeting of the City Council, of which Vladeck was a member, and the three went to see the Vladeck project. Sherwood was greatly impressed by Vladeck and his work, and the two men became friends and corresponded. Sherwood was just about to answer an appreciative letter from Vladeck on the first performance of *Abe Lincoln in Illinois* when he read in the newspapers of his death.

It is characteristic and significant that at the end of his notes in the published version of *Abe Lincoln in Illinois,* after having quoted from the classical authorities, Sherwood chose as his climactic quotation a few lines from an article by B. Charney

162

Vladeck, published in the *Locomotive Engineers' Journal*. It says in part:

One of my first and most memorable lessons in Americaniza-tion was Lincoln's Gettysburg address. When I read it and reread it and learned it by heart, struck by its noble clearness and sweeping faith in America, I felt as if the whole past of this country had been lit up by a row of warm and beautiful lights; as if some unknown friend had taken me by the hand on a dark and uncertain road, saying gently: "Don't doubt and don't despair. This country has a soul and a purpose and, if you so wish, you may love it without regrets."

Sherwood's comment on this follows:

This was written by the late B. Charney Vladeck shortly after he first came to this country, a Jewish refugee from oppression in Tsarist Russia. Vladeck had been a member of the Bolshevist Party, had voted at the meeting which had elected Lenin their leader and had served in prison for his revolutionary activities. He then emigrated to America, a man whose heart was filled with bitterness—and he learned here that those illusive words, liberty and equality, may have profound meaning. . . . Here, in these glowing words from one who had been a deeply skeptical alien, is the essence of what we like to call "Americanization" but which is actually just what Lincoln meant it to be: liberation.

Sherwood feels a burning indignation against those he con-siders callous and insensitive to the struggle in Europe, against those who seem to him indifferent to its outcome and unaware of its immense importance for us. He does not make a habit of writing letters to the papers, but after Colonel Lindbergh's first radio speech, in which the Colonel said, "We must be as im-personal as a surgeon with his knife," Sherwood wrote a letter to *Time* in which he said that the Colonel's simile was an insult to the medical profession. He went on:

If surgeons were truly impersonal (or, one might say, truly neutral) they would not heed the calls of distress from suffering humanity when they themselves were otherwise engaged in watching the ticker, or playing bridge, or writing thoughtful treatises on the insanity of their fellowmen. They would not go to the considerable trouble and risk of using their knives to remove the malignant growths in the body of civilization. They would always find comfortable refuge behind that ancient question, "Am I my brother's keeper?" What Colonel Lindbergh should have said is, "We must be as impersonal as the professional mourner, who doesn't lament the seriousness of the plague, or the number of fatalities, as long as it helps his own business."

For writing *There Shall Be No Night,* Sherwood has been on one side attacked as a warmonger, on the other hailed as a great patriot. Sherwood does not believe in democracy passively, nor does he hate fascism passively. It is as inconceivable that he would say "I hate Hitler, *but—*" as that he would say "I love democracy, *but—*." The "*but*" in either case, he believes, is a conduit admitting all sorts of poisons. He believes that permanent world peace can be achieved by a union of democracies, some such union as is described by Clarence Streit in *Union Now.* Last September, when Hitler (who, unfortunately, had never seen *Idiot's Delight*) gave the order for the bombers to take off, Sherwood felt certain that everything he believed in, the faith in the Bill of Rights and in the ideal of world citizenship that he had got from his study of Abraham Lincoln, was violently threatened. What should he do to defend his beliefs? Again and again he had the impulse to go to Montreal and enlist as he had done in 1917, but he was stopped by the thought that he would probably be put in a censorship job in the Intelligence, and that wearing a uniform in some office would be only a form of escapism. He came to believe that his obligation lay here in his own country and that the best way he could fulfill it would be to write a play which would express what he felt. He didn't know what the play would be about, or where it would be laid, until the invasion of Finland, which seemed to offer a sharp definition of the issue.

Sherwood feels that the present war began when the combination of Woodrow Wilson's tactlessness and the blindness of

Henry Cabot Lodge, William E. Borah, and other isolationists forced us to declare the policy that our World War dead had died in vain and that we would take no further interest in the international task of keeping the peace. We handed Europe over to the bankrupt statesmanship of such men as Baldwin and Chamberlain and Laval, who in the last analysis, Sherwood thinks, gave Hitler his power. In spite of all that, Sherwood remains an incorrigible optimist. He has a faith in the ultimate triumph of the democratic principle, a faith which he expresses in *There Shall Be No Night,* and which has been described by at least one critic as "whistling in the dark."

In his valedictory address to the Dramatists' Guild, made when he retired from its presidency in 1939, Sherwood had this to say:

One of the greatest virtues of the American Theatre is that it has never been strictly national. Upholding the best principles of the people whom it represents, it is unlimited by the fetishes of chauvinism, sectionalism, racism. . . . We are writers, and we are living in an age when powers of communication have achieved fabulous importance. . . . There is a new and decisive force in the human race, more powerful than all the tyrants. It is the force of massed thought—thought which has been provoked by words, strongly spoken. Words which may originate in the mind of someone in this room may be brought to people of all kinds and kindreds who are hungry for them, who may be stimulated by them to a new faith in the brotherhood of life, who may, for all any of us can tell, be saved by them.

So far, words have not kept pace with the guns. Words have not stopped invasion or organized murder, but they may still, and as a counter-attack Sherwood's words in *There Shall Be No Night* seem to be doing their part.

. . . .
. . . .
. . . .
. . . .
. . . .
. . . .
. . . .
. . . .
. . . .
. . . .
. . . .

THE
RED
AND THE
BLUE

A. E. (Joe) Kazan

1945

LIKE HIS SELF-AVOWED PROTO-
type, Casanova, and like Marcel
Proust, Avraam Elia Kazan sits in
a room writing down his remem-
brance of things past. He has already published two books, *Life
of a Kazanova* and *Sixty Minutes
Experience,* and he has the material for several more. Kazan,
who signs his works and all his
letters "A. E. (Joe) Kazan" and

167

frequently refers to himself in conversation as A.E., is a little younger than the Venetian was when he finally got around to remembering at Dux: Casanova was seventy-two; Kazan is sixty-eight. The small hotel room on West Fifty-eight Street where, for the past few years, Kazan has sat pouring out his recollections is not corklined, like Proust's, but the intensity of his preoccupation with what he has lost is the same. Like Proust again, he has had to pay for the publication of his memoirs himself. The books he has either published or only partly completed have various titles, but, like the worldly recluse of the Boulevard Haussmann, he has really written only one work; it is an endless statement of what he has enjoyed and endured. Spiritually, of course—and he would be the first to acknowledge it—this latter-day A.E., who is of Greek descent, is much nearer the Italian than the Frenchman; his life is an astonishing span of the modern picaresque—from rags to riches, and beyond that to disillusion and moralizing. A seven-dollar-a-week messenger boy on the streets of New York at twenty, Kazan became a millionaire before he was thirty. However, the Algeric analogy will lead you astray in any summary of the career of A. E. (Joe) Kazan. Virtue was not its terminal, or idealism its motive power. You will be on firmer ground if you stick, as A.E. does, to Casanova. If he has regrets, it is because he has not always done the expedient thing. The conscience that hurts him is economic; the only guilt he feels is for not having held on to his money. Toward his lapses from strict rectitude, he is tolerant. What he cannot forgive is his poverty, for which he holds himself directly responsible. Like George Bernard Shaw, he looks upon poverty as a sin, and, in a rather ducal way, he is contrite about having committed it. His detachment about himself and his contempt for his major failure are symbolized in his invention of the name by which he is known in the circles he frequents—Flat Tire Joe. "It's a good name, don't you think?" he will inquire, without wistfulness. A.E. is never wistful. He is stern, he is sardonic, he is zestful, and he has reached old age

168

without mellowness. This endows his personality with a kind of clean jauntiness. You can take him or leave him, but you don't have to be sorry for him.

In his appearance, Kazan sharply contradicts his self-applied pseudonym of Flat Tire Joe. He looks like a Morgan partner of the nineteen-hundreds (probably far more so than the Morgan partners ever looked) on the way to lunch on the Corsair with the head of the firm. His manner of dress is invariable and impeccable: a somewhat outmoded but impressive double-breasted black coat, very square and long, gray-striped trousers, gray spats, stiff-winged collar, and dark-blue bow tie with tiny white polka dots. His shirt front is dazzling white and stiffly starched. He carries a silver-headed cane. He wears a black bowler with an old-fashioned square crown. He is tall, square, white-faced, and bald, with snapping eyes and a somewhat bleak and rugged aspect. His usual expression is austere. It takes a lifetime of self-indulgence to produce a look so ascetic. Kazan sits in his hotel room mornings and early afternoons writing. About four, he usually walks to his favorite haunt, the Café de la Paix, at the Hotel St. Moritz, where he has a regular table. He is a striking figure on the street. If you passed him on his way to the Café de la Paix, moving slowly along, encased in his boxlike garments, tapping the sidewalk with his walking stick, his expression tense and unrevealing, his mind polishing up submerged facets of his past, you would think that he was the diplomatic representative of some strange country and that his avocation was abstract philosophy, which, indeed, it is.

Unless you have read his two published works, it is very difficult to have a sustained conversation with A. E. (Joe) Kazan. The full title of his first book is, somewhat after the ample eighteenth-century manner, *Sixty Minutes Experience: Modern Philosophy and Psychology: Joe Kazan's 50 Years' Experience.* This one, which he wrote for children, is bound in bright red. The second book is called, in full, *Life of a Kazanova: I Lived,*

Loved, and Learned: Joe Kazan's 50 Years' Experience, and is bound in bright blue. It is necessary to be up on both these volumes. If, undocumented, you ask him about some period of his past, he will answer, with a benign testiness, "That's in the blue." Should your question be in the realm of the philosophical, the speculative, or the psychological, he will say, "That's in the red." He is like the master of some esoteric science who will not discuss it with you until you have learned at least the fundamentals. If you ask him, for example, how he got his start in America, he will simply say, "It's in the blue." Illiterates just cannot converse with A.E.

The juvenile, *Sixty Minutes Experience: Modern Philosophy and Psychology,* is on sale in the philosophical section of Macy's book department. Macy's would not stock *Kazanova.* Presumably the buyers were afraid of the effect of this intimate autobiography on their customers. *Sixty Minutes Experience* is prefaced, again in the eighteenth-century manner, with a prospectus which says:

Father tells his experience to young ones—they do not like it— and they do not take advantage. In later years they wish they had. This applies also to sixty minutes experience paragraphs.

This book is published by the Capano Press of New York. *Kazanova* is published by the Alexander Press of New York. On the first page of each volume is a ruled square, in which appears "Compliments of," followed by a blank line. *Sixty Minutes Experience* goes even farther than *Kazanova* in its implications of generosity. The second inside page is headed "To My Good Friend," below which is a blank line for the name. The next line, waiting, like a blank check, for a signature, has the word "Author" at the end. The modesty of this device is ingratiating; it is as if A.E. could not imagine that anyone but himself would make a present of this volume. The Capano Press offers a further convenience for the careful reader of *Sixty Minutes Experience,*

170

the last page is ruled and is headed "INDEX FOR PARAGRAPHS YOU LIKE."

The two books differ in intent; *Sixty Minutes Experience* is didactic, whereas *Kazanova* is sensationally confessional. It is interesting, however, to note that the author has numbered the pages of the two books as if they were one outpouring. Thus, *Sixty Minutes,* or the red, ends on Page 120, and *Kazanova* begins on Page 121. It would undoubtedly seem odd, if you innocently picked up *Kazanova* in someone's library and found yourself, at the very start, already on Page 121. Perhaps, in a shy way, Kazan is merely trying to anticipate those hard critics of even more prolific writers—of Somerset Maugham, for example—who say that no matter how much these authors turn out, they really write only one book. This is especially true of Kazan, because he is a behavioristic rather than an imaginative writer. He embosses what he knows, has seen, and has lived through; he is materialistic and factual. Although nothing could be farther from the child's world of *Sixty Minutes Experience* than the livid realism of *Kazanova,* there is internal evidence that the two books are webbed together in the obscure caverns of Kazan's unconscious. Thus *Kazanova,* while not overtly a juvenile, is a long apostrophe to a generic nephew named Bob; it is an avuncular fireside chat from a sophisticated older man to a guileless boy. Almost every admonition in the book is addressed to this imaginary Bob. And it is not unusual, when Bob asks his uncle a question, to find such a brusque answer as "Read paragraph 127 of *Sixty Minutes Experience.*" A.E. won't talk even to Bob unless he is up on the red. It should here be noted that in the juvenile *Sixty Minutes Experience* there are no cross references to *Kazanova.* Obviously, Kazan belongs to the rather old-fashioned school of pedagogy that does not believe in pushing children too far beyond their depth.

On the title and facing pages of *Sixty Minutes Experience,* Kazan, following Fielding and Richardson, permits himself to revel in creative anticipation, as follows:

171

WISDOM OF EXPERIENCE
IF YOU WOULD BENEFIT
FROM THE EXPERIENCE OF THE
AUTHOR, AGED 67, READ THIS BOOK
SIXTY MINUTES EXPERIENCE
FULL OF TRUTH
ALSO
FOUNDATION FOR GROWN CHILDREN
THIS BOOK IS DICTIONARY OF
THE PROBLEMS OF LIFE ANYTHING
HAPPENS WILL HAPPEN:
READ IT AGAIN AND YOU WILL FIND
THE ANSWER AND THE REMEDY

Following is experience
(not advice)

Underneath this introduction is a box with the legend "This Book is obtainable at:—" The promise of the colon is not fulfilled; the emptiness that follows leaves you dangling in an irritated suspense, unless you happen to find out about Macy's.

Kazan urges anyone he meets to feed *Sixty Minutes Experience* to the children. "If they cannot read," he will say, "read to them." The book is written in the manner of *Also Sprach Zarathustra*, in chased aphorisms. Some of the epigrams suggest that the children for whom Kazan intended them must be not only grown but even precocious.

The aphorisms are all numbered. Aphorism 3 indicates that A.E. has at least something in common with the progressive school of educators: "Do not do anything you do not want to do. Ignore forcing."

Aphorism 85 is evidently for incipient politicians: "Question. What benefit does bribing bring in this world? Answer. Plenty. Very few persons refuse bribes if they are big enough and legal."

Aphorism 121 must be intended for children who are about to go into business: "Any proposition comes to you, say 'No' first, easy to change it to 'Yes,' not easy to change it to 'No.' This will protect you from better trader than yourself in business."

172

Similarly, Aphorism 25: "If you write nasty letters, mail them next day; you may change them. Mail all important letters yourself."

Kazan seldom makes the concessions usually demanded of the writers of juvenilia; he expects the tots to supplement their experience with imagination, to fill in the void of the present with the fullness of anticipation. Probably on no other basis, for example, could he counsel: "The right time to propose marriage to a lady is at a wedding. The poor lady's heart is soft and trembling."

But occasionally A.E. forgets Chesterfield and remembers Polonius, as in Aphorism 39: "Do not swear and do not use vulgar language. Your tongue will get used to it. You might call your family names."

For girl babies, A.E. has special advice: "Ladies, do not fight with your man in the morning; he cannot attend to his business and you will not have luxuries or automobiles."

Again: "Ladies and sweethearts, save your money, because for no reason your man may switch his affection to another woman with 50% less charm than yourself."

He can be hard: "Do not trust anyone until you find him otherwise; an agreeable surprise. This means you are protecting yourself."

There are echoes of Aesop: "Story: An old farmer's wife was very fond of pigeons and erected a pigeon house in back yard, and watched them every day. Neighbors asked her why she was so fond of pigeons. She said, 'I like the billing and cooing of the male pigeon and his love.'"

And echoes of La Rochefoucauld: "Definition of partner—prays his partner will become extravagant so that he can own the business himself."

And of King Lear: "Father spends thousands and lots of trouble to bring up the youngsters; when father, mother, or sister gets poor and the children get rich they do not look after father, sister, or mother; they are beasts in human clothes."

And of Cicero: "Before 50, if you just happen to be in some risky business and accumulated a fortune, quit at 50 and become 98% honest. Otherwise, you will be caught doing wrong. It requires youth, nerve, technique to do wrong. You haven't got it after 50."

And of Montaigne: "Careless remark: Bill: 'Since when are you taking all birds to a night club?' James: 'The blonde is my wife.' Bill: 'Oh, I meant the brunette.' James: 'She is my sister.' (You have embarrassed yourself.) Diplomat says, 'I saw you with two charming ladies at the club,' as ladies are charming at any age."

And of Wilde: "What is the easiest thing in life to do? Wrong."

Sometimes one suspects—and it is true of so many books for children—that the inner message of *Sixty Minutes Experience* is intended for adults, as when the author ruminates, in Aphorism 259: "What is alibi of Philosopher? When he becomes poor, he says to himself, 'Too much money is no good anyhow!'"

Perhaps the most poignant moment in the book is the author's final paragraph, in which he reflects on the advantages contemporary children have that he lacked as a child. This is his envoi to his wandering in the child's world: "THE AUTHOR SAYS: I wish this book had been printed 50 years ago so that I might have read it and gotten the benefit."

The blue, or *Life of a Kazanova: I Lived, Loved, and Learned: Joe Kazan's 50 Years' Experience,* most of which is written in numbered episodes, is surely one of the frankest self-exposures in the long history of confessional literature. In Kazan's millionaire period, he maintained apartments in New York and in Paris and sported Rolls-Royces and Isotta-Fraschinis on two continents. Essentially (like so many bachelors) a homebody, he had sweethearts in various capitals so that while he was travelling he could enjoy the illusion the Statler hotels have always striven to achieve of a "home away from home." He also helped to make himself feel at home by taking with him, wherever he went, his most prized possession, a custom-built brown velvet sofa, on which he slept. He has clung to this sofa; it is all that is left of his former opulence. It stands now in his hotel room. A vanished and fascinating world is opened for you in *Kazanova,* a world of uninhibited enterprise, of mighty fortunes made in selling rugs, of $64,000 staked on one hand in *chemin de fer,* of flying trips between Constantinople and New York, of international business amalgamations, of sybaritism in New York, Paris, Madrid, Vienna, Budapest, and Cairo.

Under the statement "This Book Is a Lesson for Adults," A.E. begins his autobiography with his birth:

Bob, I was born in the city of Cesaria in Turkey in Asia Minor. There were three of us children. My mother passed away when I was six years old. I don't remember anything about her except that when I approached to her for a kiss (she was sick in bed) they pulled me away from her.

What effect this earliest remembered trauma has had on the career of A.E. it will remain for the psychologists to expound. There is certainly no indication in *Kazanova* that it made an introvert of him. Of the childhood incidents he relates, the following is perhaps the matrix of what was to come:

Bob, at the age of nine when I was going to school, the best my family could do was to give me Turkish bologna sandwiches for my lunch almost every day. Then I became a racketeer, at the age of nine. (Compulsory.) A rich parents' son (sissy) at school. His lunch contained cheese, chicken sandwiches, cake, candy. One day I asked him to give me some of his lunch. He said no. The next day at noon I said to the rich boy, 'Let us go on the roof and have our lunch in the sun.' (Only the two of us were alone on the roof.) I grabbed his lunch box and ate half of his lunch, and I gave him half of my bologna. I also gave him a couple of slaps. I told him: 'If you don't get me extra lunch every day you will be licked by me.' The sissy obeyed me from fear. I had a delicious luncheon every day for a year. He told his mother

175

he got awfully hungry at 3 o'clock and wanted more lunch. Years after, returning to Constantinople from America (having money) I met a young man at the Tokatlian restaurant. From his name I recognized him as the boy whose lunch I robbed every day at school. For days and days I treated him, dining him, champagne, girls, etc.—never allowing him to spend money. He never guessed who I was.

The free-lunch racket waned (perhaps the sissy became virile), but A.E. supplanted it with another. The boys in Cesaria used to play a game called *ashik*, with marbles that were made out of the little bones in the knee joints of lambs. The young Kazan put lead in one of these marbles, and with this he could, at a distance of ten feet, easily break through a row of normal ones. For a season he had a steady income of what came to two American cents a week. But he was too consistent a winner, the device was discovered, and, at the age of ten, he was expelled from school. A.E. has never fought the temptation to gamble, no matter how much it has cost him; he feels that the instinct is both congenital and insurmountable. He does not believe, he says, in fighting nature.

The young Kazan went to work, at the age of eleven, as a messenger boy, carrying rugs around from one establishment to another, but, after four years of it, Kazan, Sr., felt that the boy was too smart for Cesaria and sent him off to Constantinople, a four-day journey by carriage, to live with an uncle and aunt and their children. There A.E. got a job in a drugstore, at eighty cents a week. He noticed that apparently no matter what the ailment, the doctors prescribed the same medicines, so he took to filling prescriptions himself, with an admirable uniformity. But the atmosphere in his uncle's house was unfriendly. The family slept together in one room, on wool beds—layers of matted wool piled one on top of another. A.E. had brought a wool bed with him from Cesaria, a parting gift from his father. Gradually he became aware of a diminishing altitude in his bed; he slept lower and lower, and finally he reached the floor. He could only conclude that the layers had been removed one at a time by his relatives while he was at work—whether for mere gain or as a delicate hint that he was unwelcome, he was not sure. In any case, he took to sleeping in the drugstore. Avraam had grown up in the rug business, and he soon felt the call to return to it. It was in his bones. "I know the business so well," he says, "that rugs are afraid of me." He got a tryout for a job with a leading rug merchant in Constantinople, spreading out the rugs and helping to show them, at a dollar a week. On his first day, he saw a coin on the floor—a coin worth a quarter. He picked it up and gave it to the boss. This evidence of honesty clinched the job for him. He had been forewarned that this dropped coin was a stratagem of the boss's, and he survived this first test of his probity.

A.E. calls the years from 1887 to 1897, when he left Turkey for America, his "chiselling days." It was while working in the rug establishment in Constantinople that there came to the Avraam the first impulse to go to America. Tersely, he describes, in *Kazanova,* this turning point in his young life:

Bob, one day a friend of my father's got me a job in a rug store in Constantinople (my father's trade) at a dollar a week. I slept in his warehouse. Every Saturday, lots of Armenian merchants visited his office to talk over business and gossip about America with my boss. I used to listen. They would say: This man became a millionaire in America. This man bought a chateau. This one is wealthy. I said to myself: me for America. I went to my rich uncle to get some money to go to America. (No dice.) What next? My boss was paying loads of money to have his rugs repaired. What could I do? I learned how to repair rugs and I worked at night for three years to save enough money to come to America.

Kazan was twenty when at last he sailed, by freighter. The journey from Constantinople to Marseille took nine days. He was quartered on the steerage deck, but as it was summer, this was no great hardship. His capital was forty-two dollars and several silk rugs he was to deliver to a brother of his Constantinople boss who was in the rug business in New York. The blandishments of Marseille were too much for the young adventurer. He left the freighter, squandered his capital, and then sold one of the silk rugs for forty-five dollars. When at last he got on a ship for America, he had five dollars left. He gambled four-ninety-five of this away. From a fellow-passenger, a lady, he borrowed a quarter to wire his boss's brother from Ellis Island. For two days he slept on benches there until the boss's brother appeared and rescued him.

Kazan considers the time between 1897 and 1904 the happiest of his life, because it was the only period of his business career when he had no overhead. His faculty for cleaning, repairing, showing, and selling rugs stood him in good stead. He went to work for his boss's brother in his establishment at Broadway and Seventeenth Street, and he earned extra money repairing rugs at night. He lived in a boarding house near Wanamaker's and got himself a girl. This girl the boss coveted. The boss seems to have been something of a Biblical student, for he sent A.E. on the road to sell so that he could woo the girl with an easier conscience. With A.E., he sent along another young member of his staff, who had been stealing from him. The boss told A.E. that he was sending him, A.E., along to watch the other fellow, but the maneuver was transparent to A.E. However, not counting the world lost for love, A.E. consented to go on tour. The two young men left for New England with their merchandise. Their procedure, after they arrived in a town, was to go to a music shop, say, or a hardware store, and get the proprietor to let them set up a temporary rug department in return for a ten-per-cent commission on sales. The tour was a triumph. In the communities A.E. and his companion visited there appeared to be a hunger for rugs which they had arrived in the nick of time to satisfy.

The first thing A.E. did after he sold a rug to a lady for a thousand dollars in Concord, New Hampshire, was to send a money order for fifty dollars to his father in Turkey. The sensation caused by its arrival was recounted to him years later, when he returned to Cesaria a rich man. A.E.'s father looked at the money order with skepticism, and he was assured by his neighbors that he could not get cash for it at the post office. At the post office he asked for the money in small silver coins, then brought it home and poured it on the kitchen table. The neighbors crowded in to look. The elder Kazan pointed with pride. "Didn't I tell you my son is a genius?" he said. "Look, we are rich!"

Women were as helpful in furthering A.E.'s career during the New England tour as they were later, with the assistance of overhead, in helping to undo him. In Bridgeport, an elderly lady came in and examined rugs for two hours. A.E.'s patience long outlasted that of his partner, who was always irritated by interminable shoppers. Finally the lady bought a rug for thirty-five dollars. She asked A.E. to deliver it to her house. The partner sneered, but A.E. stuck to business. He delivered the rug at dinnertime and was invited to dine. "After dinner," he recalls, "as I sat on my hostess's lap, she got on the telephone and began making calls all over Bridgeport." She sold $14,000 worth of rugs for him to her friends. "American women of that era," says A.E., "were very sympathetic if you came from Constantinople and were poor." From this one contact, A.E. got a fine dinner and $3,000 in commissions. He promptly returned to New York and quit his job. He approached a Fifth Avenue dealer with a proposal that they sell rugs at auction, so that they could influence the prices by bidding against each other when necessary. The merger was a great success. A.E. recalls vividly a pair of silk rugs of a crème-de-menthe color (he dwells lovingly on these two rugs, after a lapse of nearly half a century) which were bid up to seven hundred and fifty dollars, though they had cost him and his partner only sixty-two dollars. Those were wonderful years: America was a new and hospitable and rug-hungry land; there

179

was youth and a growing intimation of genius in finance; there were women of all ages, sympathetic to a good-looking boy from Constantinople; and, above all, there was no overhead.

A.E. was soon averaging five hundred dollars a week, but he continued to live in the boarding house near Wanamaker's. Boarding houses, he says, were a symbol of respectability. It helped establish credit to live in a boarding house; it was an index of honesty and industry. During the panic of 1907, A.E. was occupying a large room for which he had paid a year's rent in advance. When Wanamaker's began discharging salesgirls, many of them came to A.E. for help, and he helped. One of the more idyllic of his memories is of this period. The girls used to come to his room in the evening and talk and sing to him while he repaired his rugs. He tolerated no indiscretion; it did not go with the boarding-house façade; he was a Platonic pasha.

A.E.'s career, from this point, followed swiftly the pattern set by many immigrants of those days. He was in a world in which you outsmarted everyone you could, in which you vowed revenge when you were outsmarted, even though you could not help having a certain admiration for the outsmarter. One example, taken from *Kazanova*, will serve as an illustration of this phase of his life:

Bob: At the age of 23, a poor boy, I sold at auction to a lady one silk carpet for $1,700 costing me $550. This was a profit of $1,150. An artificial gentleman dealer saw this lady and spoiled the sale of the silk carpet, and the lady returned it. This was a big loss for a poor man. I registered this evil act of the so-called gentleman in my mind. Fifteen years later I was sitting in a fashionable café. This same dealer came in and sat with me at a table. I bought him a drink. He bought me three drinks and then he went out and bought me a cigar which cost fifteen cents and one for himself which cost sixty cents. Now what is the catch? He asked me to lend him $25,000. "Yes, if you send all your rugs (worth about $120,000) to my store I will lend you *the $25,000 and charge you $12,000 commission whether all the rugs are sold or not." I started working on the proposition and in a month I sold $37,000 worth and thereby collected my $25,000 and $12,000 commission. I sent the dealer back the balance of the rugs. He cost me $1,150 fifteen years ago but I got back from him $12,000 in one month. Bob, here is the benefit of not calling a fool a damn fool to his face. Bob, if you are willing to give a cigar to another friend, give same cigar that you smoke, not a fifteen cent cigar to him and a sixty cent one for you.*

There began the period of A.E.'s life that he describes in *Kazanova* as "Genius in Business and Technique." In this period he acquired more partners and he acquired overhead. His success was great, and he began to make quantities of money. His years of wealth, characterized by him in a subtitle as "High Living Days: Genius and Amoeba," lasted until the liquidation of his fortune of several million dollars in the crash of 1929. The first big step toward success came when Orlando Jones, a bookmaker, introduced him to another bookmaker, who wanted to buy some rugs. A.E. took the prospect to the largest rug dealer in New York. One of the salesmen there offered A.E. a thousand-dollar commission on the transaction, which came to $5,000, but A.E., remembering the dropped coin in Constantinople, refused, and asked only the customary ten per cent. The news of this startling heresy reached the boss, who, overcome by A.E.'s spectacular honesty, gave him a job at $4,000 a year, plus commissions. After four years of this, during which, A.E. recalls, the boss "liked him every day," he was given an account of $300,000 and sent to Constantinople on a buying trip. He bought too freely and when the home office heard about it he was discharged by cable. He promptly formed a partnership in Constantinople with a local banker named Castelli. In the next few years A.E. was involved, first in Constantinople and then back in New York, in a series of dissolving partnerships. One of them had an almost immediate but charming dénouement. A jovial partner, whom A.E. greatly liked, was caught cheating after one week. A.E. reproached him.

181

"I have been a crook for forty years," said the candid culprit. "You can't expect me to be honest in one week." In spite of the sweet reasonableness of this argument, A.E. dissolved the partnership.

From this period, too, comes an interesting account of the pastime of "rug-walking," taken from *Kazanova*:

Uncle, they tell me you used to chase customers from your store. Is this true?

Answer: Yes but only those rich customers who were egotists or better traders than myself. . . . For one of my best customers and friends I spread a large rug on the floor and he asked me what is the price. I said $800. He says, "I'll take it." (Being a bargain for him.) We were walking on the rug and I spoke to him in jokes—stories to keep him walking to the good end of the rug but he walked to the opposite end of the rug and then he said, "No, I do not want it." I asked him what's the matter with the rug. He said, "The rug is worn out." "How do you know?" I said. "You haven't touched it." He said, "I felt with my feet that it is worn out." I said, "Here's a cigar—but we won't do business with anyone who knows that a rug is worn out by touching it with his feet." But we wined and dined many times after that.

In 1912, A.E. felt himself strong enough to do without partnerships and founded his own firm, the Kazan Carpet Company. The firm had a rating of AAA in Dun & Bradstreet's, and he had so much money that it was not necessary for him to be respectable. The boarding-house era was over. He moved into progressively finer apartment houses and eventually took an apartment at the Ritz Tower and had it furnished at a cost of $75,000. The "High Living Days" period swung into its halcyon rhythm. It was then that he had his sofa made, and when he went to Paris he took it with him. (Can it be possible that this is the first record of a man taking a bed to Paris?) One evening there, he went to dine at the home of a count who was also fond of good living. On the third floor of the count's mansion was a bathroom which aroused A.E.'s envy; it had walls of exquisite mosaic and a bathtub big enough for two. A.E. couldn't get the magnificence of this bathroom out of his mind. He was like an art lover who has looked at a tantalizing picture and cannot rest until it hangs on his own wall. The next day he called the manager of Claridge's, where he was stopping, and had him, with the count's permission, visit the bathroom. A copy of it was installed in his suite at Claridge's. He kept this apartment, as well as the one in New York, all through the High Living Days.

A typical high-living day is described in Episodes 621 and 622:

In the morning my customary coffee served in my room, Masseur, osteopath or Turkish bath, alternately; besides my own gymnasium in my apartment. Every morning the barber comes at the same hour to shave me. Even if it is only to talk, the manicurist comes now and then. No worry for expenses (keep the change). A tailor comes once a month with samples and I buy a suit of clothes or an overcoat whether I need it or not.

Good organization at the store. Customers buying my rugs at any price, as I am almost a monopoly. I look at the newspapers —stocks go up. At one o'clock before I go to lunch I stop in at the stockbroker and buy 1000 shares of some stock on which I already have a tip. (To be sold at 1¼ point profit if it goes up. This profit will pay for my luxurious expenses.) And they go up. Arrive at 61st Street restaurant. Plenty of beautiful girls. Of course I am welcome to these girls because some of checks go on my account (and their sweeties are working at the time). I go with some of the girls back to the apartment, either to play bridge or dance or drink (Prohibition). Some of them jump on my electric horse and camel. Bob, I was very generous with my girls. If they went out dining and wining with a nicer looking man than myself, I forgave them. Otherwise, elimination.

This life of easy gymnastics occasionally has a more astringent note. As in Episode 638, on "The Influence of Heredity":

Bob, here's an example of how a person can inherit certain habits from his parents. When I was in Constantinople, I used to

183

visit my father every Monday in the suburbs where he lived. In his bathroom I saw a cake of soap which had been made from little scraps of left-over soap. That was economy! And I, the damned fool, had lost $5,000 the night before playing poker. Did I learn anything? We shall see. In New York, I lived at a Tower Hotel. I was wealthy and lived very expensively. Yet I also had a cake of soap made from little scraps of left-over soap. Even today I do the same thing. These are the little things that you inherit from your parents. And here's how it benefited me. A girl once came to ask me for $125 for a Chinese dog that she wanted to buy. When she happened to go into the bathroom and saw my cake of soap which had been made from little scraps of left-over soap—she left the room without carfare.

It is doubtful whether any man has ever been franker than A.E. in disclosing his failures with women. He seldom recalls an amorous episode that did not have some economic aspect. This is very hard to understand, because A.E. is a handsome, imposing man even today. Possibly, if he had remained poor, women would have been touched by his need for love, as they were in his non-overhead days, but it is hard to be sorry for a very rich man. If there is one idyl in the life of A.E., it is his nostalgic worship of the lady whose identity is veiled in his lavish numerology as Sweetheart No. 5. (He is inclined to say less about Nos. 1 through 4.) He loved and wanted to marry this girl and yet, even in this case, his nostalgia is soured a bit by the fact that, although he spent a fortune on her and wanted to send her to school and to educate her, she left him, when he began to lose his money, to marry a man who had had the good sense to remain a millionaire. He still thinks with tenderness of Sweetheart No. 5 and writes to her now and then, but she does not answer his letters.

Some of Kazan's innumerable trans-atlantic crossings during the high-living days were dictated by romance. Sensitive to the merest inflection of infidelity, he once quickly abandoned a Paris sweetheart because, in an absent-minded moment, she called him by the wrong name. To salve his wounded *amour-propre,* he sailed at once for New York, only to have his New York sweetheart make a similar unfortunate slip of the tongue. One incident in *Kazanova* is reminiscent of a painful episode in *Of Human Bondage*—when Philip gives his friend the money to go away with Mildred—and is none the less poignant for being told so pitilessly:

I made arrangements with a new manager to take care of my business as I was sailing for Europe on the Majestic. When I arrived on the ship I received from a real friend the following telegram (4 words): "You are a donkey—Bill." But after I got on the boat I changed my mind—I wanted to get off—but the first whistle for leaving had blown. The second steward, who knew me well, said, "The only way you can get out of here is to get sick"—and I got sick plenty. They had to lower the plank and I got off. This cost me $100. Now what was my idea? First, I was not doing justice to my business. Second, I wanted to go and watch my exclusive sweetheart, for her I bought a small house in the suburbs, and to see if she was in love with someone else. On two occasions I went around her house but did not have the courage to go in and see for myself if . . . I never justified my suspicions because I never found out. Damn fool—but this is love.

Kazan attributes his failure in business and his present impecuniosity to his gambling and extravagance and what might be called the "flat tire" quality in his character, but not for a moment does he regret his romantic expenditures, financial and emotional. He indulges in no sentimental what-might-have-beens even about the practical Sweetheart No. 5. And toward all women he still retains an attitude of incorrigible gallantry. If his life has been an unending immolation on the altar of Eros, he feels no remorse. In this sense he is a true Casanova, the perennial Don Juan, a perfectionist in amour. It is perhaps A.E.'s most striking and ingratiating quality that he is detached and unregenerate. He looks upon his own failings, as he does upon honor in others, with equanimity, as eccentricities of character to be observed and catalogued and appraised for their instructive value. He is constantly contrasting his brother, who is the father of Elia Kazan, the stage and screen director, with himself. This brother has been successful in the rug business, but not so spectacularly as A.E. He is respected in his business circle in New York and in New Rochelle, where he and his family live. In *Kazanova*, A.E. refers to him as "my noble brother." He applies this epithet not with irony but with real reverence. "He is a good man," A.E. will say. "Never did anything dishonorable. A good man, a thousand times better than I." But he says it in a tone of casual inventory, as if he were estimating the value of a rug or a diamond. He does not envy virtue. For the good brother's son, his nephew Elia, he has an admiring affection. He repeats with relish conversational tilts he has had with Elia.

"Once," he says, "I asked him for five hundred dollars."

"You are always telling me," Elia answered, "to save my money. How can I give you five hundred dollars and still save my money?"

"Because," A.E. said, "when you give you get back more."

A.E. won the argument and the five hundred dollars.

His nephew's increasing fame and success have not been an unmixed blessing for A.E. "Formerly, friends sometimes helped me," he says. "Now they say, 'Why should we help you? You have a millionaire nephew. Why don't you go to him?'" (In A.E.'s circle you can't be merely affluent; you are a millionaire or nothing.) There is a story that Oscar Wilde, when he was living in poverty in Paris, wrote the synopsis of a play called *Mrs. Daventry* and one day sold it to a producer, promising to write the play. He didn't write it, but he kept the advance. He repeated the process several times with other impresarios, always using the same synopsis. Finally, one of these men got someone else to write the play around Wilde's synopsis and put it into rehearsal. When Wilde heard of the impending production, he wrote an indignant letter to this producer. "By producing this play," he said, "you rob me of a certain source of income!" A.E. feels somewhat this way about his nephew's success.

The small hotel room on West Fifty-eighth Street in which A.E. has lived for nine years seems even smaller than it is because most of it is occupied by the much-travelled sofa. The sofa is the worse for wear, and its generous proportions make living in the room somewhat of a maneuver. Pressed against it on one side is a bridge table, on which A.E. does his writing. The table is covered with manuscripts. Next to the sofa, on the other side, is a huge wardrobe trunk plastered with labels: "Berengaria 1926;" "Paris 1927 to Hold on Arrival." Into the trunk, A.E. recalls, he once threw $1,500 after an alcoholic card game and didn't discover it till five years later, when he was rummaging for a collar button. The sofa, bridge table, and trunk form a small triangle. In this little triangle, most of A.E.'s existence is now confined.

Kazan's sofa was made to order by the Tiffany Studios in 1921. "I paid seven hundred and fifty dollars for it, but now I couldn't get ten dollars," he says, not ruefully but as a comment on worldly mutation. No other man has ever been so faithful to an article of furniture. Even when he lived in his apartment at the Ritz Tower, which had a magnificent bed, he slept on the sofa. Whenever he was ready to go to Paris, he would simply order his chauffeur to ship the sofa ahead. When he arrived in his apartment at Claridge's, it would be there. Now it is his workbench as well as his bed. He lies on it, collecting his thoughts, and when he is ready to set them down, there is the bridge table. The sofa, A.E. says, is his pal. It is a relationship analagous to the one between Elwood P. Dowd and Harvey.

A.E.'s degeneration into a writer took place in this way. In 1941, yielding to one of his rare bouts with apathy, he didn't go out of his room for three days. On the fourth day, the maid who does his room prodded him, "You haven't been outside the room for three days," she said. "What's the matter with you? You must be a writer!" The writing germ, a non-filterable virus, entered A.E. at that moment. By the end of a week, A.E., now dedicated, was at work on his first manuscript. His new avocation, he feels, has lifted him above the ordinary, material plane on which he had always lived. On the floor of his room are three worn rugs; he estimates their total value at ninety cents. On Christmas Day of 1944, A.E. was alone in his room with his work. He looked down at the rugs and found himself remembering that once he had had in his store two thousand rugs, each worth between five hundred and $2,000. He laughed. He went out to the Automat for his Christmas dinner, and while sitting there, drinking a glass of milk, he laughed again. It is his conversion to art, A.E. feels, that gave him the power to laugh on that Christmas Day.

A.E. takes a certain pride in the magnitude of his downfall. In 1929, he went bankrupt for a million dollars, and he still carries, and likes to display, a newspaper clipping recording this handsome débacle. Since 1929, he has done no formal work. He is an authority on the late sport of horse racing. He had elaborate formulas for betting, the most incomprehensible of which he called the "unit system." Once he evolved an intricate scheme for a betting pool with a capital of a million dollars. He perfected the plan with patient lucubration and then offered it as a sort of gesture to the Greek community in New York. It was turned down. He was rather hurt by this, because he was prepared, he says, to devote all his time to it. For a while, after the crash, he lived in the Hotel St. Moritz, and he still goes there almost every afternoon and sits on a yellow-leather chair at his regular table in the Café de la Paix. He loves the Café de la Paix. The proprietor of the hotel, a Greek by the name of Taylor, is an old friend. The waiters and clientele also know him. When he tips the waiters, they good-humoredly refuse the tips. They don't want to be tipped by their friend, they say. When A.E. arrives at the Café de la Paix, he sits down at his *Stammtisch* in one corner. He talks to his regular waiter in French. He has known this waiter for thirty years, since the days of the old Café Martin. They inevitably recall the night Stanford White was shot there. They were at the Café Martin when it happened. A.E. puts on a pair of horn-rimmed glasses, takes some long sheets of yellow foolscap from his pocket, and asks the waiter to read to him from his work in progress, *My Life at the Café Martin.* "The proprietor, Martin, was like my brother," says A.E. "What a man I was!"

Back in his room, A.E. puts in an hour before dinner at his writing. The pockets of his double-breasted black overcoat and of his jackets are stuffed with foolscap covered with writing—newly remembered stories of his past, amplifications of stories he has already told. Afflicted with graphomania, he keeps adding and adding to his reminiscences and speculations. If you visit him in his room, he insists upon your reading his works aloud to him. He will reach into a pocket and pull out a sheet of paper. "Read this," he will say, in the voice of one long accustomed to obedience. "Aloud!" When you start reading, A.E. tilts his head back and a little to one side. A faint smile curves his lips and the expression on his distinguished, strongly modelled face softens to benignity. As the sentences set in motion the stream of memory—of opulence, of power, of defeat, of voluptuousness—the benign look deepens, and it is plain that the voices he hears are mellifluous. At last the passage is finished. There is a silence. The sun lights up a column of motes rising from A.E.'s sofa to the window. He gets up and adjusts his boxlike jacket against the back of his collar. "Damn fool," he mutters. "Damn fool."

"What would you still like to accomplish in life?" his visitor asks, to snap him from his past to the future.

"You will find the answer," he says brusquely, "in the blue—797A."

It is there, on the last page, just before the addendum, which is a little manual on horse racing. It reads:

Bob asked his uncle: "Why did you start writing this book?"

Answer: "It is a good hobby, if you are lonesome, and an education. You will become a better person reading your own memoirs and experiences, and I am tired of stretching a dollar as far as it will go. I am also trying hard to make this book more successful so I will be able to reciprocate favors which I receive from my family and my friends, and will be able to establish a small orphanage and live with the children and see them happy. When they come and jump on my lap and kiss me, that is the only genuine kiss in the world with no hidden personal interest, except, of course, mothers'."

PLAYWRIGHT

Ferenc Molnar

1946

IF YOU HAPPENED TO VISIT NEW York in the winter of 1908 (or even if you lived here), you could scarcely avoid seeing *The Devil,* a play by the Hungarian playwright Ferenc Molnar. Probably for the first time in the history of the New York theatre, four companies were simultaneously performing one play. Two of the productions were in English, one

191

was in German, and one was in Yiddish. In one of the English versions, produced by Henry W. Savage at the Garden, the fascinating Devil was played by Edwin Stevens; in the other, produced by Harrison Grey Fiske at the Belasco, the part was played by George Arliss. *Judge* came out with a cover that showed Mephisto, perched on a rock, leering down on a New York street solidly made up of theatres, all of which were playing *The Devil*. A caption recorded Pluto's satisfaction with what Molnar had done for him: "I seem to be quite popular." The Devil was so popular, not only in New York but throughout the United States, that producers complained it was impossible to get leading men anywhere; they were all away somewhere or other playing Dr. Miller, which was the pseudonym affected in the play by the distinguished visitor from below. There was also a grievous shortage in opera capes and silk hats, for Dr. Miller was a formal dresser.

In the thirty-seven years that have passed since these multitudinous productions of *The Devil,* seventeen other Molnar plays have been produced in New York, a record few American playwrights can claim. In 1914, David Belasco put on *The Phantom Rival,* with Leo Ditrichstein, and it was extremely successful. In 1921, the Theatre Guild, then just getting started, took a leap into the unknown and produced his most famous play, *Liliom*. A quarter of a century later, the Guild is presenting it again—expatriated to Massachusetts—as *Carousel,* with music by Richard Rodgers and lyrics by Oscar Hammerstein II. *The Guardsman,* a later Molnar play, was the first production of the Theatre Guild that made real money. In it the Lunts acted together for the first time and had their first major success, and they chose it for their first and only film. During the next several years, Gilbert Miller put on three Molnar works—*The Play's the Thing,* with Holbrook Blinn; *The Swan,* with Eva Le Gallienne; and *The Good Fairy,* with Helen Hayes and Walter Connolly—and all three were very successful. At the moment, three theatres in Budapest are playing Molnar—*The Swan, The Play's the Thing,* and a bill of one-acters. *Liliom* and *The Play's the Thing* are also current in Vienna. Of contemporary playwrights, only Shaw, Maugham, and O'Neill, it would appear, have shown a comparable durability.

Molnar, who has been living at the Plaza ever since he arrived in this country in January, 1940, was born in Budapest on January 12, 1878, of a Jewish family named Neumann. His change of name was not an assimilationist caprice, nor was it akin to the naïve aspiration which in Boston animates the Kabatznicks to assume the dubious protective coloration of Cabot. The shift from Neumann to Molnar was a gesture of patriotic assertion rather than of escape. Until late in the eighteenth century, Jews in the Austro-Hungarian Empire were not permitted to dignify themselves with surnames. Then Emperor Josef II, in a burst of tolerance, made the pronouncement that they could wear swords and have surnames, provided that these were German and were approved by the officials. Hungary struggled against the process of Germanization until well into the nineteenth century, and even before 1867, when a decree making German the official language was revoked, a revolution took place in the nomenclature of the Hungarian Jews, whose abruptly acquired family names were often the coarse inventions of grossly comical German officials. In some cases the imposed names were scatological, in others merely ribald. Molnar's family had escaped the elephantine vagaries of official German humor, but he himself felt that he could not write under any German name whatever; he felt it would be unfair to Hungarian literature. Almost every Jewish doctor, lawyer, and businessman had somewhat the same feeling. "Molnar" is Hungarian for "Miller;" this was the profession of his favorite uncle, and he took the name over. It was a fling at nationalism.

In a preface to one edition of his collected plays, Molnar wrote a capsule biography of himself up to 1925:

1878, I was born in Budapest; 1896, I became a law student at Geneva; 1896, I became a journalist in Budapest; 1897, I wrote a

193

short story; 1900, I wrote a novel; 1902, I became a playwright at home; 1908, I became a playwright abroad; 1914, I became a war correspondent; 1916, I became a playwright once more; 1918, my hair turned snow-white; 1925, I should like to be a law student at Geneva once more.

Molnar's father was a fairly successful physician, and the son's earliest memories are of people sitting in the Doctor's darkish waiting room. The whole household atmosphere was gloomy, and the boy, to liven things up, often played practical jokes on the patients. There is the legend that one of these jokes was so vivid that it quite literally scared his grandmother to death. (Probably this is the malicious invention of someone who suffered from his practical jokes in after years. According to Molnar, his grandmother merely broke a leg.) Except for whatever excitement of this sort he was able to whip up, the first five years of his life seem to have been, as he puts it, a "hiatus." In quick succession, for the next thirteen years, he attended a number of schools in Budapest, ending his local scholastic career at the Royal Hungarian University of Sciences, where, he recalls, he got into the habit of going to the Central Café, a local Mermaid Tavern, to do his homework. There he laid the foundation for that capacity to concentrate in cafés which later made it possible for him to toss off *Liliom* at a marble topped table in one of the town's most populous restaurants, to the music of a military band. At the Royal University he studied law, concentrating on its criminal branches, and wrote a disquisition on criminal law and criminal statistics that appeared in *Pesti Hirlap,* a Hungarian political paper. He leavened these solemn activities by composing stories and light verse for a humorous paper.

In 1896, when he was eighteen, Molnar decided to devote more of his time to journalism. He presented himself at the editorial offices of *Pesti Hirlap,* where he was told that the managing editor was away hunting. On subsequent visits, he got the same story. This hunting trip lasted fourteen years; Molnar didn't meet the editor until 1910. When he did, however, he got a job.

In the meantime, piqued by the prolonged absence of the tireless huntsman, he decided to tackle plays. His first major dramatic effort, *The Blue Cave,* had been successfully produced when he was fourteen—on a stage he constructed himself at a cost of eight florins—in the basement of a friend's home. There was a lot in this play about alchemy, and the props were mostly blue bottles filched from his father's office. The play must have been controversial, for the performance ended in a riot. Molnar had to wait ten years for his next production. This was a farce called, not too surprisingly, *The Lawyer.* It was produced at the Gaiety Theatre, in Budapest, in 1902. Only the other day, forty-four years later, Molnar sold the film rights of *The Lawyer* to R.K.O. An incident of this sort brings to mind Shaw's advice to young dramatists. "Don't go in for Hollywood or radio or anything else," he adjures them. "The money you earn by these sidelines will vanish. The earnings from your old plays will support you in your old age." At the moment, Molnar is drawing six hundred dollars a week from *Carousel* alone, and occasional film sales of old works keep the wolf still farther away from the lobby of the Plaza.

Molnar never practiced law, though he went to Geneva, after he had finished with the Royal University, to continue his legal studies. In Geneva, he tried his hand at feuilletons and correspondence for the Budapest papers, and his material caught on so well that he definitely decided to give up the law. To the intense unhappiness of his family, he abandoned his studies, returned to Budapest, and set himself up as a fulltime journalist. It was as a journalist, not as a dramatist, that Molnar won his first distinction; he was the leading newspaperman of Hungary from the beginning of the century to the end of the first World War. His plays were a byproduct of his newspaper work. For a time, in *Pesti Hirlap,* he wrote a column—its name can be loosely translated as "Miscellaneous Chronicles"—which thoroughly delighted the town. It did not deal in celebrities, as most of our columns do now; it dwelt upon the caprices and currents of life, as fiction does. Many of the columns were overheard, or imagined, dialogues. One of these dialogues was a conversation between two servant girls about their men. Molnar used this dialogue again in writing the story of Julie and Marie in *Liliom*. In fact, it was the nucleus of the play. *Jozsi,* an earlier play, was also a dramatization of one of his newspaper sketches.

Molnar was very handsome in those days, and very witty. It has been said of him, as it has been said of Oscar Wilde, that his real genius is revealed in his conversation. A serious-minded friend of this period regrets that Molnar was so lavish in social extemporization. "Had he written it down instead of talking it away in all-night carousals," the man recently said, "we should have had volumes of brilliant humor." Molnar speaks French, German, and Italian fluently, as well as his native tongue, but when he arrived here in 1940 he knew little English. One night soon afterward he went to a dinner party in New York at which most of the guests, Broadway people, spoke only English. He felt painfully out of things. On the way home, he said to a compatriot, "You know, I used to dominate occasions like this one. It is terrible to have no English. True, I have learned to say quite well 'Where is my hat?,' but it does not seem to excite people." He now speaks a cultivated and easy English, and, surrounded by dictionaries in his room at the Plaza, is experiencing the adventure of writing a play in his most recently adopted language.

In 1896, when Molnar celebrated his eighteenth birthday, his native city celebrated its thousandth. It had a culture all its own. In those days, everybody in Budapest wrote, painted, or composed music. Entering a café one day, Molnar observed a gentleman at a table who was deep in a book. "There sits the greatest reader in Hungary," Molnar said. "In fact, I am not sure he is not the *only* reader in Hungary." In spite of its antiquity, its glitter, its winy gaiety, Budapest was a provincial capital. None of the city's enormous output of literature was exported. The true Austro-Hungarian capital was Vienna, a five-hour journey from

Budapest. The German-language writers and playwrights of Vienna were well known in Budapest, but none of the authors of Budapest had broken into the charmed circle of Franz Josef's city. Not one Hungarian play had been seen by the theatregoers of Rome, Paris, or New York. Molnar changed all that. In 1907, he wrote *The Devil,* and it was such a success in Budapest that it was soon translated into every major language and played the world over. Thereafter, Hungarian plays were in. Molnar's plays became Hungary's principal export, and a large demand developed for the work of his colleagues. (It is said that when, during the last war, the Russians bombed Budapest, they destroyed two playwriting factories.) The stir in Budapest when first it was realized that Molnar was an international success was enormous.

Nevertheless, Molnar stuck to his newspaper work. He had by that time written novels, sketches, and short stories, but it did not occur to him to give up his profession. Molnar's fame as a playwright later outdid his reputation as a novelist, but, like Maugham, he has practiced both crafts all his life. In between *The Hungry City,* a bitterly satiric novel on Budapest corruption, published in 1901, and his most recent work, *Farewell, My Heart,* written in New York and published by Simon & Schuster in 1945, Molnar wrote many novels. Of them all, *The Paul Street Boys,* a story of juvenile gang warfare, is considered by most Central Europeans his masterpiece. His own choice is *The Green Hussar,* the tragic love story of a chorus girl.

There does not appear to have existed, in the Budapest of that time, any line of demarcation between journalism and what is nowadays loosely called "creative work." All the novelists, playwrights, poets, and short-story writers were working for newspapers or magazines; journalism was their mainstay, and they did not feel that what they did for their employers was on a lower plane than their other work. Molnar even now calls himself a journalist. While he was still a practicing newspaperman, he once set down the following view of his calling:

Reporters in America and elsewhere go out and get the news, whereas we more often than not stay in the office or in our garrets and make the "news." By that I mean that we report the news of the mind and soul of our characters as much as we do the actions and happenings of daily life, which are, after all, the material accidents of existence rather than the significant realities of life. But some of it, I insist, is literature. True literature is life translated into letters.

By this definition, of course, *Swann's Way* and *The Brothers Karamazov* make pretty good journalism.

Not long after *The Devil* became a success, Molnar found himself the head of an informal organization known as Molnar's Gang. On one of the boulevards of Budapest, the New York Life Insurance Company had built a grandiose five-story *Wolkenkratzer,* or skyscraper. Not long afterward a restaurateur leased the ground floor and basement and called his place the New York Café. The opening of this café was something of an occasion. Molnar was given the key to the front door by the owner and, escorted by his Gang, he proceeded to the Danube and ceremonially threw it in the river, as a fairly intricate way of saying that the café would never shut its door. In the memories of its patrons, the New York Café was a fabulous establishment. It had marble columns, terraces, and bars. It had lunch rooms where the poor could sip a glass of beer and munch a roll, and dining rooms for those who wanted luxury. It had rooms with dance orchestras and rooms without dance orchestras. Because Molnar's Gang made its headquarters there, the group was known alternatively as the New York Crowd. For a newcomer with artistic ambitions to be invited to sit at Molnar's table in the New York Café was an accolade, a kind of decoration. Molnar's disapproval of a play or book or piece of music could have a serious effect on its career; his saying that a young man was talented got the young man a hearing. The New York Crowd was made up of a dozen or so of the city's most celebrated men —composers, painters, and sculptors, as well as novelists and playwrights. There was only one requisite for membership in the Crowd—talent. Molnar himself plays several instruments well, and in his youth he wrote, along with everything else, some songs and lyrics. Among his musical protégés were Viktor Jacobi, the composer, and Dr. Albert Sirmay, now the musical editor of Chappell & Company. The group travelled everywhere together. They went to dress rehearsals and first nights in a body and then repaired to the New York Café for the post-mortems.

One member of Molnar's Gang, now distinguished in musical circles in New York, was astonished when he discovered that Richard Rodgers and Oscar Hammerstein II have an office. In Budapest you worked at home, and when you had business to transact you went to one of the cafés. Each theatre had a café that was considered its own, across the street or around the corner, and when you wanted to see the manager or the director, you could be certain—unless, regrettably, he had died during the night—that he'd be in that café every afternoon. The café took care of everything: you could plan a production there, do your casting, and even, as Molnar sometimes did, write your play there; if you needed money, you could get an advance against royalties from the café manager or, if he was evasive, borrow from the headwaiter. The café headwaiters were important and apparently lavish personages. The most famous and the most lucrative was Uncle John, of the New York Café. His loans over the years to the less lucky customers took on the aspect of an annuity, appropriate to the actuarial setting. After Molnar became prosperous, Uncle John would say to him delicately, before delivering the change from a large note, "Anything on account?" Molnar would tell him how much, and the headwaiter would presumably allocate the amount to the liquidation of forgotten debts. This went on for several years. Finally, Molnar decided it was time to stop. "You've been collecting from me for several years," he said when Uncle John made his usual request. "Surely I didn't borrow as much as that from you!" Uncle John grew purple in the face; he began to shout at Molnar. "And what about all those who *can't* pay?" he demanded.

To many of the survivors of the era of the New York Crowd, a considerable number of whom are now in this country, Budapest still seems a little paradise. There are dissidents who say that the town was all right for those who could escape into the literary and theatrical Bohemia but that it had another side. There is an actress who, although not Jewish herself, was upset, when she was a girl, by the lurid anti-Semitic posters she saw on her way to school. She also remembers going on a picnic in the lovely countryside along the Danube and being shown a wood where, her companion told her, with a great longing for the return of the good old days, a considerable group of Jews had once been taken out and shot in inexact reprisal for the Communist uprising, headed by the Jewish revolutionist Bela Kun, just after the first World War. Some members of the Molnar Gang, including its leader, were conscious of these undercurrents. Threaded through many of Molnar's plays is a light, Heinesque awareness of this lurking enmity. He himself was, however, immune from persecution, and so were his friends. Immersion in the arts washed them with a shimmer of inviolability, even of honor. In 1908, official Hungary gave Molnar recognition by making him a member of the Petofi Society, a kind of national academy of arts and letters. The head of the Hungarian Democratic Party was Molnar's closest friend, and if Molnar had had serious political aspirations, he probably could have done very well. He was, in fact, actually elected a Democratic member of the City Council of Budapest, but although he attended a number of sessions, he never made a speech. "He is not a fighter," a more militant contemporary has said of him.

Those who remember the Budapest of the golden days remember not only the city but their youth as well, and this may easily heighten the town's glamour in retrospect. Just the same, life there was once beguiling, and it afforded one amenity of undeniable worth that unfortunately has never taken root elsewhere. This was the system of the Red Caps. The Budapest Red Caps did not carry baggage; they were uniformed messengers who did miscellaneous errands. They had beats and favorite corners all over the city. If you found yourself unable to pay your bill at a café and your credit with the headwaiter was overextended, you simply called the Red Cap on the corner and had him take your watch to a pawn shop. If you wanted to borrow money without security, you sent him with a note to whomever you wanted to touch. Lazy borrowers devised a time-saving system: they wrote one letter and addressed envelopes to five or six prospects. The Red Cap was instructed to deliver the letter first to the most likely. If it met with a rejection, he was to recover the letter, put it in the envelope addressed to the second-best bet, and go there, and so on until the loan was forthcoming or the list was exhausted. The Red Caps made it possible to converse in cafés with continuity even if you were insolvent.

The Red Caps were used for a hundred things. They were hired to wake up people who had slept through an appointment or to wake oneself up. There is a story of a theatre manager who sent theatrical-page items every day by a Red Cap to a newspaper editor who hated him. The editor would invariably take the material from the Red Cap and ostentatiously throw it into the wastebasket. After a while, the Red Cap would just bring in the dispatches, bow to the editor, and throw them into the wastebasket himself. Once Molnar, dissatisfied with some goulash in a little restaurant he frequented, sent a Red Cap to a rival restaurant for a goulash and ate it before the stricken gaze of the proprietor. The oldest and most cherished, if not the sturdiest, Red Cap was naturally stationed near the New York Café. He was ancient, white-bearded, arthritic, and given to procrastination. Nevertheless, he bore gallantly on the visor of his cap the legend "EXPRESS." One of these messengers was Molnar's prototype for Wolf Beifeld, whom the servant girl Marie falls in love with in *Liliom*, mistaking him for a soldier because of his uniform.

Molnar wrote *Liliom* in Siberia. Siberia was a name given to one of the terraces in the New York Café because it was patronized by Hungarian dancers who came home broke after touring Russia. It was a custom of Budapest managers to send companies of dancers to Russia. Some of the dancing girls were successful, stayed in Russia, and married noblemen. The Tsar's government was strict with the less accomplished ones. If they failed as dancers, they were not allowed to remain and improvise. The unfortunates who returned made at once for Siberia. Molnar, himself an inveterate fancier of far-off places and with an inborn hatred of the minutiae of actual travel, came to love Siberia. He arrived there one evening at his usual time, settled himself at his usual table, and ordered an expansive dinner, after which, with the café's military band going full swing in the background, he began *Liliom*. He wrote till dawn. After three weeks of exile, the play was finished. It opened in Budapest, on September 5, 1909, and failed. Molnar was by now married to his first wife. She had furnished for him an ideal writing room, with a polished mahogany desk, silver inkwells, and comfortable armchairs. Somehow, Molnar found himself not using this room to work in. It was too lonesome and it had no military band. When *Liliom* failed, Mrs. Molnar was angry but triumphant. "This is what comes of not working at home," she said. Then she reproached him for having written such trash and extracted from him a promise that he would never compound the offense. Years later, after the Theatre Guild success with *Liliom* and a general reversal of opinion about the play, Molnar recalled this vow. "It is about the only promise I ever made to a woman that I fully kept," he said.

Molnar's first wife was the daughter of Jozsef Veszi, a local newspaper publisher. This man was a great figure in the town, cultivated and gay, who kept open house and seems to have attracted and stimulated everybody who had anything to do with him. Molnar, like everyone else, loved going to his house, and he had an adoring affection for his future father-in-law. There were wonderful dinners and literary and musical parties. The man had four daughters, so Molnar married one. Possibly owing to her insistent critical faculty, the marriage did not last. There is a point, with a writer, at which candor may be excessive. They had one daughter, Molnar's only child, who is now a widow and lives with her two sons and a daughter in Budapest.

Probably because of his lighter plays, there is an atmosphere about Molnar which conveys the impression that he has had a multiplicity of wives, but he has had only three, and he is still married to the third, the actress Lili Darvas. Molnar's second wife was Sari Fedak. She was the greatest stage star of Hungary, equally brilliant in straight parts and in operetta. She was so famous at home that when Erno Rapee, the Hungarian conductor, came to America, he at first called himself Fedak, under the impression that this resplendent name would guarantee an easy success in New York. Mr. Rapee was grieved to find that the path to recognition here was somewhat more devious. After a highly publicized courtship of seven years, Molnar and Fedak, in 1922, married. This marriage celebrated the end rather than the beginning of their relationship; it has been described by a contemporary as a "farewell marriage." This seems to have been a peculiarly Budapestian form of leave-taking. It was on the occasion of this wedding that Molnar made one of his most frequently quoted remarks. When his friends came to escort him to the ceremony, they were shocked to find him wearing a gray business suit. When they upbraided him, he answered, "I dress only for premières."

By the time Molnar married Fedak, he was deeply involved emotionally elsewhere. There had appeared in Budapest a new young actress who, though only seventeen, had made a big hit in an inconsequential play. Her name was Lili Darvas. Everybody ran to Molnar to ask him to go to see her. He refused. He seemed to regard the new star as an intruder. Without seeing her, he predicted that her success would be only temporary, but instead it grew with each new play she appeared in. Molnar's friends assured him that Darvas was just the sort of actress he was writing for. Molnar's resentment grew. For a long time he refused to meet her. (Later, long after his hostility had ebbed, he explained to her. "It was your youth," he said. The emergence of a new star so young had made him aware that his own generation was growing old, that the next generation was pushing up.) The question of casting a part in a new Molnar play arose. Molnar had chosen for it an actress with whose husband, a jealous man, he had recently fought a token duel. Fedak refused to allow her to play the part and insisted that Darvas have it. Eventually, Molnar yielded. Within three years, Darvas and Molnar were married. This seems to have had the effect, for a time, of somewhat diluting their relationship. But it has survived the years and many plays and war and exile, and though Molnar and Darvas are living in separate establishments in New York, there is still a deep friendship between them. She is playing the Queen in the Maurice Evans *Hamlet,* now on the road, and during its recent run here, when, on matinée days, there was too little time between performances to go to her own flat uptown, where she was living with her mother, she had dinner with Molnar in his favorite delicatessen, near the Plaza.

Molnar's parsimony is as lengendary as his wit. His prodigality seems to be confined largely to conversation. When he was divorced from Fedak, he paid her $30,000. Before he married her, they had given many elaborate parties, on which she spent a great deal of money. Molnar had a flat of his own, but the parties were given at Fedak's flat, an arrangement which suited Molnar admirably. The $30,000 was like the payment of a long-overdue bill at a restaurant. The parties at Fedak's are still remembered by those lucky enough to have been invited. One of the regular guests was the Mayor of Budapest, who played the piano far better than Jimmy Walker and who often accompanied the famous tenor Richard Tauber. There were other parties, too. One evening, in the home of a well-known politician and his wife, Tauber was singing and the Mayor was playing the piano. Molnar, carried away by the *Stimmung* of the moment, found himself absentmindedly embracing his hostess. In his free hand he held a lighted cigar. Her husband walked over to Molnar and spoke to him. His manner was severe and his tone unfriendly. "Mr. Molnar," he said, "may I see you alone?" Molnar followed him into another room. He felt miserable, for he is a man who hates all conflict that is not verbal. "This," he thought in Hungarian, "is it!" The husband closed the doors behind them, then faced him. "I must request you, Mr. Molnar," he said, "not to smoke while Herr Tauber is singing. It is bad for his throat." It was a music-loving atmosphere.

Not the least of the diversions at the Fedak parties were the occasional quarrels between Molnar and Fedak. Molnar gave her a large but uncelebrated painting, and occasionally, to counteract the calumny that he never gave anyone anything, he would proudly point it out to the guests. One night, after a sharp difference of opinion between him and Fedak, he had the picture taken down and removed to his own flat. Later it reappeared in Fedak's flat. During the course of the next few years, this painting made many trips back and forth. When people started gossiping about Molnar and Darvas before their marriage, the opinion was frequently expressed that this time it must be real love because, it was reported with stupefaction, "he spends money on Darvas!"

Molnar himself capitalizes anecdotally on the widespread legend of his stinginess. In 1927, on his return to Budapest after his first visit to America, where Darvas was by then playing in Max Reinhardt's repertory company at the Cosmopolitan Theatre, he was given a welcome-home dinner party. A former friend who had become an enemy managed to be invited. Molnar was in good form and told a number of stories about New York. One of them concerned the night Darvas had come home to their hotel weeping. Her purse, which had more than a hundred dollars in it, had been stolen out of her dressing room. To calm her, Molnar recounted, he had said, "Don't cry. I will give you the hundred dollars." Then, surveying the table through the monocle he has always worn, he caught the look of utter incredulity in the eyes of his estranged friend. "Don't be so startled," said Molnar. "I only promised it." Recently, in New York, someone asked him whether he was able to send anything to his daughter in Budapest. "Yes," he said. "In the beginning, I sent her money through Rumania, then through an American soldier who was going to Budapest, then through the Red Cross, but now I hear that all you have do is go to the bank and just send. In fact," he added, his voice broken with factitious sobbing, "it's getting easier and easier and easier!" Molnar says that he finds a reputation for stinginess costly. When a man has a reputation for generosity, he believes, people are apt to say, "Well, he's so nice and kind and gives so much that I can't approach him." On the other hand, of a stingy man, they think, "He's so tight it will be a pleasure to nick him."

Hungary's one reader must have been hard put to it to keep up just with Molnar's output. For some twenty years before the first World War, Molnar led an industrious life in his native city. The literary program to which he determinedly adhered was: a feuilleton or a short dialogue for the papers every day, a short story every week, and a play and a novel every year. His fame grew, but in those years travel, which was forced upon him later by the Nazis, was very unattractive to him; he would not stir out of his beloved capital. No one could budge him from it, though many tried. One day, a friend just returned from America met Molnar in a café and talked persuasively of the delights of New York. Molnar sighed and said it sounded wonderful.

"If it seems so wonderful to you, why on earth don't you go?" the friend asked. Molnar made a gesture to convey the fantastic improbability of such a journey.

"Is it that you dislike boats?" inquired the friend.

"No. Although I have never been on one, I rather like the idea of boats," Molnar said.

Emboldened, the travel agent pursued his advantage. "Is it that you are afraid of the Atlantic, like Grieg?" he asked.

No, Molnar had no special prejudice against the Atlantic.

"Are you afraid of seasickness?"

Mildly, perhaps, but Molnar might take a chance.

"Is it the rail journey to Le Havre or Villefranche that puts you off?"

Tiresome, perhaps, but with a hamper of books and brandy it might be managed.

"Why, then," his companion shouted triumphantly, "don't you just pack up and go to New York?"

Molnar ordered a brandy and came to grips with the situation. "All the stages of this journey I think I might accomplish," he said, "except the most hazardous of all—the one you have not mentioned."

"What is that?" asked his friend.

"Getting from this terrace where I am sitting," said Molnar, "to the railway station in Budapest. That I cannot do. That, I feel, is beyond me."

Budapest had much of the intimacy of a small town. Molnar remembers having a political argument with a friend in his rooms on the second floor of an apartment house. The argument undoubtedly became noisy, because a passerby in the street who disagreed with one opinion came upstairs and joined in the argument. Another time, Molnar was going past Viktor Jacobi's house in a cab. He heard Jacobi playing the piano. Molnar asked the driver to stop the cab and listened carefully to the tune. Jacobi was working out a new melody. While playing cards with Jacobi in a café a few days later, Molnar started casually humming it. Jacobi went pale. "Where did you hear that tune?" he asked. "In Paris," said Molnar offhandedly. "It's quite a hit there." "Strange," Jacobi said. "I wrote it and thought it was original. I must have stolen it unconsciously."

Molnar's working habits were celebrated. He would not emerge from his rooms until early evening. Then he would stroll or ride to the New York Café, where he would dine and afterward sit till dawn, writing, conversing, drinking, and listening to the music. His courtship of Darvas made only a slight change in this routine. He would meet her after the play and take her to what would be her supper and his lunch. He would then escort her home and return to his Gang. In one of the public gardens along the Danube was a statue of Lajos Kossuth, the Hungarian patriot. It was considered improper in the New York Crowd to go home before the tiny bronze lettering at the foot of the statue was legible. There came a day when Molnar's rigorously nocturnal existence was interrupted; he was summoned to be a witness at a trial. It was borne in upon him that he had to appear in court at ten in the morning. Red Caps were mobilized to see that he got up in time, his friends bivouacked in his rooms as a further precaution, and, at nine-thirty on that grim morning, the still incredulous and foggy Molnar found himself in a carriage being driven through the streets of Budapest, unfamiliar in the unaccustomed light, to the courthouse. Molnar looked around. The streets, he discovered, were full of people bustling about at this insane hour. He was appalled. "Can it be," he asked, "that all these people are witnesses?"

During the first World War, Molnar was a war correspondent for the Budapest papers. Three volumes of his war correspondence were published, and as a result of his experiences the plays he wrote immediately afterward contained a good deal of tragedy. In the postwar period, the Molnar Gang began to dwindle and a rival gang began to form. The new one included a number of what one of Molnar's adherents described as "character enemies." It is a requirement of Molnar's nature that he constantly have on hand a pet enemy on whom to focus his lethal epigrams, and by systematically attacking people in rotation, he has been able, through the years, to build up a considerable body of opposition.

Of a mediocre painter who was an inveterate and brilliantly successful gambler, Molnar said, "Yes, he's awfully good at the roulette table, but everything he makes at night he paints away in the daytime." The authorized translator of Bernard Shaw in Germany was Siegfried Trebitsch. "What have Bernard Shaw and Siegfried Trebitsch in common?" someone asked in a literary symposium. "Neither understands German," Molnar answered. To a magazine publisher who had accidentally dropped Molnar from his free list, Molnar wrote, "Let us get my relation with your magazine clearly established. If I am not on your free list, I see it too seldom, and if I am, I see it too often."

There was a diverting group in Budapest known as the "revolver journalists." These gentlemen had mastered an unusual variety of blackmail. They all published little papers, some of them no more than throwaways. Their method had a refreshing modesty. They attempted to hold up not the bosses of big business firms but their subordinates. The procedure was simple; one of them would print an effusive article about the chief clerk or the vice-president of an organization. The tenor of the article would be that the head of the firm was a mere figurehead, that the real brains of the organization was the subordinate. The journalist would call upon the selected victim and show him the article, then ask him to subscribe for so many copies. The man would be horrified, especially if the praise was justified. "You can't print this," he would say. "It will cost me my job!" He would have to pay heavily to suppress the rave notice. A gentleman named Schweiger, one of the best-known practitioners of this art of extraction by loud praise, encountered Molnar when he was taking the cure in Karlsbad. Evidently Schweiger had run out of superlatives, for he asked Molnar for a loan. Without saying anything, Molnar threw him twenty pengos, which was less than five dollars. Schweiger was hurt. "From a Molnar, twenty pengos?" he said. "No," Molnar said. "To a Schweiger, twenty pengos!"

One of Molnar's intimates was once asked whether Molnar

was not his enemy. "No," the man replied. "Just now Molnar has Feleki, but he's got an option on me for October." Of this Feleki, a well-known, startlingly thin journalist, Molnar one day remarked pleasantly that when he was born, the nurse threw the child away but kept the umbilical cord. Feleki resented this description, and the feud between them was prolonged and bitter. A reconciliation was finally arranged; Feleki was to be brought by mediators to the New York Café for supper with Molnar. Molnar was sitting at his table, surrounded by his court. The great moment came; Feleki appeared, and the enemies shook hands; they were friends. But there was an assurance about Feleki's manner that annoyed Molnar, and he suddenly had the feeling that the reconciliation was premature. With a cordial wave of his hand, he motioned his old friend to a seat at the next table, then calmly began to eat his meal, stopping now and then to fix his chagrined and glowering enemy with his monocle.

After the first World War, Molnar began to pay the penalty for his long and undisputed dominance in his native city. The papers did not receive his plays with the unanimous fervor to which he was accustomed. They actually ventured criticism. As a result, he began to make excursions from Budapest. He went first to Vienna, where he was able to enjoy a new flood of adulation. His plays were produced in the Burgtheater, which was a national honor reserved principally for playwrights who were dead. His third wife, who accompanied him, also had a great success in Vienna. Thereafter, Molnar spent more and more of his time away from Budapest, and this defection was resented at home. Molnar's chief crime, however, was his commercial success in other countries. In the higher literary circles of Budapest, there was one sin which was beyond forgiveness. That was to be prosperous. In his memoirs, Stefan Zweig said that the same thing was true of Vienna; to make money out of literary work was considered vulgar. In either town, to make money out of America was the ultimate solecism, which confined you to a limbo from which no goods works could possibly rescue you. Molnar committed this ultimate solecism repeatedly. His enemies said he no longer wrote for Hungary, he wrote for America. It was like a Harvard halfback making a touchdown for Yale. In the cafés, they called him Checkspeare. Between 1920 and 1930, Molnar's gross earnings from his plays were, in fact, enormous—amounting to well over a million dollars—but the net was much less, averaging about $25,000 a year, which was still an imposing sum in Hungary. His fiscal relations with agents and translators were very complicated and their fees were exorbitant. From *Liliom,* not counting the substantial income he receives from *Carousel,* he has made, in thirty-seven years, about $50,000 net. He sold the film rights for $500. For a while, Molnar had a *prix fixe* of $23,000 for the foreign and film rights of all his plays. How he arrived at this figure he does not know; it just appealed to him. $3,000 of the price was an advance against the stage rights and $20,000 was an outright payment for the film rights.

Molnar's absences from his native city kept getting longer. For the two decades following the end of the first World War, while his books and plays were current all over the world, he maintained what he called his "five-room apartment"—a room in the Hotel Hungaria in Budapest, another in the Imperial in Vienna, a third in the Pupp at Karlsbad, and one each at the Danieli in Venice and the Negresco in Nice. The five staffs necessary to keep up this apartment, he used to say without vanity, were numerically and in skill on a scale few men could afford in their private establishments. He felt that even the very rich might well envy him his unicellular luxury. Molnar believed in the dispersal not only of his apartment but also of his bank balance. The sensational failure, in 1931, of the Creditanstalt, Austria's leading financial institution, was a disaster for many people. It was possible for Molnar to be philosophical about it because he had acted (or so, at least, he claims) on a pet investment theory all his own. "In case of bank failures," he says, "the small depositor is always paid off first. Therefore, if you have $100,000, all you have to do is keep two dollars in fifty thousand banks. Under this system of dispersed deposit, a great many banks will have to fail simultaneously to do you any real harm."

Molnar's political instinct is extremely keen, and for a long time before the second World War he felt that a débâcle was coming. Sitting on a café terrace with Gilbert Miller in 1936, he waved a hand toward the Danube, flowing peacefully below, and said, "This won't last, you know." All through the thirties he allowed the money his plays earned in America to remain in this country. He was deeply impressed by a lighthearted remark he once overheard in a Budapest café and has often quoted it during the years of his exile: "A Jew should never own more property than he can jump quickly over a fence with." He has also remembered another: "A Jew should never keep his money in the country where he is. He should send it to some other country. But he should always be in the country where his money is." In September, 1937, Molnar left Budapest for what may have been the last time. He spent the next year in the Venetian room of his apartment, and in 1939, when the war broke out, he was in Geneva, Switzerland, a country that had always courted visitors but was now nervous about them. It was afraid of food shortages, and there were even demonstrations against foreigners. Visitors were urged to go home, advice which it was peculiarly impossible for Molnar to act on, because the Nazis had already infiltrated into Hungary.

A companion of Molnar's Budapest days who visited him in Venice in 1938 noticed a great change in his outlook. The friend made a joke about the Jews and Hitler. Molnar said sharply, "It is bad taste to joke about things like that." This was a surprise; in the old days, the two men had joked about everything. The friend, on the defensive, said that before he left Budapest he had given five thousand pengos to help the historic boatload of Jews marooned in the middle of the Danube, on a ship that was unable to exercise one of the traditional functions of a ship; namely, to land somewhere. This gift, he argued, gave him the right to joke. But the easy mechanics of levity, which would have

212

served in the old days, served no more; the scope for comedy was shrunken indeed. Molnar was grim. The friends parted, and the pengo giver came to America. In 1939, he and a number of other exiles, including Molnar's wife, who had been here for a year and a half, sent him cables urging him to follow. The expressions on the faces of the Geneva hotelkeepers became more and more forbidding and finally Molnar sailed for New York. Gilbert Miller reserved a room for him at the Plaza. He arrived on an Italian ship on the evening of January 12, 1940, his sixty-second birthday. Darvas and four Hungarian cronies of old met him at the pier and escorted him to the hotel. They all had dinner in Molnar's room. There was a tense and agonized interval at the end, when the waiter came in with the check. For a moment time stood still. Molnar signed the check.

II

The first performance of Ferenc Molnar's tragic comedy *Liliom* (generally considered his dramatic masterpiece), at the Gaiety Theatre in Budapest on September 5, 1909, was a flat failure. The amiable ghouls who seem to hover about premières in all countries hurried to the cafés to pronounce the obsequies and to prophesy that Molnar, who was then thirty-one, was through. (This is a universal formula. A well-wisher of Jerome Kern's said to a similar prophet between the acts at the opening of the original production of *Show Boat,* "Well, do you think Jerry is through again?") For one thing, the first-night audience at the Gaiety was shocked. The playgoers came expecting to laugh. In this same theatre, Molnar had diverted them with farces like *The Lawyer,* his first play, and with sex comedies like *The Devil,* which had been a resounding international success. *Liliom* permitted them to laugh only occasionally and wryly. Moreover, the hero had the effrontery to die in the fifth scene and saunter up to Heaven. To kill off an actor might be all right in the Burgtheater in Vienna, where acute mortality was a staple; in a place like the Gaiety, it was bad form. Since that failure, *Liliom* has had two thousand performances in Budapest and almost a thousand in the United States; it has been played in very nearly every country in the world, including Japan. Under the old German system of simultaneous production in various state and city theatres, *Liliom* sometimes was being played in two hundred theatres the same week.

The resentment of that first-night audience in Budapest, and of the very few others that saw the first production, had its counterpart twenty years later in the office of a Hollywood film executive at a full-dress story conference. A playwright who had been imported from New York to do the film version presented the first draft of his scenario. What the executive had expected the playwright to provide for Liliom at the point where Molnar has

214

him kill himself has not been recorded, but he was profoundly shocked to find Liliom still dead. "You can't have a hero who dies in the middle!" the executive protested. The director of the picture, Frank Borzage, who had had conspicuous success with the silent film of *Seventh Heaven,* made the usual invocation of the classic for precedent. "The hero of *Seventh Heaven* goes blind," he said. "A blind man," countered the executive with some heat, "can still go to bed!" The limited versatility of a corpse had everyone stymied, but the writer was firm. *Liliom,* he argued, was too well known a play for him to give the hero a reprieve. Were he suddenly to endow him with an inheritance from America, making it unnecessary for him to go through with the attempted holdup that leads to the suicide, or to allow him to be startled by the evangelical influence of Janet Gaynor into sudden reform, or to rely on any of the other ingenious palliatives that were on file, he, the writer, might come in for some rough kidding from the uncontaminated playwrights who had so far been offered no contracts in Hollywood. The argument raged back and forth, but on this point the playwright would not yield. Finally, the executive, one of his major principles violated, gave in, and the conference ended. Sullen and frustrated, he nevertheless offered to drive the stubborn stickler for the death sentence back to his hotel. They rode in painful silence for a long time. The executive apparently made a frantic and futile attempt to recall a successful picture in which the hero had died in the middle before there erupted from him a startling remark. "You know," he shouted at the writer, "you're new out here, and let me tell you something! Out here you're not writing for a lot of goddam Hindus!" The playwright, as delicately as he could, insinuated from the movie man the background for this statement. It turned out that he had been plowing through a book on India and had come across the concept of nirvana. "You know," he growled, by way of summary, "those bastards love death."

Molnar's theatre is unique in our time, because it is an endless self-exploration. Shaw started with a fixed idea—Fabian socialism —which he has masterfully stuffed down the throats of his audiences while they were agape with laughter. Maugham, quite objectively and with dazzling craft, describes the society he has observed about him. O'Neill deals in cosmic symbols. But Molnar's theme is himself and he has taken his society right along with him over the footlights and confided to it expansively in stage whispers. Unlike the novel, the theatre has rarely been autobiographical; Molnar's plays are the great exception. His Budapest was preeminently a theatre town: the cafés bubbled with gossip, personal and professional; the intrigues from its bohemias overflowed onto the stage from the restaurants and boudoirs. When Molnar, who was always engaged in feuds, lampooned some current enemy in a play, the audience knew whom he was transfixing and watched the victim's expression in the stalls, much as a Boston audience stared at Alexander Woollcott during a performance there of *The Man Who Came to Dinner*. When, in a play, Molnar allowed himself to run through the statistics of an actress's infidelities, the audience was in on the count. His own life became so inextricably involved in the theatre that it was probably inevitable that he should develop, singlehanded, a theatre about the theatre itself. This genre has become popular with playwrights in England and in America, but Molnar invented it. Living in a zone in which reality and illusion overlap, he finally developed a category of plays in which he gave up all attempt to divide the two worlds and used as his theme their very indivisibility.

It may be gathered from reading his plays that Molnar loves artists, the poor, and royalty. *Liliom,* his finest play about the poor, is also a prime example of his self-analysis. Molnar's friends say that Liliom *is* Molnar. They point out the hero's, and Molnar's, constitutional inability to avow love, and the hero's vacillation between cruelty and repentance, reflecting the dualism in Molnar's own nature—the combination of the impulse to suffer and the impulse to make suffer. There is in *Liliom,* besides, a deep feeling and tenderness for the dispossessed. "Budapest was wonderful for a few," Molnar says now, in his exile in New York, where he has lived since 1940, "but for the vast majority it was something else." He has put that "something else" into *Liliom* and into his other proletarian plays, as well as into *The Paul Street Boys,* one of his best-known novels. A member of a persecuted minority, Molnar has always felt a sympathy for the underprivileged. *Liliom* had censorship trouble in England on the score that it was sacrilegious. For that matter, Molnar has never had—except for one play, *The Swan,* a comedy about royalty—much success in England. The psychological reasons for the British coolness to Molnar are perhaps traceable. The passion of love, as a dramatic subject, went out of the English theatre after Shakespeare; to treat seriously of love in the wide open spaces of the proscenium, before a lot of strangers, seems to the English a violent breach of taste. In the Budapest theatre the audiences not only encouraged the discussion but felt cheated if they could not identify the characters. The Heaven scene in *Liliom* is not the best one in the play—it is difficult to make Heaven credible on the stage or anywhere else, and even Milton was more successful with Satan that he was with God—but Molnar had to have it to make his point. The Chief Magistrate sends Liliom back to earth to see whether he can perform one good deed. He returns to find his widow and his sixteen-year-old daughter, who was born after he died, eating lunch in the yard of their country cottage. Liliom, his mild kleptomania uncorrected by his celestial visit, and eager to win his child's love, offers her a star he has stolen from Heaven. The girl, frightened by the stranger's insistence, rejects it. The incorrigible Liliom, frantic, hits her, as often in his lifetime he hit her mother. The girl goes to her mother, deeply moved and wondering:

LOUISE: Mother—tell me—has it ever happened to you—has anyone ever hit you—without hurting you in the least?
JULIE: Yes, my child. It has happened to me too.

LOUISE: Is it possible for someone to hit you—hard like that—
real loud and hard—and not hurt you at all?

JULIE: It is possible, my dear—that someone may beat you and
beat you and beat you—and not hurt you at all.

In this passage, which is the end of the play and its emotional
point, Molnar reaches a peak of tolerance in which he vicariously
forgives not only the blows he has given but also those he has
received. Now in the English theatre, hitting a woman is a laugh-
getter. The big laugh toward the end of Maugham's *The Circle*
comes when Lady Kitty says of the young man whose elopement
she has tried to prevent, "Of course, the moment he said he'd
give her a black eye, I knew it was finished." Similarly, the big
laugh at the end of *Pygmalion* comes when Higgins threatens to
let Eliza have it. In New York, possibly because the Slavic ad-
mixture is so considerable, Molnar has got away with it, but
there has been practically no immigration into England since
1066, and to anatomize the passion of love in the theatre is a thing
that nice people there no longer do.

In Molnar's day, philandering had a kind of civic status in
Budapest: it was an established institution; the cafés vibrated with
gossip, speculation, prophecy about it. Unless a man was pursuing some married woman, his day was somehow incomplete.
Molnar hit on a dramatic device which must have fulfilled all the
wish dreams of the jealous and the curious—to put the Devil
himself on the stage, in the middle of a sexual intrigue, as knowl-
edgeable as if he had been lounging under the table in every
cabinet particulier in town. Early in his career, Molnar became
aware that the Devil is good copy. He went to a performance of
Faust one evening and the notion drifted through his mind that
it might be amusing to put Mephistopheles in a white tie and
make him the protagonist of a comedy of sex. *The Devil* is the
first of his comedies to explore this notion. In this play, the prob-
ings into the mysteries of sexual impulse and motive which his
male characters carry on so exhaustively in his later plays (though

no more exhaustively, his friends say, than Molnar himself) are made by the Devil professionally, in line of duty. Even today, *The Devil* has a striking contemporaneity; Dr. Miller, which is Molnar's name for the Devil, is merely the materialized subconscious of the troubled and vacillating characters. He turns up at inconvenient moments; he mocks them when they utter sentimental nobilities; he urges them to go after what they really want when their timidity cautions them to live up to the conventions.

The first act of *The Devil* takes place in the studio of an artist named Karl Mahler. A prominent banker brings his wife to have her portrait done. The painter and the wife had been in love when they were both young and poor. They protest to Dr. Miller, when he appears, that this love has long since died, but he proves to them that this is inaccurate. He is all-knowing and persistent, and though the characters resent him bitterly, they cannot withstand his manipulations. At the end of the first act, Dr. Miller and the painter are alone. By this time the painter is deeply disturbed by his newly aroused feelings for his old sweetheart, but he still insists that his affection is only platonic. The Devil tells him a story, and here Molnar uses effectively the device of the dramatized anecdote: have a character tell an allegorical story and then make the action of the play follow the allegory.

DEVIL: Last fall, on the sixth of September—I shall never forget the date—something strange happened to me. I put on an old suit I hadn't worn for a long time, and as I picked up the waistcoat, a sovereign fell out. God knows how long it had been there. As I turned this sovereign over to look at it, it suddenly slipped through my fingers and rolled away. I looked and looked, but my sovereign was gone. I became nervous: I can't find the sovereign. I search around for half an hour, three-quarters of an hour, still I can't find it. I get angry, I get furious. I push the furniture about—still no sovereign. I call my man—we both look everywhere till it gets dark. I tremble, I perspire —I have but one idea: to get that sovereign back. It becomes an obsession. Suddenly a suspicion comes into my mind. I get up from my knees. I accuse my servant: "You have found the sovereign and put it into your pocket." The man gets angry and answers me disrespectfully. I am about to strike him when I see the blade of a knife shining in his hands. I draw my revolver (*takes a shining revolver out of his pocket and rises*) and with this revolver I nearly killed a man for a sovereign, a sovereign I didn't need and had never missed—just a found sovereign. (*He puts revolver on the table.*)

KARL (*vaguely discomfited*): I give found money away.

DEVIL: I would have given it away, but it slipped through my fingers and whatever slips through our fingers is just the one thing we want. We break our necks for it—that's human nature. And if it once slips through your fingers, you will run after your found sovereign. And, when it is too late, you will discover it was worth having—the one thing that might have made your life significant, worth living. . . .

KARL: To draw a revolver for a found sovereign! . . . Why do you tell me all this? Why? What do you want? Who sent you?

DEVIL: Nobody! No one! I am here! (*Touches Karl's forehead.*)

KARL (*almost shouting*): No! Do you hear? No! I've known her all these years, and we've been good friends only—and we'll remain good friends, nothing else. I don't want the found sovereign!

DEVIL: And if it slips away? If another man runs away with it?

KARL (*with terrified suspicion*): Who?

DEVIL (*with calm triumph*): I. Tonight. This very night. For ten thousand years I have had no prettier mistress.

The Devil whips his victim's jealousy to a frenzy by describing the minutiae of his impending conquest:

How you will run after your lost sovereign! Every hour that you wonder where she is, she spends with me. A carriage passes: your heart stands still. Who's in the carriage? . . . You see a couple vanish around a corner, clinging to one another. Who were they? A light goes out in a window. Who put that light out? We sit in every carriage, we vanish around every corner, we stand behind every window curtain. . . .

Karl, unable to stand any more, reaches for the revolver the Devil has put on the table. The Devil takes it out of his hands. Karl sits down, stunned. A butler comes in, carrying a lighted candle, then walks over to the Devil and helps him put on his fur coat.

DEVIL (*with a sad smile, in a warm tone rather like that of a father speaking to his son*): You see, my boy, one may draw a revolver for a lost sovereign.

In Molnar's Budapest, everybody was chasing lost sovereigns.

Molnar's prejudice against stockbrokers and middlemen is revealed in an especially acrimonious passage in *The Devil.* To get himself invited to a party where he can further pursue his occupation, Dr. Miller tells the wife he is arranging to have seduced, "Your husband will be delighted. I've just come from Odessa. I have good news. Wheat is rising—this year's crop turned out worse than they thought it would." The Devil derives a certain satisfaction from the speculator husband's joy that conditions which cause starvation in Russia will enable him to turn a profit, and he later refers to the husband as Mr. Wheat.

In Italy, the part of the Devil was played intermittently for thirty years by Zacconi, the greatest Italian actor of his time. Molnar's favorite theatre story concerns Zacconi. The two men first met in a dressing room in a theatre in Turin, when the actor was fifty years old. Molnar had gone there to give him some suggestions for a production of *The Devil* in which Zacconi was soon to open. The actor was sitting in his costume for the play in which he was then appearing, an old war horse he had been playing for years, called *La Morte Civile.* He was in seventeenth-century costume—buckled shoes, white stockings, short velvet trousers—and a brilliant red wig that he always wore for his part. On visits Molnar made to Italy in the course of the next several years, he saw Zacconi a number of times, and then there was a lapse of twenty years. One day, Molnar was walking with some friends along a street in Cannes when he saw a poster announcing the appearance of Zacconi for one evening in *La Morte Civile*. He was very moved, sent a message around to the actor, and immediately got an emotional note of welcome and an offer of a stage box for that evening. Molnar attended the performance with his friends. In the intermission, he went around to see the star, who was sitting in his dressing room, in his seventeenth-century costume and flaming red wig. Zacconi was now nearly eighty. The greeting was fervent; they sat and talked for a bit, and then Molnar saw tears forming in Zacconi's eyes and rolling down his painted cheeks. Molnar was distressed. "This is a happy reunion, Zacconi," said Molnar. "Why do you weep?" "I weep, Molnar," he answered, "to see that since last we met your hair has gone gray." Molnar is fond of the story because it epitomizes the world of the theatre, in which reality becomes merely a wavering reflection of illusion. The old actor, sitting in his dressing room in his flaming red wig and weeping over Molnar's white hair, had forgotten completely that for him, too, time had passed; his wig was young and so was he.

The interpenetration of life and the theatre in Budapest reached some sort of incestuous climax when Molnar's theatre began feeding upon itself and he wrote his series of theatre plays, among them *The Guardsman, The Play's the Thing, The Violet,* all three eventually produced in New York, and *The Prologue to "King Lear,"* which has not been done here and is probably the best of the lot.

"Is there anything," says the Critic to the Actor in *The Guardsman,* "that you can't believe if it's necessary?" The Actor has just allowed his wife, the Actress, to persuade him that the Russian guardsman was not at her apartment the afternoon before, although, since the guardsman was actually the Actor himself in a disguise, he knows very well he was there, and the Critic's rhetorical question serves as still another illustration of the half-world between reality and fantasy in which actors live. Later, when the Critic upbraids the Actor for crying over his wife's willingness to be unfaithful with the character he has impersonated, he whimpers, "I can't help it. I'm so used to shedding real tears on the stage that I can't always restrain them at home."

In Molnar's *The Prologue to "King Lear,"* one of the characters is an actor cast in the role of Lear. He cries when the husband of the wife he has been pursuing comes backstage to accuse him of dallying with her; the husband is unconvinced by his tears, and the actor says:

> Anyone can cry. But to us it is like the throat to the man who swallows knives. We practice crying so long that it no longer pains us; else acting would destroy us. Do you know where the fault lies? In that crying fails to move us even when we might relish the pain of tears. That is why I find no relief—in crying privately.

When Molnar wrote *The Guardsman,* he was told by friends that no one would accept the fact that a wife wouldn't recognize her own husband, no matter how ingenious the vocal and physical makeup. Molnar brushed this argument off; he said, "The theatre exists to lie—except in essentials. If an audience will accept a bit of painted canvas as a forest, they'll accept this. They'll believe she didn't recognize him because I say she didn't." Technically, *The Guardsman* is a model of dexterity. Molnar tosses off this thin and perilously unbelievable story with great ease. In the midst of a quarrel between the Actor and his wife, Molnar innocently introduces a theatre-loving creditor who comes to the Actor's home to dun him for a bill. The Actor puts him off with a couple of passes for the following night to the show in which he is playing. The Actor's quarrel with his wife rises in intensity. The creditor departs, but a few minutes later sends back a message; he has found out that the Actor won't be appearing the next night and is returning the tickets because he doesn't want to see someone else in the role. The message is tossed into the Actor's rising spiral of emotion, and at the top of it he hears himself declaring, "I say, you know it's mighty decent of a simple fellow like that to refuse to go to the theatre when I'm not acting. Believe me, that makes me feel good." A moment later he is back writhing in his unhappiness.

The theatre in Budapest was evidently not respectable; it was truly bohemian. Actors didn't write political columns or address their publics over the radio in the manner of elder statesmen. And their café society was quite separate from society. Eleanor Perenyi, in her recent book about Hungary, *More Was Lost,* tells how shocked her noble husband was when, newly arrived from America some ten years ago, she asked to meet Molnar. "Molnar does not go into society," said Baron Perenyi apologetically. "Neither does Bartok or, I'm afraid, most of the people you would like to know." The writers and artists were content to lead their own café life. A passage in the first act of *The Guardsman* indicates the relaxed atmosphere of theatrical Budapest. The Actor is discussing with the Critic—an old family friend, mildly and vainly in love with the Actress—the background for his suspicion about his wife:

ACTOR: I can't keep it to myself any longer. I've got to tell someone. Listen!

CRITIC: What's the trouble?

ACTOR: You know who—*what* Marie was before I married her?

CRITIC: I know—I mean I suspect, at least.

ACTOR: We both knew whatever there was to know. Why should we be ashamed to speak of it? She had many lovers—very many. If I should count merely those whom I knew personally—Hartung, Zellenberg, Krauss . . .

CRITIC: Don't bother. I made the inventory long ago. There were nine.

ACTOR: Counting me?

CRITIC: Without you.

ACTOR: Pardon me! There were seven.

CRITIC: You haven't counted Hochberg.

ACTOR: And why should I? That was only malicious gossip. Then there was Kohazy. He was madly in love with her, but she couldn't endure him.

CRITIC: Very well, then—seven real cases—one gossip—and one she couldn't endure—nine altogether.

ACTOR: Seven!

CRITIC: Nine!

ACTOR: I cannot allow anyone—not even you—to cast aspersions upon my wife—there were seven.

CRITIC: Very well, we'll say seven. And even those seven we can't be sure about. The only thing we can be sure about is that I wasn't one of them.

ACTOR: I'm sorry. I'm sorry, old man, but don't weep over it now. There are more important things to talk about.

During this passage, the Budapest audience was presumably in a mathematical fever, supplementing breathlessly with its own additions and subtractions.

One afternoon, in a hotel in Vienna, where Molnar was then living with his third and present wife, the actress Lili Darvas, he was entertaining a male visitor in their suite. Darvas was in the next room, from which there presently emanated violent protestations of love, in German. Molnar's visitor pretended not to hear them, but they soon became too obvious. "My wife is rehearsing a love scene with Dr. Hock, the German director," Molnar explained. The visitor, evidently thinking that Molnar had pulled this explanation out of thin air, still looked embarrassed. Molnar saw there he would have to do something drastic to put the man at his ease—to show not only that his wife was innocent but that he had absolute confidence in her. Molnar suggested that the visitor and he join Darvas and Dr. Hock in the next room, then threw open the door without knocking. Among Budapestians, entering your wife's room without knocking was the highest possible tribute. The incident gave Molnar the idea for *The Play's the Thing*. Adapted into English by P. G. Wodehouse, it was produced in New York by Gilbert Miller, with Holbrook Blinn as Turai, the playwright, and was an enormous success. In addition to instructing his audience in how to get out of such an embarrassing situation in case they should find themselves in it, Molnar offers in this play a living manual of playwriting; the secrets he confides this time are not only erotic but professional. The action takes place in a castle on the Italian Riviera. It is 2 A.M. when the play begins. Turai, his collaborator, Mansky, and Adam, a young composer, are standing at an open window, looking at the sea and smoking:

TURAI: I was just thinking how extraordinarily difficult it is to begin a play. The eternal problem of how to introduce your principal characters.

ADAM: I suppose it must be hard.

TURAI: It is—devilish hard. Up goes the curtain, there is a hush all over the theatre, people come on stage. Then what? It's an eternity—sometimes as much as a quarter of an hour—before the audience finds out who's who and what they are all up to.

MANSKY: I never saw such a fellow. Can't you forget the threatre for a single minute?

TURAI: No. That's why I'm such a successful dramatist.

MANSKY: Life isn't all theatre.

TURAI: Yes, it is—if you write plays. You know what Alphonse Daudet says in his Memoirs? When he stood by his father's deathbed, all he could think of was what a wonderful scene it would make for the stage.

MANSKY: It's silly to let your job become an obsession.

TURAI: Well, that's the theatre. Either you master it or it masters you. And of all the brain-racking things in the world, beginning a play is the worst. That's where your tech-

226

nique comes in, my boy. Take this scene here, for instance. We three—curtain goes up on three ordinary men in ordinary dinner jackets. How is anybody to know even that this room we're sitting in is a room in a castle? And how are they to know who we are? If this were a a play, we would have to start jabbering about a lot of thoroughly uninteresting things until the audience gradually found out who we were.

MANSKY: Well, why not?

TURAI: Think how much simpler it would be if we were to cut out all that stuff and just introduce ourselves. (*He rises and addresses the audience.*) Ladies and gentlemen, good evening. We arrived tonight to spend a couple of weeks at this castle. We've just left the dining room, where we did ourselves remarkably well with some excellent champagne. My name is Sandor Turai. I am a playwright. I have been a playwright for thirty years. I make a very good thing of it. I bow and step back, leaving the stage to you.

Molnar leaves it to them for only a minute; then he takes charge again, and ends by writing a play within a play to get his heroine out of her dilemma.

In *A Prologue to "King Lear,"* Molnar gives the shadow characters created by Shakespeare so much authority that the so-called actual characters have to acknowledge their own lack of substance and scramble off, beaten, into the dim makeshift of reality. It is a long one-act play, which has become standard in the Central European repertory; it is usually presented with Molnar's one-acters *Marshal* and *The Violet,* as a triple bill called *Theatre.* The scene is the empty stage of an august state playhouse, an hour before the curtain time of a performance of *King Lear.* The situation is also standard: the star, Banati, who plays Lear, arrives in a panic because he knows that the angry husband and a friend are pursuing him. The actor who plays the Duke of Burgandy, already in his makeup when the panicky star arrives, summons

227

the stagehands, the fireman, the costumer, and the electrician to protect the star from his pursuers when they rush in. But the husband, a Dr. Erno, and his friend, a Dr. Kiss, break through the cordon. It is a piquant detail that Dr. Kiss is also after Dr. Erno's wife. The husband was just about to have it out with him when he was diverted by the more immediate threat of the actor, and Dr. Kiss joined in the pursuit in a sort of abstract indignation. The husband is a bespectacled pedant who teaches literature in a university. By the time he and his friend come onstage, Banati is already in his King Lear costume and makeup, and the idea of the play is that the benign majesty of the makeup, and the implicit evocation of the spirit of Shakespeare, make it impossible for the husband to vent his anger on the actor. The actor, too, once his beard and crown and costume are on, transcends his mundane personality and treats the fuming husband with the Olympian dignity with which he ordinarily deals with his stage daughters. Even when he risks dispelling the aura by telling the husband how he met the wife in the zoo (what is there about zoos that makes playwrights think that they are incubators of flirtation?), Dr. Erno cannot disabuse himself of his awe. He attempts to whip up his anger and fails:

> I am trying to analyze this unique situation into which I, a civilized being, have been swept. My wife's seducer hides from me behind a mask and stands before me in the guise of a majestic figure, an unhappy mythical king and father, whose fate has so often stirred me. And above it all, over and above my comparatively specklike grief, hovers the tremendous Shakespearean sorrow that verges on madness. Over both of us the spirit of that giant British poet holds relentless sway. It is Shakespeare of whom Taine said that he was overshadowing and creative, unfathomable, overbearing, immoral, and extraordinary—the greatest figure that has ever revealed the whole gamut of form and has conjured living characters into our ken.

To this Burgundy replies:

228

I consider Shakespeare an ordinary drunken actor and theatrical director. His plays were written by Bacon.

This irreverence diverts the unhappy professor into an impassioned denunciation of the Baconian theory, in the course of which he spouts an array of authorities. He keeps trying to whip up his anger against the actor, and he keeps failing. Finally he gives up:

ERNO (*advances menacingly but is repulsed by Lear's majestic gesture*): Oh, how dreadful to be so restrained by culture. Terrible! Are you familiar with Sir Thomas Lucy?

LEAR: Never had the pleasure.

ERNO: Sir Thomas Lucy was the English nobleman who gave Shakespeare a beating. Think of it, sir! Shakespeare himself! You are merely the image of King Lear—just hair, cosmetics, tin, mask, and actor . . . but that was Shakespeare himself! As a historian, I thoroughly despise and brand Sir Thomas Lucy, but, as a man, I envy at this moment his objectivity.

This objectivity is beyond Dr. Erno; he eventually goes away, reconciled with his wife and fairly happy, though he realizes that his experience with the actor is still too poignant to permit him to see that evening's forthcoming performance of his favorite tragedy.

Molnar remembers wistfully the reign of Franz Josef. His affection for the Emperor was not snobbish; it was a matter of temperament. He loved the imperial climate because it was exceedingly mild. Franz Josef, so Molnar seems to feel, was an amiable monarch who had no prejudices and who believed in living and letting live. "Why shouldn't men of my generation be monarchists?" Molnar has inquired. "The first time we got drunk, the first time we made love, the first time we painted the towns of Vienna and Budapest red, there was an emperor on the throne. What is more natural than that we should believe we

229

would again be able to make love, again get drunk with impunity, again be able to paint the town red, if only there was an emperor back on the throne?" This is to regard the Emperor as a kind of Voronoff and is perhaps expecting too much of him.

Molnar's infatuation with royalty is responsible for a series of plays, the most famous of which is *The Swan,* a satire on the mechanics of dynastic marriage. The head of a dethroned family, an energetic and frustrated woman whose passion it is to get her family back in the royalty business, is entertaining in her household the young heir apparent to a throne, in the hope that he will marry her young daughter. The young man is maddeningly indifferent. In the household is an attractive young man who has been engaged as tutor for the princess. The dowager mother conceives the idea of having her daughter flirt with the tutor in an attempt to make the visiting heir apparent jealous. Once this banality has been stated (Molnar even allows one of his characters to comment on it), it is treated with remarkable freshness and feeling. The attitude of the mother toward the tutor is exactly the attitude of Higgins toward Eliza Doolittle in *Pygmalion*— that the subject's own feelings about the experiment are not to be taken into consideration. No one will ever see a more dehumanized scene than the one in *Pygmalion* in which Higgins and Pickering come back home with Eliza after her successful début at the Duchess's garden party. They never speak to Eliza; they simply discuss her as if she were not in the room and, between yawns, tell each other what a bore the experiment was. Such a scene could have been written only by a man temporarily crazed by a passion for phonetics. Molnar's princess is far more human; when she sees the suffering in the eyes of her guinea pig, she forgets her bargain with her mother, breaks down, and tells all. She loves the tutor, who loves her, too, and the memorable second-act curtain comes down with her kissing him publicly. This was also Molnar's kiss, blown to a princess who was as susceptible to unpremeditated love as were his own plebeian friends in the cafés.

Every playwright writes the same success twice, but the second time it is usually a failure. Molnar tried to repeat the success of *The Swan* with *Olympia,* and the second play was one of his poorest. "Only a mediocre writer is always at his best," Maugham has said, and many of Molnar's plays are tenuous or strained. Even his failures, however, contain at least one scene that is notable and that only he could have written. *The Delicate Story,* the last play by Molnar to be produced here, and an unsuccessful one, contains such a scene. A delicatessen keeper is given a police summons for his wife. Distressed, he goes to the police station to find out the reason. The scene is in the office of the police captain. The storekeeper's calling card is brought in, and when the captain reads the card, he says angrily:

> Henry Cristof. Henry Cristof—nothing else. No occupation, no address, nothing. How am I to know what kind of man he is? A bootblack? A banker? He simply prints his name—as if everybody was expected to know. Just like that: Henry Cristof. As if he were Henry Ford. This world is full of strange people.

The delicatessen man is ushered in, and the captain berates him for the lack of detail on his card. Cristof explains that it is a visiting card, not a business card. But the captain, while the poor storekeeper simmers anxiously, wondering what his wife has done to get a summons, insists on rewriting the card. He fills it in with Cristof's occupation, address, and telephone number. He gets a creative satisfaction from this. Then he tells the delicatessen owner that his wife and a man were caught making love in a parked car, and finally, before dismissing the distressed husband, orders him to have his card reprinted according to his specifications. "You're not Henry Ford," he says. "You must resign yourself to that."

Although Molnar does not, like the bastards in India, love death, he saw so much of it as a correspondent in the first World

231

War that he felt he had to take it into account. He put it on the stage in a series of fantasies. In *Heavenly and Earthly Love,* adapted by Edna St. Vincent Millay and produced here by Arthur Hopkins under the title of *Launzi,* the heroine, after an episode which has shattered her emotionally, spends the rest of the play pretending to be a corpse. She has her father build her a catafalque on which she lies during Act II, and in Act III she puts all the other characters to the inconvenience of also pretending that she has died and is an angel in Heaven. At the final curtain, she commits suicide, which seems redundant. In *The White Cloud,* a play not yet produced in America, several soldiers in the first World War are killed on the Galician front. The play shows what effect the news of their deaths has upon their families. The children of the dead soldiers, who had been neighbors, become obsessed with the idea that their fathers are on a white cloud at the top of a nearby mountain, and the rest of the play takes place on the cloud. *Mima,* another fantasy, gave David Belasco a field day; for its production here, he transformed his theatre into a Plutonic machine shop. The play concerns the operations of the Magister, described in the stage directions as "a super-devil, an engineer, and inventor who has just completed a machine which is intended to wipe out all goodness in the heart of every man and woman in the world above." Privately, Molnar, as he is careful to point out, is an excessively timid man, but in these fantasies he takes enormous chances.

In Molnar's novels and plays, people on the fringes of misery clutch at the hope of love, the hope of happiness, but there is always the intimation of morality. Since Budapest was the capital city of the borderland between the East and the West in Europe, a borderland in which bitterly opposed ideologies have often clashed and in which there has always been war or the threat of war, it is no wonder that Molnar has divided his attention between gaieties now vanished and death. In his serious plays, the characters are irked by love, but they are also beckoned by death. In many of his amorous triangles, the third figure is hooded.

In this country, Molnar is scarcely known as a novelist at all, but in Europe he has a considerable reputation. Possibly his most celebrated work there is a novel, *The Paul Street Boys*. In it, too, death plays an important role. It is a story of juvenile street-gang warfare. Molnar is vastly interested in children. He has said that of all human beings, children are the most cruel, but *The Paul Street Boys* is no *Innocent Voyage*. For one thing, these children are mostly very poor. They are nevertheless cruel enough, especially to one of their number, a boy who is terrified by the fighting in which his companions are engaged. This boy, eroded by the sense of his inadequacy, by his loss of face with his comrades, embarks on a daring adventure beyond his physical equipment. He falls ill as a result of it. The book is populated only by children until the final chapter, when the boy is brought home mortally ill. The boy's father, Nemecek, is a tailor. As the boy lies on his deathbed, an impatient customer comes into the shop to try on a suit. From the next room, the boy's final delirium, as he lives over again the titanic battles fought in a vacant lot, comes through to the father while he is trying to please the fussy customer. This is the kind of counterpoint that occurs over and over in Molnar's plays and with which, when he is at his best, he manages to convey a sense of the erratic, grotesque, and comic interplay of ordinary life. Molnar's awareness of poverty is intimate and personal, just as Shaw's is abstract. Shaw is undoubtedly justified in bracketing himself with Shakespeare as the other great playwright of the English language, but Shakespeare is a bit more realistic with his poor characters than Shaw is, and so, for that matter, is Molnar. The poor in Shaw's plays have never missed a meal; they are like his well-off characters except that they drop their aitches. But Molnar's have a salivary reality; you feel their glandular reflexes while they stare through plate-glass shop windows at the confectionery. It is the difference between *Das Kapital* and Dickens. The tailor in *The Paul Street*

Boys goes to work at once on the brown jacket his customer orders; the thought comes into his mind that the money he gets for it will pay for his child's coffin. While he sews, he does not permit himself to look at the bed in the next room, because "he was afraid that a glance in that direction would discourage him and would make him fling everything—Mr. Csetneky's brown jacket—to the floor, and then throw himself beside his darling child." When the child has died, the tailor goes to the bed and sinks beside it, weeping: "But even now," Molnar writes, "he was not unmindful of Mr. Csetneky's handsome brown jacket; he slipped it off his knee, so as to prevent it from being stained by tears." Molnar understands the pressure on people who have to go on making a living even when they are dying.

III

Since January 12, 1940, Ferenc Molnar, the Hungarian author of more than fifty volumes of plays, novels, short stories, essays, war correspondence, and children's stories, has spent most of his time in one long, narrow room at the Plaza, with an incomplete collection of his own works. On the bookshelves beside his one window, which looks out on the fountain in the Plaza, are a mere twenty of the fifty volumes in the Hungarian set of *Molnár Ferenc Müvei*. He managed to find room for these twenty in his luggage when, a few short jumps ahead of the Nazis, he fled Budapest; the rest he had to leave behind. On his shelves he also has some French, Italian, German, Finnish, and Serbian translations of his novels. Molnar is apologetic when he shows you his bookshelves; he is aware that their contents are somewhat monotonous. The library in his abandoned apartment in Budapest contained five thousand volumes, some of them by other authors. All but a few of the books were eventually confiscated by the Nazis. On the walls of the room at the Plaza are Gauguin prints. Behind a massive and polished desk is an armchair with a deflated balloon cushion. Molnar has long since given up the attempt to keep it pumped up and has allowed it to relax permanently in flat discouragement. On the floor beside the desk, like a faithful mastiff, is his unabridged Webster, given to him last Christmas by his compatriot Sir Alexander Korda.

Leading off this room is what Molnar calls his "combination library-kitchen;" this contains a small electric stove and a set of shelves intended for kitchenware but bulging with manila envelopes stuffed with manuscripts and piled compactly to the ceiling. The detritus of a long and international career trickles out of the manilaed walls: caricatures of Molnar clipped from German, English, Hungarian, and Italian magazines, commentaries on his work by Central European critics, notes on the backs of Berlin and Vienna hotel menus, clippings of interviews with

235

him in several languages, and playbills of countless Molnar productions. Of these last, one has a particularly sad aura. The late Joseph Goebbels, before his intolerance hardened, permitted the Jews of Berlin a ghetto theatre in which they could put on plays, provided all the participants, including the author and the audience, were Jewish. One looks at this playbill and see the actors in a performance of Molnar's *Delilah*. There they are, in the cheap newsprint, being seductive and winning, flirtatious and amatory. Pinned to this playbill is a long and serious review of the play, clipped from a ghetto newspaper. It is written as though the critic were unaware that he, as well as the actors he admonished, would soon be swept away.

Molnar's theory of hotel life is simple: get the cheapest room in the best hotel, and eat in the best cheap restaurant in the neighborhood, preferably in a "grocery," his name for a delicatessen. His favorite locally, a small but excellent delicatessen with booths in the back, is at Fifty-eighth Street and Sixth Avenue. There he lunches almost every day and dines several times a week, often with his devoted Hungarian secretary, Miss Wanda Bartha, who, he says, is his best literary adviser and best friend. Molnar is well satisfied with the Plaza. It provides him, he figures, with a staff of twenty-six well-trained servants. For Molnar, who is an exceptionally frugal playwright, there is an added advantage to hotel life. He suffers from insomnia and has been an addict of sleeping powders for thirty years. He usually goes to bed with a book rather early, takes his powders, and waits for sleep to overcome him. Often he falls asleep without turning out the light. This negligence, he says, would be very expensive if he lived in a flat of his own. There is, however, one flaw in his Plaza existence. Telephone calls from this hotel cost eleven rather than ten cents, and he is irritated by the sociability of some of his Hungarian visitors, who are very casual about using his telephone.

Molnar has always hated walking, but his American doctor has prescribed this form of exercise and he does his stint by walking around and around the block on which the Plaza is situated. A methodical man, he notes down in a book at the end of each walk the number of times he has circumnavigated the block and how long he has been outdoors. Whether afoot or in a car, he rarely gets more than a few blocks from the Plaza. Sometimes he will go out of his orbit to dine in one of the fashionable restaurants his friends patronize, but it is a wrench for him to forego his regular booth in the Fifty-eighth Street delicatessen. In whatever restaurant or private house he finds himself, he does not rely on the cutlery set at his place; he carries a sharp penknife, which he uses to cut his meat.

On the way to his delicatessen, Molnar usually passes Bergdorf Goodman, and he usually stops to gaze at the mannequins in its windows. They have perhaps a special interest for him because one of his plays, *Riviera,* was laid in a fashionable shop; its plot revolved about the weary and underpaid shopgirls and clerks at the moment when they were putting Riviera costumes on their mannequins. By watching the Bergdorf Goodman windows, Molnar follows the changes of season and fashions. He prefers this to the more direct method of attending dinner parties, because an engagement to attend a dinner party, even if it is several weeks off, destroys for him the entire interim period. He knows that no matter what happens, he will still have to squeeze through the funnel of that dinner party. A few years ago, Molnar found out, by way of Bergdorf Goodman's windows, that Christmas was coming; an elegant mannequin, unharassed by the turmoil of Christmas shopping or any other pressures, held his attention until she disappeared to change for New Year's Eve. Molnar wrote a children's story about this mannequin and called it *The Blue-Eyed Lady.* It was published by the Viking Press. "Just think what he could do if he ever got as far as Radio City," a Hungarian friend of his remarked afterward.

In further obedience to his doctor's instructions, Molnar, who is sixty-eight, has lately given up smoking, drinking, and rich food. This asceticism, he says, is a tribute less to will power than

237

to a fear of dissolution. The mortuary customs in America, which smear death with the obscenities of makeup, revolt him, and he wishes to delay the event as long as possible. Like many men who live in their imaginations, Molnar is, as he admits himself, cowardly. In 1944, after one of Hitler's most threatening secret-weapon speeches, Molnar became convinced that the bombing of New York was imminent. When a less cautious friend suggested that he might at least wait for more tangible evidence, Molnar said, "Tomorrow one million people will be leaving the city. The stations will be crowded. I must leave tonight." With his secretary and two impressionable friends, he departed that night for Lake Placid. The quartet sat the blitz out there.

Owing to his timidity, Molnar is a nervous motorist. When he had a car and chauffeur in Budapest, he tried the experiment of installing a horn in the back, so that he could blow it in tight situations. The division of command did not work out; it resulted one day in the chauffeur's getting rattled and running into another car. Molnar was only mildly shaken up, but he lost confidence in his chauffeur and eventually switched over to cabs. During the odd and dangerous episode of the revolution of Bela Kun, following the first World War, the streets of Budapest were not safe. Molnar had a little seat built on the running board of the cab he regularly used, and rode around sitting on that and talking to nonexistent passengers inside to give thugs an impression of numbers. During that period, Molnar rarely went out, however; he used to telephone desperately to his friends to come to see him. One night a newcomer was brought along—a man of enormous stature. At the end of the evening, Molnar went up to the giant and shook his head with a worried expression. "You're so tremendous. You're so strong," he said. "Aren't you afraid to go home alone? Aren't you afraid you'll attack somebody?"

Molnar tells a story about the Bela Kun days that is a tribute to the tenacity of playwrights. A communist author of that time was trying to peddle a play around Budapest. He went to producer after producer, but no one would put it on. When the

Bela Kun regime was established, this playwright became a member of the cabinet. The play went into rehearsal. But the regime didn't last long enough for it to open. Time, as they say, passed. In 1945, the communists came back to Budapest as conquerors. The play is on.

Though scattered in Paris, London, Hollywood, and New York, the Hungarian émigré colony is a closely knit community. At its center is Molnar. For all the Hungarian exiles, Molnar, whom they call Feri, is the wise man and elder statesman. Most of the Hungarians who shuttle busily between London and Hollywood visit him when they arrive here and go to say goodbye to him when they leave. There are not only theatrical and film people but also novelists and journalists. His leadership of the Budapest group known as the New York Crowd—its headquarters was the New York Café—has survived the transposition to New York itself.

In Molnar's revolving circle are Sir Alexander Korda, who put the British film industry on the map when he produced *Henry VIII,* and was knighted for it; Michael Curtiz, the Hollywood director; Dr. Albert Sirmay, now music editor of Chappell & Company, who was in charge of the music for a cabaret Molnar ran in his youth; Gabriel Pascal, the conduit between Bernard Shaw and the movies; Emmerich Kalman, the composer; Alexander Ince, the producer and publisher; Erno Vajda, the author of *Fata Morgana;* Geza Herczeg, the author of *The Wonder Bar;* and a great many others, including several Austrians and Germans, such as Kurt Weill, Ludwig Bemelmans, Ernst Lubitsch, Otto Preminger, and Alfred Polgar (the Viennese critic who supervised the translation of most of Molnar's plays into German), who have been taken into the group as honorary Hungarians. Today the circle includes a great many people who didn't know Molnar in his younger days, and a newcomer still considers an invitation to sit down at Molnar's table an accolade, even though the table is not in the New York Café but in the

Fifty-eighth Street delicatessen. Molnar's routine is so definite that his friends can reach him at any hour. They know when to go to the Plaza and when to go to the delicatessen. Some one of them is always asking him for advice. A few weeks ago, the Hungarian director of a play written by another Hungarian came to him and complained that he was unable to cast the leading role properly. "What type do you want?" asked Molnar. "I need an actor who looks like Oscar Karlweis," the director said. "I need someone with Karlweis's comic intonation, with Karlweis's charm, with his walk, with his timing, with his gestures." "Why, then, don't you get Karlweis?" inquired Molnar, not unexpectedly. The director recoiled. "For this part, Karlweis!" he said. That is the kind of thing Molnar has to handle all the time.

The Hungarian émigrés are bound together, it would appear, by a kind of invidious camaraderie. They coöperate in the face of a common calamity, but they relish telling stories about one another's duplicities. A Hungarian will recount to you, as though describing a skillful piece of legerdemain, how a Budapest husband, separated from his wife and ordered by the courts to pay her fifty dollars a month, faithfully paid her every time and then called on her, enjoyed an excellent dinner at her house, and won the fifty dollars back from her at pinochle. "This was Budapest!" the Hungarian will say ecstatically. Or there will be the story of the composer whose long and unsatisfactory pursuit of an ambassador's wife was interrupted when her husband was suddenly transferred to Berlin. The composer packed his bags and prepared to follow, but his impresario, anxiously awaiting delivery of a score, counselled restraint. "What will you gain?" he argued. "Supposing you succeed? What then? After all, you will admit, the chief benefit you will derive will be from telling about it in the café. Well, tell it anyway and save the trip!" The composer found the argument irrefutable and rushed to a café.

In their new environment, with its naïve standards, the more exuberant Hungarian refugees seem to have acquired a zestful perspective on their national traits. "If you have a Hungarian

240

for a friend," an objective Hungarian will say, "you don't need an enemy." Another will tell you that a recipe in a Hungarian cookbook starts with the brisk injunction "Steal two eggs . . ." Another will say, "Hungarians are enemy aliens even in peacetime." They will go as far as to quote the German saying, "A Hungarian will sell his country out, but he won't deliver it." When a friend of Molnar's was asked whether it was true that Molnar was writing his memoirs, the friend replied, "He'll never do that, because he can't attack himself." Another Hungarian, contemptuous of the otiose existence led by his luckier compatriots in Hollywood, says that a movie producer finally had to put up a sign in the writers' building saying "You must work here. It is not enough just to be Hungarian." This man also tells a story about Emmerich Kalman, who, a while back, arrived in Hollywood to write the score for an M-G-M musical and was received with a maximum of graciousness by Louis B. Mayer. The studio, Kalman was informed, was prepared to do its utmost to make his stay on the lot happy. He was offered, among a great many other things, a choice of librettists from his native Hungary. "If you like," said Mayer, "you may have Melchior Lengyel." Kalman was transported. It didn't seem possible; to come to Hollywood and to work with Lengyel, for whom he had had, since his childhood, an admiration amounting to worship—it was too much to expect. "Or would you prefer Erno Vajda?" Mayer asked. It appeared that to work with Vajda had been the secret ambition of Kalman's life. Was it to be achieved at last? Beaming, Mayer kicked open still another door in the fabulous Metro stables. "How would you like Bus-Fekete?" Kalman was overcome. His admiration for Bus-Fekete was inexpressible. "Of course, Mr. Kalman," Mayer went on, "if you wanted to, you could have an American Hollywood writer." "Good," said Kalman quickly. "I'll take the Hollywood writer."

All the backbiting and self-criticism among the expatriate Hungarians seem to fall into a design of mutual aid. When a Hungarian actor is after a part in a play, other Hungarian actors do everything they can to see that he gets it, and the journalists, playwrights, and producers are helpful in the same way. When an important Hungarian scientist was mentioned in the papers in connection with the development of the atomic bomb, there were ripples of satisfaction all through the colony. Perhaps it is because each success by a compatriot serves as a hopeful augury. Another cause of their closeness is that they all speak the language of exile. And they all look back on Budapest as the happy hunting ground where naughtiness was conventional and a keystone of manners, and, shuddering a bit in the more astringent atmosphere in which they now find themselves, laughingly adapt themselves to the quaint regime.

Even Hungarians who could not tolerate one another at home stick together remarkably well in exile. There is the Hungarian editor of a scandal magazine who for fifteen years bedevilled Molnar, Korda, and other well-known Hungarians. Molnar says that this editor was almost as effective as the oncoming Nazis in driving him out of Budapest. Molnar alone supplied the mephitic publication with enough copy to keep it going for years; his marriages and his romances were the editor's lifeline. Whenever the magazine languished, Molnar gave it nourishment. The editor spared nobody; in one issue he attacked Gundel, the thoroughly respectable proprietor of the most famous restaurant in Budapest. The restaurateur, distressed, came to Molnar and said, "I must answer this man. I must write a letter of denial to the papers. I must do something!" "I advise you to ignore this scorpion," Molnar said. "But if you must reply to him, print your statement on the back of your own menus. They have a far larger circulation than his paper." When, a couple of years ago, the editor came to New York, lost without his vehicle of vilification, bereft of his sheaf of poisoned arrows, Molnar, Korda, and a few other distinguished Hungarian exiles invited him to dinner. They don't know why; they just did. At this dinner, says Molnar, the unemployed executioner experienced such an expansion of the soul that he forgave them all.

Molnar's émigré disciples have to derive what comfort they can from the edged benevolence of his humor. Unsuccessful young compatriots come to him with their hopes, successful ones with their accomplishments; he is openly skeptical about both. Young or old, they also come to him with their disputes. Then he quotes one of his favorite lines, which is from Saint Augustine: "If two friends ask you to be judge in a dispute, don't accept, because you will lose one friend; on the other hand, if two strangers come with the same request, accept, because you will gain one friend." It was so worldly of a saint, Molnar remarks appreciatively, to notice this. He is pessimistic about the state of the world and about the individual destinies of his countrymen. "We are all dead, we refugees," he says. "We walk around, shadows among shadows, ghosts of what we were, in a world that does not know us and that we only faintly comprehend." But most of the refugees feel far from dead; the successful ones swim lustily in the stream of artistic activity, the unsuccessful ones exert themselves mightily to get into the stream. Molnar's own moribundity is highly active; since his arrival here he has written half a dozen plays, two novels, and one juvenile, and has found the time, besides, to be extremely helpful in converting *Liliom* into the immensely successful *Carousel*. This success affords Molnar only a mitigated pleasure. The fact is that Puccini wanted to use *Liliom* for an opera libretto. Molnar refused, on the ground that *Liliom* would disappear as a Molnar and survive as a Puccini, the same fate that befell Murger's *Vie de Bohème*. Later the Theatre Guild tried to persuade him to allow George Gershwin to do an operetta version, and again he refused. Would it have been better to let Puccini have it? Was it a mistake to turn down Gershwin? Will *Liliom* survive *Carousel*? From the contemplation of such questions, Molnar suffers a certain erosion.

Inevitably, Molnar's thoughts now hover about the past. He sits in the Fifty-eighth Street delicatessen, surrounded by his Hungarian friends, and one reminiscence leads to another. Soon they are all back in Budapest, in the great days of the New York Café and of the Gaiety Theatre, where Molnar opening nights were major events. Old dramatic criticisms are recalled, bygone performances are analyzed, Gundel's wonderful menus are recited, old quarrels are refought, and forgotten *mots* scintillate again. Many of Molnar's fondest reminiscences of Budapest have New York associations. He tells about the time Eva Le Gallienne went to Budapest after playing Julie in the original New York production of *Liliom*. Molnar took her to see the amusement park around which he had written the play. When she saw the merry-go-round, with its barker high-pressuring customers—when she beheld the actuality behind the illusion—she wept. Another American star, Bertha Kalich, who also visited Budapest, was even more tender-hearted. In his overoptimistic youth, Molnar had fallen wildly in love with a well-known actress. Without being unduly encouraged, he confidently set about finding a rendezvous, so that, when the moment came, he would be prepared. He went to Buda (Budapest's "old town") and there, on a dark alley, he found what appeared to be the ideal place. It was a noisy, dingy two-room flat, but since it was on the dark alley, one could get in or out of it without being noticed. Molnar engaged this flat at once. The rendezvous never materialized, but he lived in the flat for twenty-two years. When Miss Kalich came to Budapest, she expressed a wish to see the place he lived in and Molnar took her to his flat. She tried, while she was there, not to show her horror, but after she returned to America, Molnar was touched to hear that she was attempting, overcome by pity for his manifest poverty, to arrange a benefit for him.

When Margaret Perry, a daughter of Antoinette Perry, the theatrical director, visited Budapest, she took with her a letter of introduction from her mother to Molnar. Molnar responded by inviting her to dinner and at the appropriate time he called for her accompanied by a dark and younger man, who, he explained, was a gigolo who danced much better than he could. The three of them had a happy evening in an open-air restaurant.

The gigolo would give Miss Perry a whirl, then bring her back to the table, and Molnar would pick up the conversation where he had left off.

Molnar likes to recall his first visit to this country, in the winter of 1927. He came over principally to be with his third wife, Lili Darvas, who was playing in Reinhardt's repertory company here. Molnar remembers an audience with Calvin Coolidge. Gilbert Miller escorted him to Washington and, to fortify him for the White House call, took him to breakfast with a friend who had an excellent library and the kind of cellar specialists collected during prohibition. Miller's friend handed Molnar simultaneously an excellent brandy and a copy of a Molnar play to autograph. Molnar drank half a dozen brandies and signed half a dozen of his plays. When the man's collection of Molnar plays was exhausted, there was a lull in the hospitality, and Molnar, glancing at the shelves, saw a beautiful volume of Shakespeare. "I have the knack of imitating Shakespeare's auto-graph," he told his host. He quickly found himself inscribing *Hamlet*. By the time he and Miller, who had been joined by the Hungarian Minister, Count Szechenyi, arrived at the White House, they were relaxed. Coolidge was not talkative. Molnar remembers a prolonged silence after the introductions. Finally, behind his hand, the President inquired of Miller, "What does this man do?" (Molnar spoke no English, but Coolidge didn't know it until Miller told him.) Miller described Molnar's activi-ties. "Yes," said Coolidge, "but how does he earn his living?" When this was made clear, the President inquired of Molnar, "What is the political and economic situation of Hungary at the moment?" Count Szechenyi translated the query to Molnar. Molnar said to the Count, "As you know, my knowledge of these matters is limited. But I will keep talking to you for a few minutes as if I were explaining the political and economic situa-tion of Hungary to you exhaustively and with authority. You can tell him anything you like as coming from me." Molnar then re-counted to Szechenyi a few choice items of Budapest gossip and the Count presently transmuted them, for the President, into a discourse on politics and economics. By the time Molnar left, Mr. Coolidge was impressed by the fact that a man whose livelihood depended on activities so marginal should have so acute an insight into graver matters.

Molnar was in this country six weeks on that visit, during which he celebrated his fiftieth birthday. He remembers his stay mainly as a blur of parties and theatregoing. The only tranquil occasions were when he went to Reuben's at three o'clock every morning to meet Max Reinhardt. They would sit there talking until dawn. "It is very healthy to get a few hours' sleep before breakfast," Molnar once remarked, and after these nightly sessions with Reinhardt he was always careful to get them. The graph of the relationship between Molnar and Reinhardt was extremely angular. Reinhardt was the first person Molnar had told about his idea for *Liliom,* years before. Reinhardt was very enthusiastic and implored Molnar to write the play. Reinhardt, says Molnar, had immense charm and was a wonderful listener, but he never actually heard what you said. He had a remarkably mobile face, which registered keen attention; his absorption was complete, but it was in what he was thinking rather than in what you were saying. As Molnar outlined the story of *Liliom,* the dancing light in Reinhardt's eyes and the mobility of his expression doubtless followed the parade of some private drama of his own. At any rate, a year or so later, after Molnar had written *Liliom,* he sent it to Reinhardt, who was then the leading producer of Europe. For a period of two years he got no answer. Finally, Molnar sent him a telegram which said, "It is a great honor to be produced by you, but not to be produced by you is no honor at all." Molnar turned the play over to a more responsive producer, and Reinhardt and he did not speak to each other for thirteen years. Then, after they were on good terms again, there was the matter of Lili Darvas's contract to play the Nun in *The Miracle,* when Reinhardt's company was first coming to this country, in 1923. Darvas, then a radiant young actress who had made a great success in Budapest, seemed to Reinhardt the ideal Nun. He offered her a handsome salary to go to America with him and offered, besides, to pay for English lessons, to help her establish herself as an actress here. The contract was signed, the departure date set. But Molnar was very much in love with her, and he persuaded her into thinking she was ill. A confirmed hypochondriac, he was able to create a valetudinary atmosphere at will. Darvas went to a hospital. Molnar, having deprived Reinhardt of his star, was not to be mollified; he broke off with Reinhardt again, this time for three years. That was not difficult; Molnar, on occasion, has found it possible to break even with a friend he has not inconvenienced. The Hungarian playwright Heltai was a close friend and the distinguished author of serious plays in verse. One night Molnar had a horrid nightmare; he dreamed that he was being publicly executed. Just as the hangman was about to slip the noose around his neck, he looked down at the crowd milling around the foot of the scaffold. Right in front, looking up at him with an expression of uncontrollable glee, was Heltai. When Molnar woke, the memory of this look of joy on Heltai's face remained with him. Molnar, churning with anger, did not speak to Heltai for five years.

There are only two periods of his life that Molnar remembers as completely blissful. One of these lasted two weeks and the other six. The first was spent in *custodia honesta,* the second in a hospital. This *custodia honesta* was a form of punishment that only Budapest could have devised. It was not common imprisonment; it was more like being a house guest. For certain minor infractions of the law, a man was put into a room in a municipal building and told to stay there for a specific period. The door was left unlocked; he was on his honor. When Molnar was a young man, he fought a duel, with pistols. He and his antagonist emerged without the least injury. Swords were not customarily used in Budapest duels, because with swords you might get hurt, whereas with pistols you could make an impressive noise and all you had to do was miss. Duelling of any sort was against the law, however, and Molnar was sentenced by the chief magistrate of the city, who was a companion of his and a great admirer of his plays, to spend two weeks in *custodia honesta,* the regulation penalty. Molnar kept putting off serving his sentence, but finally a pained and peremptory message came from his judge. "This time, my dear Molnar, you really have to go," it said. Once incarcerated, Molnar was dismayed because the sentence was so brief. His room overlooked the Danube and a rose garden. From the sentries walking up and down outside, he got an unparalleled sense of security. There were no telephones. No one could get at him, and he was free of all obligation to do anything himself. It is a jewelled fortnight in his memory. Once Molnar was out, the tribulations of love beset him again and he took an overdose of veronal. It was the fashion then in Budapest to commit mild suicide, and Molnar succumbed to it. He had been drinking heavily and he rather overdid it. He was rushed to a hospital and his arrival caused a romantic flurry among the nurses. "This is the boy who tried to kill himself for love," the nurses whispered, and for six exquisite weeks they pampered him. "It was the only failure that I ever enjoyed to the hilt," Molnar once said.

Like many other wits, Molnar remembers his own *mots* word for word. He frequently recalls his reply when he was asked how he happened to become a playwright. He said, "In the same way that a woman might become a prostitute. First I did it just to please myself, then I did it to please other people, and now I do it just for money." He has written over forty plays, and he continues to turn them out by a kind of automatism. He has just finished a new one—based on an old notion—that is in his earlier comedic, ironic vein. It is about a nonexistent character, like Harvey, and is full of minute comic invention. One of his favorite plays is one that he has never got around to writing but to which he keeps adding amusing scenes in his head. It is concerned with Napoleon, about whom Molnar has accumulated a vast lore. It supposes that in his youth, in Corsica, Napoleon fell madly in love with a girl whose father put up a great resistance to the match. Napoleon, to show that he can overcome opposition, marries her. He settles down and becomes a successful cloth manufacturer, eventually engaging in a fierce textile war with England. His wife deceives him and, in a rage, he denounces her. "I am only a provincial businessman," he shouts, "but had I followed the impulse I had before I married you, to enter the world arena—had I become a great soldier or a great figure in Europe—you would not serve me so!"

Molnar even likes to recall other people's *mots*. He generously points out that many famous remarks made by others have been attributed to him, attracted by the centripetal force of his reputation as a wit. There was a Berlin banker named Fürstenberg, whom Molnar never met but whom he knew well because of three celebrated *mots,* which were all the man possessed that was not confiscated by the Nazis. Fürstenberg telephoned another Berlin banker, whom he did not like but had to see on a business matter. The man said he would have to look through his engagement book before he could make an appointment. Fürstenberg heard the surf of the pages being ruffled in the man's book. No free time in January, February, or March. The third of April was his first free afternoon. "On April third," said Fürstenberg, "I have a funeral." On the overnight express from Berlin to Vienna, the understanding was that you could, if you wished, have a first-class sleeping compartment to yourself; the upper was simply not made up. One night when the train was crowded, the conductor implored Fürstenberg to surrender his upper to an elderly baron, who otherwise would not be able to get on the train. "Give me the night," Fürstenberg countered, "to think it over." On one of his birthdays, Fürstenberg received a present of a huge, silver-framed group photograph of his family, including all his cousins and in-laws. He found the ideal use for it. He gave it to the porter of his apartment building. "Study this photograph well," he said, "and whenever any of these people show up, I am out."

There was, Molnar also enjoys recalling, a dreadful man in

Vienna named Haas, an inveterate first-nighter and a fountain of malice. At one opening, just before the curtain rose, somebody asked him a question, involving some esoteric family relationship, which he couldn't answer. The moment the first curtain came down, he rushed to his questioner. "Your question cost me a sleepless first act," he said. The remark killed the play.

Opening nights in Budapest and Vienna were festive; the boxes would glitter with uniforms and tiaras. A Frau Baroness von Pollack was always present on these occasions. One time, after the curtain fell on a dingy play about poor people, the Baroness, according to Molnar, felt let down. "It's no play for a première," she said.

Molnar adapted an enormous number of French plays into Hungarian. Once he was given a comedy by de Flers and de Caillavet to work on, and was asked to hurry; he started on it late in the afternoon, worked all night, and had the adaptation finished by morning. Of the many plays he adapted, he remembers only one distinctly, and that one only because of a line in it which, he says, illustrates perfectly his notion that the theatre should exist for entertainment. The line came in the course of a courtroom scene; a young Frenchman from the provinces was up before a Paris judge for examination. He gave all the standard data—birth, date of marriage, and so on—and the judge asked him if he had any children. "Nine," said the defendant. The French birth rate was then rapidly falling, and the judge showed considerable astonishment at this statement. "Nine!" he exclaimed. "Did you say nine?" "Yes, Your Honor," the husband explained glibly. "You see, there was no theatre in our town."

Among the contents of Molnar's combination library-kitchen is a copy of the London *Graphic* for August 22, 1931, which has a full page of caricatures by Autori, a popular artist of the period, gently lampooning the celebrities attending that summer's Salzburg Festival. There are Reinhardt, A. P. Herbert, Anita Loos, Moissi, C. B. Cochran, Bruno Walter, and Molnar, who looks very elegant leaning against a pillar and staring impersonally at his surroundings through his monocle. Somehow or other, the world it calls up seems remoter than Spy's; the near past has been so irremediably splintered by events that it is farther away than the more distant one. Molnar, already white-haired when Autori sketched him, was plump, cool, assured, foppish; now he is much thinner, and though he still wears the monocle, his expression is mellowed and kindly, and his sharp brown eyes, still young and vivacious, are lit with a tragic impishness. His skin is clear and his face almost unlined. Today, Molnar is a grandfather. His daughter, his only child, who lives in Budapest with her two sons and a daughter, is a widow; her husband was put into a concentration camp by the Nazis and died there. Her children were taken in and protected by a family of peasants. Molnar is very much moved by this. The nobility and the peasants, he says, did not join in the persecution of the Jews in Hungary; it was largely the work of the middle class. Molnar's first wife, and the mother of his daughter, is Margit Veszi, who is now in Hollywod and a successful film writer. His second wife, Sari Fedak, who was a great stage star when Molnar married her, became a violent Nazi and is now a prisoner of the government in Budapest. His third wife, Lili Darvas, from whom he is amicably separated, is on the road in this country, playing the Queen in the Maurice Evans production of *Hamlet*.

When summer comes now, it brings Molnar no suggestion of Salzburg Festivals; he simply leaves the Plaza for Montauk Point, where he spends the season in modest lodgings. His wife and his friends visit him there. Except for these trips, he has left New York only a few times since coming to live here. He went to New Haven for the opening of *Carousel,* and once he ventured to Mount Kisco for a weekend at Billy Rose's. Packing is for him a long and elaborate ritual. He has a special medicine

251

case for his pills and sleeping powders. When he went to Rose's, he declined a dinner invitation for the preceding Thursday night because he had already started packing. Every spring used to find him in Venice, in a small corner room in the Danieli Hotel, looking out toward the Campanile. His favorite people in the world are the Italians and his favorite city in the world is Venice. His niche in the Danieli was one of the rooms of what he called his "five-room apartment," which he maintained in hotels in Budapest, Vienna, Karlsbad, Venice, and Nice. Venice was a dead city, a mercifully silent city, and every night he would come back to his room, look out over the motionless canal, then get into bed and wait for the midnight bell. It would come, twelve liquid strokes, the last a pianissimo, a lullaby. In Venice, he recalls, he gave excellent advice to Gilbert Miller, who visited him there almost every spring. The plague of Venice, as of all Italy, was the beggars. Mussolini abolished that plague, but he automatically created another. All the beggars became peddlers. They legitimatized themselves by selling something. When you sat in St. Mark's Square with your apéritif, they bedevilled you to buy corn to feed the pigeons, dark glasses to shield you from the sun, and maps of the city. Molnar advised Miller to supply himself with these commodities before he arrived at the café. This worked magnificently; they sat in peace, a map of the city unrolled on the table, a bag of corn at their feet, and dark glasses handy. When, this spring, it was suggested to Molnar that now, with the war at an end, he could return to his beloved Venice, he dismissed the idea. The time for that is past, he thinks. He feels that he can no longer afford to spend his strength in travel.

Molnar regards this country as a fascinating experiment, and he is glad to be permitted to watch its operation. He has taken out his citizenship papers. He adored Roosevelt. Last summer, while he was at Montauk, he satisfied the masochism that is one side of his complicated nature by reading the tabloid columnists. "Every day," he remarked, "they disinter him so that they may once more spit upon him." His friends mildly reproach him for reading the newspapers so much; his preoccupation with political news, they say, interferes with his work. Asked one day whether he was quite happy here, Molnar said, "Yes, I am happy, but quite happy, that I am not." He has the poise of a man who, in spite of wars, persecutions, and imperious personal drives, among them the almost searing dualism of the impulse to suffer and the impulse to impose suffering, has yet managed to make his life, on the whole, pretty much what he has wanted it. He manages still. The five-room apartment is now reduced to one, but its window looks out on the lovely back of a graceful girl. On moonlit nights the Plaza fountain murmurs in silver and the spring evenings filter in, soft, beguiling, and without memory.

ABIGAIL E. WEEKS MEMORIAL LIBRARY
UNION COLLEGE
BARBOURVILLE, KENTUCKY

814.52
B421

Behrman.

Suspended drawing room.